example, significantly explains the relative importance of financial markets. This book is the first that provides an overview of the field of culture and economics and will be of use to postgraduate researchers in the field of economics and culture.

Eelke de Jong is Professor of International Economics at the Radboud University Nijmegen, the Netherlands.

Routledge Advanced Texts in Economics and Finance

Financial Econometrics
Peijie Wang

Macroeconomics for Developing Countries, second edition
Raghbendra Jha

Advanced Mathematical Economics
Rakesh Vohra

Advanced Econometric Theory
John S. Chipman

Understanding Macroeconomic Theory
John M. Barron, Bradley T. Ewing and Gerald J. Lynch

Regional Economics
Roberta Capello

Mathematical Finance
Core theory, problems and statistical algorithms
Nikolai Dokuchaev

Applied Health Economics
Andrew M. Jones, Nigel Rice, Teresa Bago d'Uva and Silvia Balia

Information Economics
Urs Birchler and Monika Bütler

Financial Econometrics, second edition
Peijie Wang

Development Finance
Debates, dogmas and new directions
Stephen Spratt

Culture and Economics
On values, economics and international business
Eelke de Jong

Culture and Economics

On values, economics and international business

Eelke de Jong

Routledge
Taylor & Francis Group
LONDON AND NEW YORK

First published 2009
by Routledge
2 Park Square, Milton Park, Abingdon, Oxon OX14 4RN

Simultaneously published in the USA and Canada
by Routledge
270 Madison Avenue, New York, NY 10016

Routledge is an imprint of the Taylor & Francis Group, an informa business

Typeset in 10/12pt Times New Roman by
Graphicraft Limited, Hong Kong
Printed and bound in Great Britain by
CPI Antony Rowe, Chippenham, Wiltshire

British Library Cataloguing in Publication Data
A catalogue record for this book is available from the British Library

Library of Congress Cataloging-in-Publication Data
Jong, Eelke de, 1955–
Culture and economics : on values, economics and international business / Eelke de Jong.
p. cm.
ISBN 978-0-415-43861-2 (hardback) — ISBN 978-0-415-43888-9 (pbk.)
1. Culture—Economic aspects. I. Title.
HM621.J67 2009
306.3—dc22
2008043617

ISBN10: 0-415-43861-6 (hbk)
ISBN10: 0-415-43888-8 (pbk)

ISBN13: 978-0-415-43861-2 (hbk)
ISBN13: 978-0-415-43888-9 (pbk)

Dedicated to my wife Ike

Contents

List of figures and tables

Figures

Tables

Preface

This book results from research and teaching activities during the last decade. It started with my research on the relationship between independent central banks and inflation stabilization. I wondered why these two are connected as is found in the empirical literature. In my view there should be a common, hidden third factor which can explain this relation. When dealing with this issue, I read a book by Geert Hofstede. His dimension of Uncertainty Avoidance is so much related to the disadvantages of high inflation as these are described in the literature, that I thought, maybe culture is the third factor I am looking for. This resulted in my first research project on the influence of culture: De Jong (2002). After some years Radislav Semenov joined me. He had defended a thesis on cultural dimensions as major explanatory variables for differences in governance structures in industrialized countries. Jointly we have written some papers on culture, corporate governance structures and financial systems. In a later stage Robbert Maseland was appointed as a PhD student in my chair. He focused on the Asian values debate, in which one argues that the high levels of growth in parts of East Asia can be attributed to Asian values, such as thrift and hard work. Radislav and I used existing economic theory for finding plausible relations and tested these by cross-country regression analysis, using Hofstede's cultural dimensions. Robbert's first degree is in Third World Studies, which uses insights from sociology and anthropology. Consequently, his approach stands in the tradition of anthropology. As a team the group thus contained a nice diversity of approaches which were complementary to each other.

After a view years we started a course entitled Culture and Economic Behaviour for students of the Master in Economics at Radboud University Nijmegen. Since no adequate book was available, we arranged this course around a series of papers, book chapters and lecture notes. An advantage of this set-up is that it exposes students to texts from academic journals, one of the objectives of the Masters program. A disadvantage, however, is the lack of a systematic overview of all aspects of the field (history, theory, empirical methods, and applications). Existing books with culture and economics in their title appeared to be a reflection of the particular author's research and do not provide an overview of the subject. Hence, we decided to write a book which would cover most aspects of culture and economic analysis. Moreover, we wanted to use the book for teaching students the possibilities and limitations of various methods, put forward some critical remarks on the existing literature, and offer suggestions for future research. During the academic year 2006/2007 parts of our envisaged book were used for the Master's course and an interdisciplinary Honours course, Culture and Economic Behaviour. In the meantime the team expanded with Sjoerd Beugelsdijk, who has written a thesis and several academic papers about social capital, trust, and international business.

This book has at least three aims. First, it briefly sketches the history of culture and economics: from the role of values and morality in the work of Adam Smith and in that of many authors during later centuries, and the gradual disappearance from the economics literature during the first part of the twentieth century to its return to the economics discourse at the beginning of the 1990s. The second aim is to provide an overview of the state of the art in culture and economics both with respect to contents and methodology. Finally, the discussion of the literature is used for assessing various methods and providing suggestions for future research.

This book is aimed at all readers interested in economics and culture, and in particular at researchers and students, who want to obtain an overview of the field. Hence, the book is well suited for specialized courses in culture and economic behaviour, both at the intermediate and graduate level. Moreover, suggestions for future research in the last chapter may inspire researchers.

I would like to seize this opportunity to thank some people for their contribution to this book. First of all, I am grateful to students and colleagues with whom I cooperated throughout the years on this subject for sharing ideas and criticism, especially those who authored a chapter of this book (Sjoerd Beugelsdijk and Robbert Maseland) and those who co-authored papers on culture and economics (Radislav Semenov, Roger Smeets, and Jeroen Smits). A number of people commented on previous drafts of individual chapters or provided advice on some topics: Frank Bohn, Maureen Lankhuizen, Esther-Mirjam Sent, Martin van der Velde, Bob Reinalda, and Bert-Jan Verbeek. Lisa Berntsen's and Koen van der Heiden's assistance with some tedious work such as checking the references is gratefully acknowledged. I am also grateful to The Nijmegen Institute for Mission Studies and, in particular, its director Frans Wijssen, for providing a 'hiding place' during the summer of 2008, so that I could work on the book without being interrupted by administrative duties. A Replacement Grant (No. 400-07-711) by the Netherlands Organization for Scientific Research (NWO) is gratefully acknowledged.

Finally, I would like to express my heartfelt gratitude to my wife Ike for her unwavering support during the years. In the spirit of this book's theme, we share a common culture, which has added significant meaning to our joint endeavours.

Malden, The Netherlands
September 2008

Abbreviations

2SLS	Two Stage Least Squares
CAPM	Capital Asset Pricing Model
CD	Cultural Distance
CEEC	Central and East European Countries
CEO	Corporate Executive Officer
DDR	Deutsche Demokratische Republik
ECB	European Central Bank
ESS	European Social Survey
EU	European Union
EVS	European Values Survey
FDI	Foreign Direct Investments
FLMP	Female Labour Market Participation
GDP	Gross Domestic Product
GLOBE	Global Leadership and Organizational Behaviour Effectiveness Research Program
HDI	Human Development Index
ICAPM	International Capital Asset Pricing Model
IDV	Individualism
ILO	International Labour Office
ISSP	International Social Survey Program
IV	Instrumental Variables
LETS	Local Exchange Trade System
LTO	Long Term Orientation
MAS	Masculinity
MNE	Multinational Enterprise
OLS	Ordinary Least Squares
PDI	Power Distance Index
UAI	Uncertainty Avoidance Index
UBN	Unsatisfied Basic Needs
UN	United Nations
USA	United States of America
WVS	World Values Survey

Chapter 1

Introduction

Since the early 1990s culture has entered economic analysis again, whereas it was totally absent from mainstream economics during most of the second half of the twentieth century. At that time the dominant view in economics was based on rational behaviour, and did not take the context of the decision-making process into account. The disappointing results of this approach as well as developments in the world economy (the Asian miracle and the transition of previously centrally planned economies into market economies) triggered an awareness of the relevance of the context in which people make decisions. Of course there has always been an undercurrent in economics which emphasized the importance of the context for decision making. Adherents of behavioural economics, with researchers such as Herbert Simon, Richard Nelson, Sidney Winter, and later Daniel Kahneman and Amos Tversky are examples in this respect. Moreover, other disciplines of social science studied the influence of morals and attitudes towards economic behaviour and economic success. Examples are Banfield's (1958) study on the moral basis of the backward society in Southern Italy and McClelland's (1961) book on the role of achievement motivation in persons' and countries' economic success.

Within economics the urgency of considering culture as an explanatory factor was first felt in two fields where researchers were confronted with cultural differences namely development economics and international business.[1] Since the majority of the researchers studying the development of underdeveloped countries are citizens from industrialized countries they are easily confronted with differences between their countries of birth and the societies they investigate. The larger these differences, the more likely researchers are inclined to explain them by culture (see DiMaggio 1994: 33). The lack of progress in economic development is thus easily seen as resulting from a backward culture, and unexpected economic progress is related to specific values of a foreign culture. Southern Italy has been treated by researchers as an example of the former and Japan (and South East Asia in general) as an example of the latter. This easily leads to the use of culture as an explanation of last resort; explaining what the researcher cannot understand: a remnant. In Chapter 3 we briefly deal with this use of culture. For now it suffices to mention that in the 1990s an increasing number of academics and practitioners became aware of the importance of cultural differences for investigating foreign societies or intervening therein. Within the World Bank this understanding leads to initiatives such as the World Faith Development Dialogue and the Bank's Culture and Development Program.

International business scholars were among the first to acknowledge the relevance of cultural differences for international transactions.[2] The research of the role of culture in international business was greatly enhanced by the publication of Hofstede's (1980) study on the international differences in work-related values. In this study Hofstede analyzes a questionnaire's answers on work-related values from employees of IBM in 40 countries. From these answers he derives four cultural dimensions. Subsequently, these dimensions have been used for analyzing the success and failure of the entry mode of multinational enterprises: whether to start a new activity in a foreign country by means of a new factory, a joint venture or a subsidiary. Later an index summarizing cultural differences – the Kogut-Singh index – and a measure of mutual trust between inhabitants of different countries were used to explain bilateral trade flows, a topic traditionally more intensively studied by international economists than by researchers in international business studies.

Later, cultural explanations were offered for several topics in economics. Cultural dimensions of both Hofstede and Schwartz were used to explain cross-country differences in, among other things, labour market regulation (Black 1999, 2001a, 2001b, and 2005), financial systems (De Jong and Semenov 2004, Kwok and Tadesse 2006, Licht *et al.* 2001), ownership patterns (De Jong and Semenov 2006a), and the degree of central bank independence (De Jong 2002). Putnam's (1993) study on the relevance of generalized trust for the working of democracy in Italy triggered an interest in the effects of trust on the functioning and performance of economies. This research was greatly enhanced by the release of several waves of the World Values Survey and the European Values Survey, which contain the well-known question on generalized trust, which reads: 'generally speaking, would you say that most people can be trusted or that you can't be too careful in dealing with people?'. The answers to these questions have been used for explaining differences in economic growth (Knack and Keefer 1997), the quality of government (Tabellini 2008b), and several other issues to be discussed in Chapter 8. The increasing interest in culture is also visible in the more prominent place the topic plays at international conferences. At the 2007 Annual Meeting of the European Economic Association, for example, the presidential address, the Alfred Marshall lecture and the Joseph Schumpeter lecture, all dealt with culture or related issues.

Despite this growing interest in the role of culture in economics, to my knowledge no book is available which contains an overview of the subject. Jones (2006) provides an historical overview but does not discuss the literature mentioned in the previous paragraph and other studies using quantitative measures. Other books only deal with a particular topic, which could be a particular sector (Austen 2003), or a particular measure of culture (trust in Bornschier 2005). The aim of this book is to fill this gap and to provide an overview and critical assessment of the literature.

This book's structure

The remaining chapters are organized in four groups: the history of culture and economics (Chapters 2 and 3), methods and methodology (Chapter 4), applications (Chapters 5–9), and concluding remarks (Chapter 10). The history part deals with the departure of culture from economic science and its re-emergence. We explain the importance of culture in economics by developments in economic science and by changes over time in the economic and political environment. Chapter 2 sketches the role culture, ethics and morals played in the writing of economists from Adam Smith onwards. In the nineteenth and twentieth century economics moved towards more formal approaches. This led to a view of economics as economizing: agents are assumed to optimize an objective function subject to constraints. Intangible factors such as culture are left out of the analysis. The success of the formal approach is most likely partly due to the success of the use of formal analysis for solving logistic problems during World War II. Subsequently, the intellectual climate resulting from the Cold War prevented critical investigations into the diversity of the market economy and thus into the appropriateness of this one-size-fits-all assumption. Chapter 3 sketches the developments which led to a re-emergence of culture in economics. Once again attention is paid to the forces from the inside of economics as a scientific discipline and developments in the political economic circumstances. The view of economics based on optimizing agents appeared to be unsuccessful in explaining actual behaviour, and thus gave rise to approaches which take the context, including culture, into account. Such a move was also greatly enhanced by the availability of large cross-country databases on values and attitudes. Moreover, the Asian Values debate, the fall of the Iron Curtain, and the failure of the one-size-fits-all approach of development organizations, were all events which triggered the idea that values could be of importance for economic success. Chapter 3 ends with a description of the way culture has re-entered economic analysis. Three versions of the Culture and Economics approach can be distinguished: culture as explaining the residual, culture as constraints on economic behaviour and culture as preferences. The latter two approaches regard intergenerational transmission of values as the most important mechanism by which values are formed.

The part on methods and methodology (Chapter 4) deals with methodological considerations and methods used in empirical research of the relation between economics and culture. Methodological issues dealt with are: the definition of values used; means by which one can derive empirical measures of values; and the much debated issue whether countries are the appropriate units for empirical studies on culture and economics. Surveys are by far the methods most frequently used for obtaining information on values. Chapter 4, therefore, discusses various aspects related to conducting surveys, such as: the choice of the sample (matched or representative); the way questions are asked; the language used, and the methods available for enhancing the similarity of the questions' contents across different languages. Many studies make use of the cultural dimensions derived from the surveys by other researchers, especially, Hofstede and Schwartz and the recently completed GLOBE-project. Appendix 1 summarizes these studies and discusses their main differences. It also briefly describes two important measures of values derived from the World Values Survey: the two cultural dimensions derived by Inglehart and the trust-variable.

This book's main part concerns applications of the methods described in Chapter 4, and consists of Chapters 5 through 9. Intergenerational transmission has been argued to be the most important way by which individuals form their values during the first twenty years of their lives. If correct, the preferences and behaviour of second generation immigrants will partly reflect the attitudes typical for their parents' country of origin. For the United States some datasets include information about the country of origin of the respondents' parents. Chapter 5 starts with a review of the results of this epistemological approach. The rest of the chapter is devoted to cross-country studies of the relation between culture and institutions for the financial sector, labour markets, and welfare systems. These results are used for investigating whether the resulting national system of institutional arrangements is a coherent one: are the institutions of each subsystem complementary to those of the other subsystems and are they correlated with the same set of values? Meanwhile we discuss two methodological issues: the selection of countries in the sample and the possibility of a changing pattern between culture and institutions over time.

Chapter 6 is devoted to studies on the relation between culture and economic performance: economic growth and income per capita. Two themes stand out in this chapter. First, we consider the role of politicians in shaping public opinion in such a way that it favours their policy. Often these politicians refer to a 'golden' period in the past. Second, attention is paid to the endogeneity problem between culture and economic performance and the way economists deal with it.

Whereas Chapters 5 and 6 have considered various ways of approximating culture, Chapters 7 and 8 each deals with a particular proxy of culture. Chapter 7 considers religion, which is by many authors considered a very important element of culture, in particular for pre-industrialized societies. Issues dealt with are the supposed claim by Weber that Protestant values stimulate economic growth, the discussion through history about an interest ban both in Christianity and Islam, Islamic economics and identity, and whether the values associated with a particular religion are so homogenous that religion can be used as a proxy of culture. The historical study of Biblical and Christian views on paying interest forms a nice opportunity to shed light on the causality between culture, in the sense of values, and economic circumstances.

Social capital, including trust, is the other cultural variable to which we pay extra attention. Both these concepts are widely used in empirical studies on culture and economic performance. Chapter 8 argues that it is necessary to break down the concept of social capital into two levels. At the aggregate level social capital is deployed as a cultural construct related to norms of cooperation. At the individual level social capital is treated in a social-structural way related to networks. We study the cause and effect structure and the internal dynamics on both levels of analysis.

The previous chapters dealt mainly or exclusively with differences between societies. Chapter 9 focuses on the effects of cultural differences between societies on international activities. The main hypothesis in that chapter is that unfamiliarity with the working of formal institutions and unease with informal procedures (culture) hamper international transactions. Studies are reviewed which consider the effect of cultural differences in international trade, foreign direct investments, the entry mode of multinational enterprises, portfolio investments, migration, and political cooperation. Besides these various international transactions, we discuss the appropriateness of proxies of cultural differences between countries, such as the widely used Kogut-Singh index, difference in languages and genetic differences.

Chapter 10 contains the concluding remarks and some guidelines for future research in the field. One of the conclusions is that whereas in some other disciplines culture is a very broad concept, in economics culture is understood as values, which according to many definitions of culture constitute the core element, but just the core, of culture. Hence, the books subtitle: On values, economics and international business. The next section discusses these broad and narrow definitions of culture.

Definitions of culture

This section presents various definitions of culture, their use in social sciences and potential relevance for economic analysis. The American anthropologists Kroeber and Kluckhohn, for example, published 160 definitions of culture (Bodley 1994). These definitions can be very broad in the sense of containing almost all aspects of social behaviour. Anthropologists tend to use a broad definition of culture. The nineteenth-century British anthropologist Edward Tylor (1958 [1871]: 1) writes: 'Culture or civilization, taken in its wide ethnographic sense, is that complex whole which includes knowledge, belief, art, morals, law, custom, and any other capabilities and habits acquired by man as member of society'. Another broad definition can be found in The American Heritage Dictionary of the English Language (2000: 4th edn updated in 2003), where culture is defined as

> (a) the totality of socially transmitted behaviour patterns, arts, beliefs, institutions, and all other products of human work and thought; (b) these patterns, traits, and products considered as the expression of a particular period, class, community, or population (such as the Edwardian culture, Japanese culture, the culture of poverty); (c) these patterns, traits, and products considered with respect to a particular category, such as a field subject, or mode of expression (such as religious culture in the Middle Ages, musical culture, oral culture); and (d) the predominating attitudes and behavior that characterize the functioning of a group or organization.

These definitions have in common that they refer to the entire social system; the 'complex whole' and the 'totality'. By stressing the entirety, these definitions lack focus and become open-ended. If the entire system is a unit, can subsystems be distinguished and if so by what criterion? How are these aspects expected to be related? Can the different cultures be compared and in which sense? This type of definition easily leads to the creation of different categories, as the list of different cultures in the second definition illustrates. But these categories as such do not give any direction for explanation. In my view, a problematic feature of these definitions is that they contain both the possible sources of behaviour (e.g. beliefs), the behaviour itself and its results. In a similar mood the famous anthropologist Geertz writes 'They [his essays] all argue, sometimes explicitly, more often merely through the particular analysis they develop, for a narrowed, specialized, and so I imagine, theoretically more powerful concept of culture to replace E.B. Tylor's famous "most complex whole"' (Geertz 1993: 4).

More narrow concepts of culture still vary with respect to the issues explicitly mentioned as culture's elements. According to Geertz himself, (1993: 89) culture 'denotes an historically transmitted pattern of meanings embodied in symbols, a system of inherited conceptions expressed in symbolic forms by means of which men communicate, perpetuate, and develop their knowledge about and attitudes towards life'. A similar definition is penned by Kluckhohn, who writes that 'culture consists in patterned ways of thinking, feeling and reacting, acquired and transmitted mainly in symbols, constituting the distinctive achievements of human groups, including their embodiments in artifacts: the essential core of culture consist of traditional (i.e. historically derived and selected) ideas and especially their attached values' (Kluckhohn 1951: 86, n. 5). These two definitions explicitly mention symbols as part of culture. Kluckhohn explicitly mentions values, which is central in some other definitions of culture. Boyd and Richerson (1985: 2), for example, describe culture as 'the transmission from one generation to the next, via teaching and imitation, of knowledge, values, and other factors that influence behavior.' Hofstede (2001: 9), whose cultural dimensions are frequently used in empirical studies on culture and economics, derives a concise version of Kluckhohn's definition by treating culture as 'the collective programming of the mind that distinguishes the members of one group or category of people from another'. Finally, Inglehart's definition explicitly introduces the idea that culture is complementary to the directly observable aspects of society. It reads '(b)y culture, we refer to the *subjective* aspect of a society's institutions: the beliefs, values, knowledge, and skills that have been *internalized* by the people of a given society, complementing their external systems of coercion and exchange' (Inglehart 1997: 15).

These more narrow definitions have some common features: i) values are essential, ii) they refer to a group, iii) they refer to a trend or pattern, and iv) the cultural elements are humanly devised aspects that are transmitted from generation to generation. All definitions refer explicitly or implicitly to values. In addition to values, symbols, symbolic forms, and other factors are mentioned as elements of culture. Hofstede (2001: 11) has visualized the relationship between values and the other elements of culture by an 'onion diagram', in which the core consists of values and the outer layers of, what he calls, practices: rituals, heroes and symbols. Values refer to 'a broad tendency to prefer certain states of affairs over others' (ibid: 5). They can be held by individuals and by collectivities. Culture refers to a collectivity, and thus to collectively held values. Rituals are collective actions that are technically unnecessary for achieving the desired ends. Heroes are persons who possess characteristics that are highly prized in a culture and thus serve as models for behaviour. Symbols are words gestures, pictures and objects that carry often complex meanings recognized only by those who share the culture.[3]

The reference to a group illustrates that culture is a feature of a collectivity and not of an individual. 'Culture is public because meaning is' Geertz (1993: 12). The group is unspecified and can in principle be any group: a nation, a firm, a particular department, an occupation, an ethnical or religious group, etc. The culture of each of these types of groups can differ considerably. Hofstede (2001: Chapter 8), for example, reports that the features of organizations' culture differ considerably from those of national cultures. Whereas national cultures differ primarily with respect to their values, organizational cultures appear to differ primarily in their practices. Hofstede and co-authors suggest that these differences can be ascribed to the fact that people enter organizations when they are adults and nations at the time of their birth. Adults have already acquired particular attitudes and values which are difficult to change, whereas babies' mindsets have still to be developed. A survey of research on cultures of organizations, social classes, nations, and poor consumers is given by DiMaggio (1994). An individual can of course belong to different groups, a nation, occupation, etc. In many studies nations are taken as the group to be analyzed. This practice has been heavily criticized as neglecting different subcultures within a nation. In Chapter 4 we deal more extensively with this criticism.

A second feature of culture is that it refers to a trend or dominant belief or perception within a group. This suggests that the members of the group can have different opinions. Culture focuses on the trend, the mean or average opinion. Such a procedure suggests that every member has an equal weight in the formation of the group's trend. Of course it could be that some dominant members, political leaders for example, have a greater say in the formation of opinions than ordinary members. In those cases it is necessary to consider the power distribution within the group (see also Chapters 6 and 7).

Finally, all definitions of culture refer to a humanly designed phenomenon which is transmitted from generation to generation. Hence, it is not created by nature and it also does not result from physical constraints (DiMaggio 1994: 28). Culture refers to the learned aspects of life. Younger generations learn these values, beliefs and traditions from the older ones. In the section Culture as Preferences in Chapter 3 we deal more extensively with this intergenerational transmission.

Culture is not equal to identity. Identity refers to people's feelings about belonging to a particular group. The group identity consists of cultural practices and not of sharing common values. People sharing common values can even claim to have different identities and fight each other. Examples are groups within a country; the Flemish and the Walloons in Belgium, and religious groups in Northern Ireland. An identity needs another group. It refers as much to the group one does *not* belong to as the group to which one is regarded as being a member. Particular persons can have different identities depending on the situation they are in, and thus in another group they can feel distinguished from other groups, even the one they were in previously. So, within The Netherlands, I am a Frisian (born in the province of Friesland), and I am certainly not from Holland (two other provinces). When in Europe I am a Dutchman, and it is OK if you think I am from Holland, because many foreigners use Holland when referring to The Netherlands. When in the United States I can understand if you think I am from a small European country (which could be Holland or Denmark). Within a group of persons from different professions I am an economist, etc.

An important difference between the authors concerns the aim of the cultural analysis. On the one hand anthropologists, of whom Geertz is a good representative, see their work as interpretive; in search of meaning. An anthropological study is only one of many interpretations and not always the first one; the people living in a culture always possess the first order interpretation of their culture (Geertz 1993: 15). These researchers are explicitly not looking for laws. In contrast, many authors in the field of Culture and Economics are searching for relationships between culture, economic institutions and activities. Regression analysis is a frequently used tool for finding patterns between empirical measures of culture on the one hand and those of institutions and economic performance on the other. These authors are explicitly searching for generally valid laws.

DiMaggio (1994: 27 and 28) distinguishes two forms of culture, which will prove to be very useful when discussing the relation between culture and institutions. The first form of culture is constitutive (categories, scripts, etc.) and enables transactions by providing understanding and meaning. The idea is that people cannot enter into transactions unless participants know (understand) each other and share a common understanding of the objects about which they communicate. The other form of culture is regulatory. It consists of norms, values, and routines, which constrain the individuals' freedom of action. Consequently, individuals know the behaviour they can expect from others. Since norms limit selfish behaviour mutual trust can be built, and thus reduce transaction costs.

In the preceding text we have discussed various definitions of culture, their features and effects. Although there are fewer definitions of economics, the other central issue of this book, two views on economics can be distinguished. The first one focuses on the subject studied by economics. An example of such a definition is given in the quote: '(b)y the economy, I refer to institutions and relations of production, exchange and consumption' (DiMaggio 1994: 28). The other definition refers to the method supposed to be used in economic analysis. Then economics is the social science which assumes optimization by economic agents. Economics applied in the latter tradition assumes general rules to be valid all over the world. The analysis does not consider the context within which decisions are made. Since culture is about the context, culture does not enter such an analysis. The next two chapters describe the development of culture in economic science.

Chapter 2

A history of thought about culture and economy

Robbert Maseland

This chapter attempts to provide a history of thinking about the relation between culture and the economy. As we will show, any history of thought about the relation between culture and the economy is also a history of the relation between two versions of economics. Ever since the late nineteenth century, there have always been (at least) two economic sciences (Polanyi 1944). One is the formal economics that we all know from our studies, focused on marginal analysis of individual choices. This is economics in the sense of the study of economizing. The other is the substantive tradition in economic science, focusing on the study of the economy: those segments of society that ensure production, consumption and distribution of goods and services. Whereas culture has no role to play in the former, it has always been a topic of interest in the latter. The fate of culture in economic thought is therefore inextricably tied up with the continuing struggle for dominance between those two paradigms. As long as 'substantive economics' was on top, in the form of the institutionalism of authors like Veblen, Commons, or Galbraith, for example, culture could be sure to receive attention. Wherever formal, neoclassical economics reigned, culture disappeared.

This chapter tells the story of this continuing clash about the inclusion of the social and cultural context in economic thought, starting from the late nineteenth century until the current revival of interest in culture and economy. The second section starts out with the work of the man usually credited as the father of the culture and economy debate, Max Weber. The subsequent section then goes on to discuss some of the predecessors of this debate. Thereafter we discuss the emergence of economics in the formal sense. The next section discusses American Institutionalism, for a time a leading paradigm in (substantive) economics. The chapter ends with a description of the onslaught of formal economics after World War II, which sealed the fate for a role of culture in economic thought.

The birth of cultural economics

The start of the debate about culture and economy is usually attributed to Max Weber (1864–1920). Weber, who held chairs in economics at Freiburg

University and the University of Heidelberg, was a leading figure in the intellectual climate of early twentieth century Germany. He has had an enormous influence on the social sciences that is felt even today. Weber is best remembered – at least among economists – for his seminal work 'The Protestant Ethic and the Spirit of Capitalism' published in German in two parts in the *Archiv für Sozialwissenschaft und Sozialpolitik* 1904–1905. In his essay, the development of the economic system of capitalism in Northwest Europe and North America is linked to ethical principles found in (certain sub-branches of) Protestantism.

According to Weber, Protestantism encouraged purposeful, worldly activity. Rather than moving away from the world – a tendency present in many other religions such as Catholicism and Buddhism – Protestants acquired the notion that society was imbued with a God-given rationality. Each person had been assigned a task in this rational structure. The idea of work as a calling is thus typical for the Protestant ethic. Being called to a certain role in society, performing this role well was a way of honouring God and his creation. Hard, purposeful work and the acquisition of wealth were encouraged by Protestant ethics. Enjoyment of one's wealth, however, was not. Wealth could all too easily cause people to become idle and indolent. Therefore, wealth had to be invested in worldly, purposeful causes, allowing people to respond to their calling even better. The combination of the idea that it is good to work hard to acquire worldly riches and the notion that it is bad to consume and enjoy this wealth was conducive to capital accumulation. The step from such ethics towards a secularized spirit of capitalism was only a small one. According to Weber, it is this spirit that has set Northwest Europe and North America apart and has turned them into capitalist societies.

The idea of a relation between the moral values present in a society and its economy has been enthusiastically received by many scholars, who have pursued research projects along this line ever since (e.g. Tawney 1962 [1926], Granato, Inglehart and Leblang 1996, Harrisson 1992, Harrisson and Huntington 2000). Part of the appeal of Weber's thesis was that it seemed to provide a counterweight against the historical materialist approach of Marx (more about this below). Weber has often been interpreted as a proponent of the view that ideas shape material conditions rather than the other way around, as Marx wanted it (although Weber's true argument was a lot more complex than that (Giddens 1974)). To many a liberal and Christian scholar, this was a decidedly more attractive position.

Another part of the appeal of the Weber thesis is that the story of Protestant origins of the capitalist society could easily be interpreted by lesser minds as proof of the superiority of Protestant religion and culture. Thus, the thesis entered as explanation and justification of economic and political inequality in the world. Non-Protestant societies were poorer, because they had the wrong religions and values. Catholics within Northwest Europe were backward for the same reasons. Societies outside Europe and North America, characterized by religions and ethics that were even further removed from the Protestant ideal, were doomed if left to their own, ill-informed ideas and values. Administration by enlightened, Protestant colonial masters was thus necessary, for their own benefit. Such ideas motivated many colonial administrators (read E.M. Forster's *A Passage to India* or Multatuli's *Max Havelaar*, for example, or the 'benevolent assimilation proclamation' by President William McKinley upon the colonizing of the Philippines by the US in 1898[1]). In such a context of perceived superiority of Northwest European culture and religion, cruder interpretations of the Weber thesis blended in well.

It should be noted that such ideas were not limited to colonial administrations. The Weber thesis has been expropriated by many an early nationalist movement in colonized societies as well. In this line of thought, the idea that (Protestant) Western ethics and culture was superior and responsible for the political and economic dominance of Western powers was taken over. However, rather than accepting these cultural differences as an immutable given, nationalists such as Za'ba in British Malaya saw in this a battle cry for moral and cultural change of their own people.[2] Only by becoming more like their colonial rulers, could colonized societies grow strong enough to stand up and gain independence. Even today, such ideas continue to influence the debate; it has been argued that much of what has become known as 'Asian Values' in recent decades is in fact little more than a radicalized Protestant ethic (Lee and Ackerman 1997: 36). The explanation for East Asian economic success is thought to lie in their being actually more Protestant than Protestantism. Weber's thesis thus continues to frame much thinking about culture and development (Alatas 2002).

That is not to say, of course, that such ideas can be found directly in the work of Weber himself. For one thing, it should be noted that Weber's thesis is not about a relation between moral values and economic growth or development. *The Protestant Ethic and the Spirit of Capitalism* deals with the historical origins of a particular economic system (capitalism), without an assessment of the pros and cons of this system. There is no mention of capitalism being good for development or growth. There is even less mention of Protestants doing better than members of other religions once capitalism has taken hold in society. Little in *The Protestant Ethic* supports the interpretation that capitalism is confined to Protestant parts of the world.[3] There is only a historical explanation of why capitalism emerged first in Northwest Europe and North America. Weber is perhaps the starting point for the debate about culture and economy, but it has been a misinterpreted Weber that inspired many of the contributions to the field.

Ancestors of cultural economics

Max Weber's ideas about the relation between ethics and economy as a subject for empirical inquiry were perhaps novel, but the connection between morality, culture and economy itself was not. Weber wrote within a tradition of thought that defined economics as science of production, consumption, and distribution. Since social and cultural considerations had an impact on the organization of these issues, they were included in the analysis. Economics was not confined (yet) to the study of the behaviour of *homo oeconomicus*. Morality, culture, beliefs, and religion were not thought to lie outside the domain of the economic scholar.

This substantive tradition in economic thought goes back to Adam Smith, seen by many as the founding father of economic science. In his time, Smith was less known for his thoughts about the economy than for his views on morality. Almost two decades before he published his famous *The Wealth of Nations* (1981 [1776]), Smith had made his name with a book titled *The Theory of Moral Sentiments* (1976 [1759]). In this book, Smith argued that the force of mutual sympathy was what held society together. Because people are naturally inclined to put themselves in each others position, they will not ruthlessly take advantage of each other but behave in an orderly, moral manner. Inborn inhibitions felt by individuals thus result in a peaceful and progressive society. That implies that we need no external source of moral authority to ensure peace and order; people's inclinations towards mutual sympathy are normally sufficient. In this respect, *The Theory of Moral Sentiments* can be interpreted as a defence of individualism. It showed that individualism would not result in war of everyone against everyone, but in a morally developed society.

The Wealth of Nations (1981 [1776]) carries much the same message. In this book, Smith also argued that the inclinations of individuals were enough to ensure a beneficially functioning society. Now, however, the focus lay not on a moral but an economic order. Smith's famous 'invisible hand' was an organizing mechanism that sprang from the limitedly self-interested behaviour of individuals. It ensured that, if individuals were left to pursue their own interests, wealth was created for society as a whole. In other words, the 'invisible hand' of *The Wealth of Nations* performed much the same role as mutual sympathy in the *Theory of Moral Sentiments*. It legitimized and propagated a society in which individuals were left free to act upon their own ideas and inclinations, rather than being controlled by authorities from above. Seen in this way, *The Wealth of Nations* cannot be seen as a book purely about economics in the sense that we use the word now. *The Wealth of Nations* envisages an entire social order, including motivations, moral inclinations and social institutions. The discipline it founded was called political economy – but, from the present perspective, it could also be called moral economy or even cultural economy. Economics in the sense of the formal analysis of rational decision making by individuals it is not. Even the title of the book indicates that economic science is interpreted substantively here – it is not about how individuals make choices, it is about how societies produce wealth. There is no clear and fundamental separation of moral, political and economic behaviour in Smith.

This substantive view of political economy as a discipline naturally covering social institutions and morality also informs the works of Karl Marx. In his magnum opus *Das Kapital* (1978 [1867]), Marx analyzes the capitalist market economy comprehensively, from a historical perspective. As in Smith's work, the focus lies on the historical emergence analysis of the economic system he saw before his eyes – capitalism – rather than on the study of a de-historicized type of individual behaviour. To Marx, the essence of this system is that it is geared towards capital accumulation. Capital is used to produce more capital. This occurs through the exploitation of labour, which is made possible by the fact that capitalists have a monopoly on the means of production. For the right to use the capitalists' machines, tools and factories, labourers have to give up part of the value they produce. The way in which the capitalist system is structured thus creates a conflict between labourers and capitalists.

To Marx, the object of economic analysis is the entire system of relations that make up this basic structure of exploitation of labour by capital. Hence, ideas, beliefs, and social–political institutions also play a role. This role, however, is secondary. In Marx's view they are part of a judicial and political superstructure of society that is built upon a material structure. The material structure of capitalism – privileged control over means of production by capitalists – determines the superstructure. The state, for example, is seen as an extension of the capitalist class, defending property rights and the capitalists' exclusive control over capital. Since structure determines superstructure, the evolution of the mode of material production is mirrored by changes in beliefs, values and institutions (Marx 1978 [1867]: section 1, footnote 33). This pattern is called the principle of *historical materialism*. It is this idea that the Weber thesis has been positioned against.

The principle of historical materialism has been adopted by many Marxist scholars, perhaps most prominently by Antonio Gramsci. Like Weber, Gramsci focused on the role of ideas and beliefs more than Marx had done. Unlike Weber, Gramsci took over the Marxist notion that ideas and beliefs were reflecting and supportive of the political economic structures in society. He argued that the economic oppression by capitalist classes infiltrated intellectual thought and ideology, causing intellectuals to develop a discourse that legitimized and supported capitalism. As a result, violent class struggle could be averted and dominance by capitalist classes could be maintained. Rather than sources of independent and objective reflection, to Gramsci intellectuals were an instrumental part of the system of capitalist exploitation. The entire system of domination, economic, political, and intellectual, is what Gramsci called *hegemony* (Gramsci 1980 [1977]). The idea of hegemony can be found in thinking about culture and economy until today. Especially with regard to economics, the view that much theory is little more than a justification of capitalism rather than a critical reflection upon it has continued to be expressed regularly (see for example the contribution of Seligman in American Economic Association 1899, Bourdieu 1998a, 1998b).

Even more important than the idea of historical materialism itself is the fact that to Marx, and even more so in Smith, beliefs, values and institutions were part of the economic system and hence part of any economic analysis. There was no explicit reference to a relation between culture and the economy (though Gramsci, writing in the early twentieth century, comes close) because the two were not considered to be clearly different issues. Economics dealt with the analysis of the economy, and values, norms, beliefs were naturally part of that.

Sibling rivalry

If Weber worked in a tradition in which what we now call culture was an indispensable part of the object of economic analysis, what reasons do we have to call him the founding father of cultural economics? What made *The Protestant Ethic* different from *The Wealth of Nations* or *Das Kapital*? The answer to that question is: the context. When Smith wrote, social and cultural factors were naturally part of economics – if there was such a clearly demarcated field already in place. At the time of Weber's famous essay, a new interpretation of economics had emerged that placed culture firmly outside the object of economic analysis. Because there was a clearly demarcated field of 'economics' now, of which culture was no part, for the first time it began to make sense to talk explicitly of a relation between culture *and* economics. Before that, the thought that culture and economy were two different things had not entered the scholarly mind.

The birth of formal economics

What was this new conception of economics and where did it come from? The marginalist revolution, as it was called, sought to make economics into a formal science, with the maximization of subjective value as its central object. Not social structures, the production of wealth, or the exploitation of labour were the focus of economics: it was to be about the satisfaction of subjective preferences of individuals. This allowed formalization and the use of mathematical methods. From a few assumptions about how individuals make choices to pursue their self-interest, one could deduce insights applicable to any time and place. This kind of economics was thus not about the economy, as a specific system of production and consumption in time anymore. It was about economizing – how individuals could optimally weigh costs and benefits and maximize subjective value.

In Britain, this new, version of economics was pushed by Francis Ysidro Edgeworth, William Stanley Jevons and Alfred Marshall. Probably the most important proponent of this new, marginalist interpretation of economic science was not part of this Anglo-Saxon group of neoclassical thinkers, however. It was Austrian Carl Menger who did perhaps the most to develop and defend the principles of formal economics. The reason for this is that Menger, working in the German language setting, was up against a very powerful bloc of economists vehemently opposed to this formal interpretation of economics – the German Historical School. Menger was forced to develop the methodological defence of formal economics explicitly and thoroughly.

The debate between Menger and the proponents of the German Historical School, most notably Gustav von Schmoller, is called the *Methodenstreit*. In this debate, German historicists held that economists ought to study historical documents and statistics in order to derive insights about economic mechanisms from them. Much like classical economists such as Smith, they saw as the economic object a historical system of production in time. Unlike Smith or Marx, German historicists, were not inclined to believe in universal principles in economics. Different societies were characterized by different economic institutions and principles, and these also evolved over time.[4] Insights were time and society-specific.

Against this, Menger held that it was possible to develop economics as a formal science. Economics should be about developing rules about human behaviour from a few fundamental principles. Through such rigorous logic economics could come to insights that transcended time and place. The fundamental principles that Menger proposed were self-interest, utility maximization, and complete knowledge. The focus, in other words, lay entirely on the choices of the individual and his subjective perception of what was valuable. To Menger, the individual was to be the starting point for any analysis of social structures and relations. The formalism advocated by Menger lent itself very well for mathematical methods. Especially in Britain, the use of mathematics as a means to develop economic theory found some enthusiastic disciples in the likes of Edgeworth and Marshall. Menger himself, however, was not very fond of mathematical methods, which he thought were not equipped to deal with the essence of economic phenomena, but only with quantitative relationships between them.[5] Nevertheless, both Menger and the marginalists in Britain agreed upon the development of economics as a formal science focusing on individual choice and subjective utility. Economics was the science studying economizing rather than the economy. Social structures, religious beliefs, or collective values lay outside its domain.

American institutionalism

This formal interpretation of economics did not go unchallenged. In Germany, the social-economic studies of Max Weber, who was strongly influenced by the Historical School, formed an important counterweight.

Marxism continued to have its own share of followers. At the time, the most serious challenge to neoclassical economics came from the United States, however. It was in the United States where scholars like John Commons and most importantly, Thorstein Veblen, formed a distinct school that came to be known as *Institutionalism*. Institutional scholars were immersed in German historicist thinking, without fully embracing its premise of historical contingency. Veblen, for example, launched a strong attack against classical (and neoclassical) economics in his 1898 essay 'Why is Economics not an Evolutionary Science?' In this paper, he claims that neoclassical economists' fondness for 'pure theory' results in economics as a 'theory of the normal case' (Veblen 1998 [1898]: 409). With its premises about individual decision making and action, neoclassical economics set the standard of what behaviour should normally be like. Rather than analyzing the world before them, neoclassical economists developed an ideal behaviour[6] which functioned as a benchmark for the real world. In this, economics stood out as backward amid more progressive sciences such as anthropology, psychology and, most crucially, biology, which Veblen saw as a model. Whereas such modern sciences are evolutionary, focusing on explanations of dynamic processes in terms of cause and effect, economics still clung to a metaphysical vision of the world in which the world is the way it is simply because that is the normal, natural order.

Although emphasizing the importance of a historicized economic science, Veblen did not go along completely with the German historicists either. He dismissed the historicists' focus on interpretation and understanding in favour of development of objective, positive theories about historical processes. Veblen sought a theory of historical change as an evolutionary process, grounded in universal biological categories and their interaction. In some ways, it could therefore be argued that Veblen proposed a formal economics as well. Yet, this formalism – if it may be called such – was entirely different from the formalism of neoclassical economics. For one thing, it was not grounded in principles about individual decision making, but on biological laws. But more importantly for our story, it did not imply a demarcation of an economic object as different from social, historical, psychological and cultural factors. Economics was still the science that studied the entire system of relations and institutions that made up 'the economy'; i.e. those parts of society in which production and consumption were organized. Reading a work like Veblen's *Theory of the Leisure Class* (1899) from a twenty-first century point of view, one would have difficulty in saying whether this is economics, sociology, anthropology or history. It is in fact, all of them – American Institutionalism never adhered to the strict demarcation of economics that the marginalists had developed. It explicitly argued that drawing from psychology, biology and theories of culture was necessary for an understanding of the economy. Changes in economic institutions, for example, to Veblen occur through changes in 'the individual's habitual view of things', while 'economic activities, and the habits bred by them, determine the activities and the habitual view of things in other directions than the economic one' (Veblen 1897: 391). Economic behaviour, perceptions, habits and institutions – they are all interconnected and to be analyzed together. Economic mechanisms cannot be separated from the political and social system in which they are embedded.

Institutionalism, for some time, was the main school of economics in the United States. Apart from Veblen, institutionalism brought forward some famous names such as John R. Commons, Wesley Mitchell, and later, John Kenneth Galbraith. The formal definition of economics propagated by marginalism was not yet accepted as the norm. Over time, this would change, however. In spite of the individual excellence of the authors it brought forward, institutionalism began gradually to lose influence, until after World War II, the idea of economics in the formal sense had all but taken over the debate.

The supremacy of formal economics

Where economics before World War II had been – like any social science – a discipline in which various perspectives coexisted and vied for dominance, economics from the 1950s onward became a decidedly homogenous affair. The formal interpretation of economics had taken over the discipline successfully, pushing substantive economics aside. Also, mathematical methods begun to dominate the field (for a full account of this latter development, see Weintraub 2002). All this implied that the attention to culture in economic thought withered.

There are various reasons for these developments. Part of the interest in mathematics in economics was directly related to the war. For one thing, the war had not only been an enormous military effort but also entailed a logistic operation on an as yet unprecedented scale. This had required a huge number of people involved in planning and data analysis. Mathematical modelling had proven highly successful in these operations. Thus, after the war ended, the idea of production and distribution as something that could be caught into models had become accepted. It is no surprise that many of those who went on to become famous economists had served their war years in environments like the Statistical Research Group (Friedman, Stigler), the Office of Strategic Services (Rostow, Barnett) or the Combined Shipping Board (Koopmans). These experiences added to the belief that mathematical modelling could be a useful tool in economic analysis and policy (Weintraub 2002: 224). Ideas like this inspired people like Jan Tinbergen to develop highly complex econometric models as instruments for planning.

In addition, events in Europe had caused a lot of young academics to flee to the United States, especially Jews from various European countries. Since these people were not immersed in the linguistic and cultural tradition of their new home country, they preferred the universal language of mathematics as a means of communication. Using mathematical reasoning was the one way in which they could overcome their disadvantages of being recent immigrants (Weintraub 2002: 217). The turn towards mathematics thus not only caused a loss of interest in culture but was often partly motivated by a wilful decision to ignore the cultural setting. Even if they had wanted to, new immigrants were probably not able to write the kind of historicized, in-depth economic accounts about their new country that were preferred by Institutionalists and the Historical School. Knowledge of the cultural context of the economic processes they sought to understand was their most vulnerable point. They were probably all too happy to be able to leave it aside.

Politics was probably another factor in the ascendancy of formal, mathematical economics. The war had left various political legacies. First, experiences with authoritarian regimes had bred a generation of intellectuals with a deep distrust of state intervention in social and economic life. Second, the end of World War II had been the start of the Cold War, which fuelled these tendencies further. Both these developments stimulated the emergence of a monolithic economic science, positioned against the Marxist economics propagated in the communist bloc. The stress on the benefits of the market and the focus on individual choice that was present in neoclassical theory fitted this political message better than the often (slightly) anti-market, social structure focused approach of institutionalism. Indeed, various authors began to interpret neoclassical analysis of the market economy, with its stress on individual choice and knowledge, in terms of freedom and democracy; the idea that the free society was a market economy began to be propagated (e.g. Hayek 1980 [1948], Friedman 1962). Although on the one hand, all this shows that post-war economic theory was deeply immersed in a set of liberal values and ideology, on the other hand, it fuelled a desire to develop social sciences on an (superficially) apolitical and amoral basis. The ideological commitment to individual freedom and subjective decision making caused economists to stay away from factors like culture and moral values. Those were things for individuals to sort out for themselves, and they were none of the economist's concern. The rise of this neoclassical paradigm heralded the fall of any role for culture in economy.

Closing the ranks

What happened to those scholars who had been working in the substantive tradition of economics? Some of this tradition, of course, simply disappeared. A few, increasingly isolated individuals remained committed to an institutional version of economics – John Kenneth Galbraith being a prime example. Most of this tradition, however, did not so much disappear as was reclassified. Recall, for example, that Max Weber had held a chair in economics and devoted his most important works to analysis and the theory of economy. Yet, if one asks anyone nowadays who Max Weber was, it will turn out that he is remembered primarily as a sociologist rather than an economist. Practically no economics textbook devotes any attention to him; all sociology textbooks do. Thorstein Veblen continues sometimes to turn up in economics textbooks, but as someone who has come up with some exotic exceptions in economic theory rather than as someone with a comprehensive vision about economic science.

What happened was that the formal interpretation of economics became not only a school of thought in economics, but transformed into a definition of the economic discipline itself. One of the most popular definitions of economic science is the one penned by Lionel Robbins in 1932, in which he says that

> 'Economics is the science which studies human behaviour as a relationship between given ends and scarce means which have alternative uses'.
> (Robbins 1932: 16)

Economics had come to *be* about economizing, rather than that economizing was but a perspective from which one could do economics. Studies of any other topic or process came to belong to sociology, psychology or something else. Thus, the substantive tradition disappeared from economics and found new shelter in the sub-disciplines of economic sociology and history.

A last haven for culture: development economics

The substantive tradition with its attention to culture did not disappear entirely from economic thought. There was one area of economics in which culture continued to play an important role. This was the new research field of development economics.

The idea of something called development economics itself only came about after de-colonization processes set in all over the world. Before that, some attention to development problems had already begun to be paid by economists, but this work focused mainly on less developed areas in South-Eastern Europe and was not considered a special sub-discipline (e.g. Rosenstein-Rodan 1943). Part of the interest in the development of this region sprung from a political concern to maintain these areas in one's sphere of interest during a time of global conflict. Similarly, the Cold War triggered a great deal of attention to the development of newly independent former colonies. International aid was partly inspired by strategic objectives. It was also morally inspired though: the rise of social-democracy, an increasing guilt about colonization, and feelings of international solidarity formed important motivations to be concerned with development.

The economic theory dealing with developing societies that emerged over time was decidedly distinct from mainstream theory. This had various reasons. For one thing, developing societies were obviously facing some shared problems that were rather different from the ones experienced by developed economies. More importantly, however, the idea of separate development economics with different principles and ideas was probably fuelled by a tendency to see non-Western, Third World countries as fundamentally different from the West. In fact, the objective of development economics and aid was for those 'Others' to become more like us. Development was modelled after the experiences of Northwest European and North American countries. Developing countries had to overcome their differentness and start to resemble the modern West.

Since people in the former colonies were so obviously 'different', it followed that normal economic ideas about rational choice and purposive behaviour did not apply to them. It thus became important to try and understand the irrational ways in which 'they' made decisions. After all, if one could get people in developing countries to get rid of their traditional modes of thought and backward culture, then their development was possible. Culture, beliefs, and values, was thus an indispensable part of development studies. Whereas the economic model of rational man was sufficient to study behaviour in Western, developed societies, it did not apply in the rest of the world. Here, culture and traditions ruled the day.

Such ideas implicitly found their way into development economics. It was the one area in which economics was still about the question of how society ensured production, distribution and consumption rather than about individual choices. It was also the one area in which answering such questions made people turn towards politics, social relations, and culture. The dominant paradigm in development economics in the 1950s and 1960s, modernization theory, dealt with much more than economic development. Modernization included a move towards bureaucratization, democracy, and a modern mindset geared towards market behaviour (McClelland 1961, Nash 1964). It implied a move away from traditionalism.

If one is searching for any thoughts about culture in economic science in the decades following World War II, development economics is the place to be looking for it. However, even there, the substantive interpretation eventually had to make room for the onslaught of formal economics. From the 1970s onwards, development economists, disgruntled with the lack of progress made by most developing societies and frustrated by ill-functioning bureaucracies and red tape, began to launch an attack against the prevalent ideas in development economics. The core of their message was that instead of development planning, international aid and inclusive theories of societal change, it was necessary simply to apply mainstream economic insights to developing countries as well. The blessings of the market that had brought the First World affluence were to be exported to the Third

World. The most explicit attack against development economics came from economist Deepak Lal (1983, 1985), who argued that there was no need for a separate development economics. Normal – that is neoclassical – theory would suffice.

This attack, which was known as the neoclassical counterrevolution, heralded two decades of neoclassically inspired policies and thinking about development, culminating in the (in)famous Washington Consensus (Williamson 1990). The removal of culture from even this last corner of economic thought seemed to seal the fate of culture in economics for once and for all. Yet, as the rest of this book shows, culture was to unexpectedly bounce back again in the 1990s.

Summarizing remarks

The historical overview in this chapter has sketched the development of thinking about culture and economy over time. Generally, the debate about culture and economy was thought to have started with Max Weber. Weber's *The Protestant Ethic* was indeed one of the first major works that made the connection between culture and economy an explicit focus of analysis. Part of the reason for this explicitness is that in Weber's time, it was no longer self-evident that any comprehensive work in economics paid attention to issues like institutions, values and beliefs. Classical economists – from Smith to Marx – had not considered 'culture' to be something lying outside their domain. At the end of the nineteenth century this had changed; a new understanding of economics had surfaced, defined not as the study of the economy but as the study of economizing. From that moment on, the history of economic thought can be seen as a history of struggle between two rival conceptions of economics, one formal and one substantive. The history of thought about culture and economy has been directly linked to the fate of the substantive version of economics. Formal economics, focused on individual choice and rationality, had no place for issues like culture and institutions. Substantive economics, concerned with a complete understanding of those segments of society that we call the economy, had.

The exact development of this struggle varied between contexts. In the United Kingdom, the formal definition of economics soon became dominant, helped by the influence of neoclassical scholars like Marshall. On the continent, Weber's contribution heralded the beginning of the end for studies of culture in economics as much as it was the beginning of a debate. For the first time, culture was considered something special and in need of a methodological defence which could consider the relations between ethics and economy. Weber's substantive understanding of economic science was on the wane. In spite of his popularity and influence, Weber's work would soon come to be reclassified as sociology rather than economics.

In the United States, substantivists put up a longer fight. The institutionalist school of economics, with prominent economists like Veblen, Mitchell and Commons continued in the tradition that saw economics as the science studying the economy rather than the science studying individuals economizing. For a while, institutionalism formed the main school of thought in economics in America. Eventually, however, it shared the same fate as substantive economics in Britain and Germany. Formal economics acquired a near-monopoly on economic thought after World War II, and substantive authors came to be considered more relevant for sociology or history than for economics. This development reached its summit in the neoclassical counterrevolution from the end of the 1970s onwards. The dominance of neoclassical thinking that characterized economics in the 1980s implied a near complete neglect of 'soft' factors like culture, institutions or history. This turned out not to be the end of the story, however. Surprisingly, perhaps as a reaction against the bareness of this approach, this was the context from which the current interest in culture and economics sprang. This is what will be discussed in the next chapter.

Chapter 3

The re-emergence of culture in economics

The previous chapter described how after Word War II, economics became a science about economizing in the sense of optimizing under constraints. This development can be attributed to factors internal to the science of economics and to political economic forces at the time of World War II and the Cold War. In this chapter we will argue that the re-emergence of culture in economics once again can be ascribed to forces from inside economic science and developments in the political historical context. The increased use of mathematics in economics did not deliver what some had hoped for. On the contrary, in many cases theory opened more questions and counter-intuitive results than it delivered answers. The end of the Cold War had two important influences: it ended the rivalry between the market and centrally planned economies, and it opened the discussion on the way to establish a market economy. The first made it possible to discuss varieties of market economies. The second forced academics and politicians to discuss the essential elements of a market economy and the way by which one would realize such an economy.

Within economic science and policy advice these developments lead to a rediscovery of the central role of institutions and culture for economic development. New schools within economics came into being: institutional economics, evolutionary economics, behavioural economics, etc. None of these sub-disciplines exclusively focuses on the role of culture. All, however, allow for culture to play a role in addition to other factors for explaining economic phenomena. Thus, one can speak of an economics and culture view: culture is added as an explanatory factor to an existing economic theory.[1]

In this chapter we set out first to discuss the developments within the economic science and actual politics that lead to a re-emergence of culture. Thereafter the several ways by which culture is incorporated in economic studies is discussed. We discuss the disappointing results of the mathematical approach to economics, then the political decisions that led to an increased awareness of the relevance of culture, and finally the ways by which culture is incorporated in economics.

Some trends in post-war economics

In some respects defining economics as economizing can be considered a great success. The microeconomic method of optimizing under constraints became widespread in social sciences. Paul Samuelson's *Foundations of Economic Analysis*, first published in 1947, served as a catalyst for optimizing under constraints as an appropriate method to study almost all economic problems. On the other hand this procedure led to theoretical problems and to sophisticated models which in the end did not provide much insight into actual behaviour.[2]

Samuelson derived demand and supply curves by framing the consumers' and producers' decision making as a result of maximizing a utility function or a profit function under constraints. The next question is: Will these demand and supply curves, which are derived from microeconomic decisions, lead to an economy-wide equilibrium? The results on these economy-wide questions are mixed. One was able to prove that in competitive markets the general equilibrium equations had some solutions. However, it proved to be impossible to show that there is just one (unique) solution, that the economy will converge towards equilibrium, and that the characteristics of the equilibrium could be found once the data of preferences, endowments and technology had been given. Other questions concerned were: could existence of equilibrium be proved for imperfectly competitive markets? Could general equilibrium theory be used for underpinning money and macroeconomics? In addition, inspired by the ad hoc character of some macroeconomic functions, especially in the 1970s and at the beginning of the 1980s, many were of the view that macro relations were in need of a microeconomic foundation. The models used were characterized as representative agent models: only one or a few type(s) of economic agents were thought to represent the economy. A fundamental problem with these types of models concerned the difficulties with the aggregation of individual relations. It proved that despite well-behaved functions at the individual level, the aggregate functions were to a large extent arbitrary. This is one of the impossibility results of the Sonnenschein-Mantel-Debreu theory. Moreover, researchers in the field used complicated mathematical tools, so that 'the average practitioner increasingly became disenchanted with and unable to understand and use general equilibrium theory' (Rizvi 2003: 382).

The unsatisfactory results of the general equilibrium theory stimulated researchers to take another route. Rational choice game theory was one of these alternatives. Some of its advantageous features are its ability to study strategic interactions and to deal with imperfect competition. Unfortunately, the common solutions concepts of these models (the way the game is played) are dependent on unrealistic common-knowledge assumptions.

> Common knowledge means that each player knows that each player knows (and so on) each player's rationality and structure of the game.

> With such an immense structure of knowledge being assumed, the idea of strategizing, which involves guesswork in the face of knowledge, is nearly rendered incoherent.
>
> (Rizvi 2003: 386)

Under these common knowledge assumptions, new information cannot generate trade between rational agents, even in the presence of asymmetrical information. Partly due to these unrealistic assumptions and results researchers moved towards evolutionary game theory. In these games players follow fixed rules, which are not the result of any optimizing behaviour. Different types of rules are used and the population changes as unsuccessful types are replaced by more successful ones.

A similar development can be observed with respect to the Rational Expectations Revolution which took off in the beginning of the 1970s. In rational expectations models, expectations of endogenous variables are obtained by minimizing the variable's forecast error. As part of this procedure agents are assumed to know the model and its parameters' exact value. Under these assumptions the agents do not make any systematic forecast error and in the absence of stochastic shocks the expectations are always perfect, hence the term perfect-foresight models. An unstable equilibrium is a typical feature of these models. When a shock hits the model, a new equilibrium has to be determined. In principle an infinite number of equilibriums and corresponding paths through time are possible. Only one of these equilibriums and paths are stable. This stable path is called the saddle path. The rational agents select that particular equilibrium which is reached by following the saddle path. In order to select that particular path from the infinite number of possible paths, they are assumed to foresee developments into the far future and understand that all other paths will not lead to the new stable equilibrium.[3]

An advantage of rational expectations models is that these expectations are forward looking: they depend on expected events (exogenous variables) to come, whereas previous forms of expectations were backward looking. Essentially, the latter were often weighted averages of past observations. This forward-looking feature of rational expectations models enables an investigation of announcement effects and of various degrees of credibility of economic agents (especially governments). However, the price paid for these improvements was high. As might have become clear from the preceding, in rational expectations models agents are assumed to know almost every issue already: they know the economic world including the exact parameter values, and are able to calculate the paths into the future when an external shock hits the economy. So learning, which is such an important element of expectations formation, is totally absent (De Jong 1988). Similar to the common knowledge assumptions in rational-choice game theory, rational expectations models assume that economic agents possess an unrealistically high level of knowledge about the working of the economy. Acquiring such a high degree of information and understanding of the economy exceeds by far the cognitive capacity of human beings.

The concept of bounded (or near) rationality takes into account humans' cognitive limitations. These limitations concern the capacity for 'discovering alternatives, computing the consequences under certainty and uncertainty, and making comparisons among them' (Sent 1998: 36). Under these conditions, the use of fixed decision rules and rules of thumb can be rational in the sense of cost efficiency. Moreover, agents can differ due to their prior belief in particular rules and relevant factors. Consequently, instead of one representative agent, these models generally contain (often two) or more types of agents. Multiple equilibriums are a common feature of these types of models. The equilibrium chosen can depend upon the private agents' expectations of policy makers' future actions and on the type of heuristics used by the majority of private agents.

Bounded rationality is an element of behavioural economics, which tries to incorporate elements from psychology into economics. It started in the 1950s by authors like Herbert Simon, Richard Nelson, Sidney Winter, and others (see Sent 2004: 741). These old behavioural economics 'focused on discovering the empirical laws that describe behaviour correctly and as accurately as possible' (Sent 2004: 742).[4] As such it presented itself as an alternative to the rationality assumption of mainstream economics. The new behavioural economics, which started in the beginning of the 1970s, takes the rationality assumption as a benchmark and analyzes departures from this standard instead of presenting an alternative approach. Kahneman and Tversky are important authors in this field. They found that under uncertainty, decision makers often make use of heuristics and systematically biased judgements. Furthermore, they discovered that choices can be influenced by the way the problem has been phrased and structured. Based on these two findings they developed the prospect theory, which is a descriptive theory and not an optimizing one such as neoclassical theory. According to prospect theory individuals take their present endowments as a reference point when valuing alternatives. The value function is convex for losses and concave for gains and initially steeper for losses than gains (see Kahneman and Tversky 1979).[5]

Many of the results in behavioural economics are found by means of laboratory experiments. These experiments enable the researchers to control the conditions under which the subjects make decisions. Many of these experimental results suggest that agents act less rational (in the sense of obtaining the highest profit) and less selfish than assumed in standard economic theories. The insights of the new behavioural economics were much more easily incorporated in mainstream economics than those of the old behavioural economics. Maybe this success is due to the fact that the new behavioural economics is less remote from mainstream economics: it takes the results of mainstream economics as a starting point. Another factor could be that in the mean time the failures of the mainstream approach had become more evident.

The neoclassical model assumes a universal structure and thus disregards the context within which agents make their decisions. Economists belonging to the New Institutional Economics emphasize the importance of the institutional context for decision making. Institutions are defined as the 'humanly designed constraints that shape human interactions' (North 1990: 3). These constraints can be formal (laws and written rules) as well as informal (codes and conducts in use by a group of persons). These institutions structure the environment of economic agents and thus reduce uncertainty. The reduction of uncertainty decreases the costs of making transactions and enables transactions, where these previously were impossible due to, for example, lack of information about the creditworthiness of the counterparty. Hence, like culture (see Chapter 1) institutions are expected to facilitate and stimulate economic activity. These institutions are formed during a long period, often centuries. The informal institutions form a natural link to include culture in the analysis (see the section Economics and Culture).

In conclusion, the approach by which economics is restricted to economizing ran into a dead end. Only a few results could be confirmed and attempts to find solutions for various problems resulted in complicated methods and models, which could be understood only by a select group of researchers. Moreover, the assumptions used in rational choice and rational expectations models imply an unrealistically high level of acquiring and processing information. These disappointing results and unrealistic features of the neoclassical framework opened the doors for other directions, such as behavioural economics and institutional economics. All these theories acknowledge the agents' limited cognitive capacities. Under these conditions, different types of agents are naturally included in the model. Often multiple equilibriums are possible and agents are likely to follow heuristic rules. The equilibrium and rule selected will depend on prior information and prior beliefs. This feature opens the door for incorporating culture in the models, as we will see in the section Economics and Culture. Before that we briefly describe how this development towards pluralism within the economic science nicely corresponds with changes in the political economic situation.

Post-war trends in the political economic situation

The heyday of the economizing approach of economics corresponds with the years of the Cold War. The great debate was whether a market economy would deliver better results than a centrally planned economy and variants thereof. Developing countries experimented with import-substitution policies, which were characterized by high degrees of regulation. Moreover, during the first post-war decades the economies of many industrialized (in particular continental European) countries were quite intensively regulated. Increases in wages and in prices of goods (in particular those of food) were limited by law. Financial markets and international financial flows were restricted. The discussions were ideological (free markets versus state regulation) or of a more or less technical nature; the lag length by which economic policy measures are felt in the economy. Within economics, no attention was paid to the relationship between values and economic institutions and performance.[6]

The Asian miracle can be regarded as the first important post-war event that triggered a discussion about the relationship between values and economic growth. From the mid 1960s to the mid 1990s income per capita increased by 7 per cent to 10 per cent annually in some East Asian countries (namely Taiwan, South Korea, Hong Kong, Singapore, and Malaysia). These extraordinarily high levels of economic growth were unexpected. In the mid 1950s, former British colonies such as Sri Lanka and India were named as candidates for successful economic development. Sri Lanka, for example, was at the time of its independence (1948) an open country with a relatively high living standard. During the first decades of its independence it followed an import-substitution policy, which led to a closing of the economy and economic slowdown (Ganeshamoorthy 2003: Ch. 5). The six New Industrialized Countries (NICs) on the other hand followed a policy which prepared their industries for competition on the world markets.

Their economic success triggered a debate about the determinants of this growth. Those who believe in free markets as vehicles for economic growth emphasized the export oriented industrialization of these countries. In their view the success can be ascribed to the fact that these countries' governments had prepared their industry for worldwide competition. So, although especially during the first years, domestic industry was protected by import duties, the ultimate goal was to put it under the pressure of world competition and thus to let competition determine the success of industries. Others (structuralists, for example) however, emphasized the determining role the state of these countries played in selecting and supporting the exporting industries. Moreover, many of these companies were owned by states, state-related organizations or private persons with close connections with government or party officials. This crony capitalism provides more evidence in favour of state-led growth than of growth led by free markets.

This undecided debate about the determining factors of the Asian miracle, provided fertile ground for a third explanation, namely that particular Asian values were conducive to economic growth. Values such as group spirit, mutual assistance and thrift were claimed as having provided the correct incentives for economic growth in these countries. Often these values were argued to originate from the region's dominant religion Confucianism.

According to Hill (2000) the discussion on Asian values, was started by Western scientists. During the late 1960s and the 1970s the discussion in Singapore focused on themes of national consciences and identity and not on Asian values. In 1979 three influential books on Asia and Asian values were published by Western scientists. As a result, Asian values, and in particular values originating from Confucianism, were considered important for explaining the economic success of Asian countries. Confucian ethics were considered to play a similar role as Max Weber had claimed for Protestant ethics about a century earlier. They facilitate hard work and stress social obligations. During the 1980s the Singapore government stimulated the knowledge of Confucian values by means of a Moral Education project. In a similar move the Malaysian authorities stimulated a modern version of Islam which was also labelled as a 'highly Protestantized form of Islam' (Lee and Ackerman 1997: 36). Later on the Malaysian Prime Minister Mahathir emphasized the Asian nature of these values (Maseland 2006a: Chapter 5). Hill (2000: 188) concludes that for Singapore the entire project of Confucian and Asian values had 'much in common with the "invention of tradition" which has historically accompanied nation-building'. Of course the Asian crisis of 1997 gave a blow to the distinctiveness of Asia and its growth path and so also to the relevance of typical Asian values. For our discussion, however, it is important that at one time – the end of the 1970s to the 1990s – it triggered the attention for the relevance of non-tangible factors such as culture.

The fall of the Iron Curtain in 1989 provides another event suggesting the potential relevance of culture. As such the fall of the centrally planned economies was regarded as evidence of the superiority of the free market economy, so that the discussion was not about the best system but about the best way to implement a market economy. Was a shock therapy by which one would introduce market regulation as soon as possible the best way, or would a more gradual approach be preferred? Those in favour of a quick transformation consider an economic system as a rationally designed set of institutions, which is valid worldwide. The models underlying this policy advice do not contain adjustment costs, so that a quick move towards this optimal structure is the best policy. Many of the contributions in Blanchard *et al.* (1994) adhere to this view. The adherents of a gradual approach argue that any economic system will function appropriately if the country's inhabitants are acquainted with the rules and know how to use the institutions. It will take time for the citizens of the post-communist countries to adapt their behaviour from a setting where private initiative is not expected nor rewarded to one that relies on private initiative (Murrell 1995). The years under communism have led to a culture in which the state is expected to take care of and decide on almost every aspect of life. A gradual adjustment is needed to change this dominant culture of passive involvement into one that relies on active participation.

The fall of the Iron Curtain also triggered a renewed interest in the essential aspects of a market economy. Then it appeared that the market economy was not as universal as claimed by some; almost every industrialized country had its own variant. This stimulated the literature on varieties of capitalism and comparative economics, with names such as Albert (1993), Amable (2003) and Hall and Soskice (2001). This literature discusses the differences between the economies, whether subsystems (labour market, educational system, financial system) are complementary and how historical events have led to the present system.

In the 1990s the universal validity of a particular model of the market economy also came under attack due to the failure of the one-size-fits-all approach of the World Bank. Within the Bank and related development organizations this led to an increased attention to diversity and to non-economic factors such as culture and religion for economic development. Examples are the World Faith Development Dialogue hosted by the World Bank and the World Bank's Culture and Development programme, which is a Dutch-supported initiative that is based on the thesis that, in order to be effective, development processes to reduce poverty must understand culture, or take culture into account, for two reasons: culture shapes the 'ends' of development that are valuable to the poor; and culture influences how individuals, communities, and institutions respond to developmental changes.

The developments described above attack the view of a universally valid economic system that operates efficiently in every context. Moreover the Asian values debate and the discussions about the best way to implement a market economy in previously communist countries suggest the relevance of values and traditions for the design of economic institutions and economic growth.

Economics and culture

The developments within economic science and within several economies (Asian tigers, demise of centrally planned economies, and failure of one-size-fits-all approach) have led to a re-emergence of culture in economic analysis. The way this renewed attention for cultural factors was introduced into the analysis can best be explained by starting from the optimizing approach in economics.

According to the optimizing approach individuals' decision making can be modelled as optimizing an objective function under constraints. Hence, this approach contains at least four elements: an objective function, constraints, the optimization procedure and the results of this optimalization process. A common element of all cultural approaches is that they question the optimization procedure as this is modelled in neoclassical theory: rational choice and rational expectations, for example. All cultural approaches explicitly or implicitly assume that the limited cognitive ability of humans have to be taken into account when modelling human actions. They differ in the way they incorporate culture in economics. Using the element of the optimizing approach, three approaches of culture and economics can be distinguished: culture as a deviation of the result, culture as constraints and culture as preferences.[7]

The first approach treats culture as a rest factor explaining the difference between a theory's predictions and the facts. It takes the optimizing approach as its theory and confronts its predictions with reality. Considerable and systematic differences between theory and reality are contributed to non-rational factors, such as culture. Many of the contributions to the Asian Values debate belong to this approach. The unexpected success had to be explained by non-rational factors. Essentially, culture is treated as an afterthought and no theoretical arguments are provided for explaining the role culture plays. The two other approaches – culture as constraints and culture as preferences – claim a theoretical framework for incorporating culture in economic analysis.

Culture as constraints

The culture as constraints approach can be seen as an offspring of New Institutional Economics, which emphasizes the importance of institutions for the functioning of economies. Institutions are defined by Hodgson (2006: 2) as 'systems of established and prevalent social rules that structure social actions. Language, money, law, systems of weights and measures, table manners, and firms (and other organizations) are thus institutions.' Institutions structure social action and thus 'enable ordered thought, expectation, and action by imposing form and consistency on human activities' (idem: 2). They enable individuals' actions by imposing constraints on each participant's behaviour. Consequently, North (1990: 3) defines institutions as 'the humanly devised constraints that shape human interaction'.

Institutions work only if they are embedded in shared habits of thought and behaviour (Hodgson 2006: 6 and 13). North divides institutions into formal institutions, such as written rules and legislation, and informal institutions: unwritten codes of conduct that underlie and supplement formal rules. The latter correspond with our definition of culture and Williamson's embeddedness. In the following, institutions are considered to be formal institutions. The institutional framework of a society is a function of shared mental models of its members (Denzau and North 1994). Institutions (and thus, indirectly, culture) will to a large extent determine the costs and benefits of different choices. At the same time, how agents perceive and interpret information and by which criteria they choose their actions will be determined by their mental models, and thus by cultural norms. Hence, culture will influence the production process, the form and regulation of

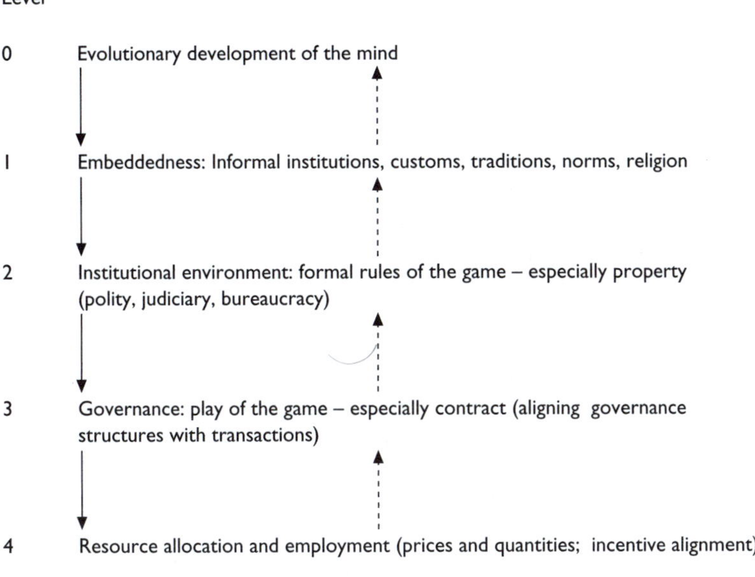

Adapted from Williamson (2000), Figure 1.

Figure 3.1 Culture as constraints

exchange and consumption (DiMaggio 1994). For example, several authors have argued that a market society requires a certain set of values, such as individualism and achievement. Within the group of countries with a market economy, differences in state–society relations are deeply rooted and the result of national history (see DiMaggio 1994: 38). In general, any stable economic system has a compatible and supportive cultural system that legitimates that system (Inglehart 1997: 15).

This view of institutions that on the one hand are embedded in shared beliefs (culture) and on the other hand influence economic behaviour is schematically presented by Williamson (2000). Figure 3.1, which is a slightly adapted version of Williamson's figure, shows the various levels of social analysis distinguished by Williamson. The first level (called level 0 by Williamson) is not included in Williamson's original figure but is mentioned in his text only. It concerns the evolution of the mechanisms of the mind; the research object of evolutionary psychologists and cognitive science researchers. The other four levels are: embeddednes, institutional environment, governance, and resource allocation. Social embeddedness consists of norms, customs, traditions, mores, and religion. According to Williamson, the latter plays an important role at this level. The characteristics of this level are called informal institutions, referring to the fact that they are created spontaneously. In this study we refer to it as culture. The next level consists of the institutional environment which contains formal institutions, such as constitutions, laws, and property rights. These institutions design the various functions of the government as well as the distribution of powers across different levels of government. The institutions of governance concern informal rules used by private agents for settling disputes directly. Since court proceedings are costly (both with respect to time and financially), well-functioning governance structures reduce transaction costs by creating order and thus mitigating conflict. Level four concerns resource allocation and employment. Prices and quantities adjust so that the markets reach an equilibrium. This is the research topic of neoclassical economics.

Besides defining the different levels of social analysis, Williamson formulates his view on the relations between them, in particular the dominant way of causation. In principle, the various levels influence each other in both directions. However, Williamson thinks that the effect of each higher level on the one beneath it dominates the reverse causality. In Figure 3.1 this difference in influence is illustrated by the bold versus dashed arrows. Each higher level is considered to function as a constraint on the developments of the level beneath it. Moreover, the higher levels are expected to change less frequently than the lower ones. This change can be gradual but events such as wars and economic crises might trigger a quick reform and 'a sharp break from established procedures' (Williamson 2000: 598). He thinks that in general a change in culture (embeddedness in his jargon) takes 100 to 1,000 years,[8] whereas formal institutions can change between 10 and 100 years.

Culture as preference

According to all variants of the culture as preference approach, beliefs and preferences systematically differ between groups of individuals and these differences contribute to explaining differences in performance across groups. Hence, culture is defined as 'the systematic variation in preferences or beliefs' (Fernández and Fogli 2007: 1), 'the collective programming of mind, which distinguishes the members of one group or category of people from another' (Hofstede 2001: 9), and 'a system of attitudes, values, and knowledge that is widely shared within a society and transmitted from generation to generation' (Inglehart 1997: 15). Common to these definitions are preferences or values as 'broad tendencies to prefer certain states of affairs over others' (Hofstede and Hofstede 2005: 8).

In principle, the same levels of social analysis can be distinguished as has been done by Williamson (see Figure 3.1). Some studies distinguish fewer levels. De Jong (2002: Fig. 1), for example, does not consider the development of the mind and governance as separate levels. A central issue

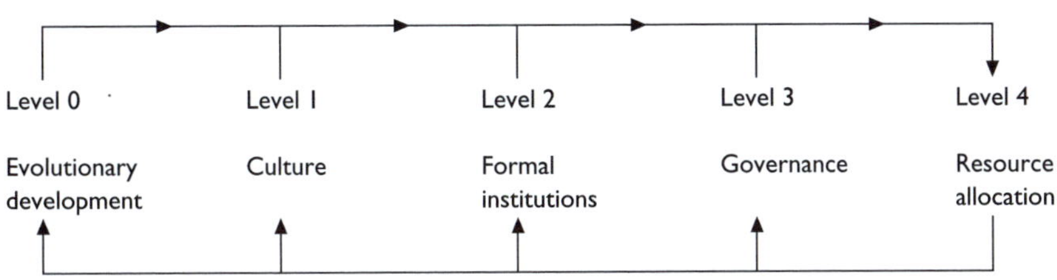

Adapted from Williamson (2000), Figure 1.

Figure 3.2 Culture as preferences

in this approach is that culture can be considered to represent values and beliefs. These values and beliefs influence the perception and design of institutions and the objectives of economic actions. In this manner culture directly and indirectly (through institutions) influences economic behaviour and the outcome of economic processes. Thus culture determines economic performance, which corresponds with the same way of causality that Williamson regards of importance and with the assumption of exogenous preferences. Many authors of the culture as preferences school, however, at least implicitly assume that causality can also run in the other direction: economic performance and the working of institutions can change the dominant perception held by the members of a group. No particular way of causation is assumed to dominate the other. In Figure 3.2 this is visualized by drawing the levels horizontally with order and by the arrows going both ways.

Although many authors of the culture as preferences approach do not explicitly study the way preferences (values) are formed, they explicitly or implicitly assume that preferences are endogenous. In this respect, this approach differs from mainstream economics. Intergenerational transmission is regarded as the most important way by which values are formed.[9] Findings of psychologists and physiologists (some references are provided in Denzau and North 1994) suggest that to a limited extent the structure of a person's mental model is genetic, but for the most part it is developed from experience, and most importantly through an ongoing communication with other individuals. Early childhood is important for acquiring values. During the first ten to twelve years of life a human being quickly and largely unconsciously absorbs information from his environment (see the literature cited in Inglehart 1997: 34). Basic values are the most important information obtained (Hofstede and Hofstede 2005: 8). In general, parents play a crucial role in the formation of these values. Fernández and Fogli (2007: 2) even conclude that 'cultural transmission will be mostly intergenerational rather than from the whole of society (e.g. schools, media, etc.)'. For a dataset of US households, Knowles and Postlewaite (2005: 14) find that children's saving behaviour is significantly affected by the parents' attitudes towards saving. This effect is strongest for the older children and the mothers' attitudes.

Although there are as many parenting styles as there are parents and children, common patterns that distinguish one society from the other can be distinguished too. Small (1998) describes the different parenting styles in varies societies: the pre-industrial societies of the !Kung San in Botswana, and the industrialised countries of Japan and the United States of America. These parenting styles differ because of differences in what parents feel will best prepare their children for the life ahead. Differences can refer to physical skills but also to attitudes expected by the society in which parents and children live. Both Japan and the United States are rich and industrialized countries. They differ in their appreciation of independence and group success versus individual success. In collectivist Japan, mothers encourage infant and child dependency, whereas in individualist USA mothers encourage their babies to spend time separate from adults and become independent individuals. These parenting styles both reflect and enhance cultural differences between societies. As a consequence, significant aspects of mental models will be similar for people living in the same society. These mental models are formed by the way children are raised and their experiences during adulthood. Hence, mental models have a layered structure. Deeper layers are formed in early childhood and are regarded as very stable. This shared deeply held values and beliefs in the society thus change gradually through intergenerational population replacement instead of conversion of already socialized adults (Inglehart 1997: 15).

External shocks to an economy and gradual economic development will influence both institutions and culture. Examples of external shocks are wars and periods of great uncertainty. The mobilization rates of man during World War II are found to have a lasting effect on female labour market participation in the USA (Fernández *et al.* 2004). Girls who were 7–12 years old in 1942 and lived in states with a relatively high mobilization rate of man during World War II show a higher labour force participation in 1980 than women of their generation from states with lower mobilization rates. These women did not work during World War II, so that it is not their experience but their expectations about a woman's role or the return on investing in market skills that explains their higher labour market participation (Fernández *et al.* 2004: 1278). The years of hyperinflation in some continental European countries during the 1920s form an example of a period with great uncertainties. During these years the middle class lost a great part of their savings. As a result they owned less financial assets, came to depend more on their labour income and sought more social protection. This started a process that led to less protection of minority shareholders and the creation of pay-as-you-go pension systems instead of funded pension systems after World War II (Perotti and Schwienbacher 2006).

Gradual economic development also leads to changes in economic institutions. The classic bureaucratic institutions of industrial society, which were part of the earlier stages of industrial society, are inherently less effective in high technology societies with highly specialised workforces. This explains their decline during recent decades (Inglehart 1997). The fall of the centralized economies of the former communist countries can be ascribed to this increasing inefficiency of hierarchical institutions. A less dramatic example is that due to the low inflation rates in industrialized countries with an independent central bank, the central banks in other countries are also made more independent from political forces.

Economic structures and economic performance have an impact on values in a society (see e.g. Bowles 1998 and Inglehart 1997). Central in Inglehart's reasoning is that values change in an intergenerational way. He assumes that people place the greatest subjective value on those things that are in short supply; the scarcity hypothesis. The values change gradually because one's basic values reflect the conditions that prevailed during one's pre-adult years. Although it usually changes slowly, culture can change through the interaction with the environment, among which the economic situation in a country is of primary importance. Ingelhart (1997) argues that the high level of income per capita in the industrialized world has brought much certainty to the great majority of the population. This has led to a large shift in values from those associated with the level of living – such as achievement or hierarchy – to greater emphasis on the quality of life.

Bowles (1998) distinguishes five ways by which economic institutions can influence preferences: framing, motivations, and effects on the evolution of norms, on task performance and on the process of cultural transmission.[10] Economic institutions frame choices. Experimental research, for example, reveals that the more a situation approximates to a competitive market with anonymous buyers and sellers, the less other-regarding behaviour is observed. Economic institutions can influence motivation. A contract assigning a reward to an activity often reduces the internal motivation for that activity. Economic institutions affect the evolution of norms. Market-like systems reduce the need for solidarity and compassion and thus can give rise to a more individualistic norm. These arrangements are also less susceptible to collusion and propagate transparency. Task performance affects values and economic institutions affect task performance. For example, a longitudinal study of job redesign of Swedish workers revealed that workers whose job had become more passive also became more passive in their leisure and political participation and workers with more active jobs became more active (Karasek 2004). Finally, institutions influence the structure of social interaction, child-rearing and socialization practices and thus the process of cultural transmission. Some of these effects are intentional in that adults (parents and teachers) want the children to acquire the knowledge and competences required for their future role in society. Bowles's main argument is that preferences are endogenous.

In the preceding text the culture as constraints and the culture as preferences approaches are presented as two different ways of incorporating culture into economic analysis. They are, however, closely related. Several authors refer to preferences as well as to constraints when discussing culture; '(p)references must be internalized, taking on the status of general motives or constraints on behaviour' (Bowles 1998: 79); 'culture . . . encompasses both facets of Level 1 institutions, as constraints and as motivational factors' (Licht *et al.* 2005: 233); 'Culture can influence both the individual's objectives and his perceptions of the constraints' (Dieckmann 1996: 299), and Inglehart, whom we regard as belonging to the culture as preferences approach also writes 'to be effective in legitimating the system, cultures set limits to elites as well as mass behavior' (Inglehart 1997: 15).

Other authors, on the one hand, describe culture as very resistant to change and on the other hand as endogenous to economic and social development. Hofstede, for example, regards national values as 'facts, as hard as a country's geographical position or its weather.' (Hofstede and Hofstede 2005: 13). But Geert Hofstede also writes

> The future of short- and long-term orientation is difficult to predict. Will Asian cultures with increasing affluence become more short-term oriented? Will the necessity for an increasing world population to survive in a world with limited resources foster more long-term orientation?
>
> (Hofstede 2001: 370)

With respect to Individualism, Hofstede notes a 'strong relationship between national wealth and individualism . . . , with the arrow of causality directed, . . . from wealth to individualism' (Hofstede 2001: 255). Whereas the first quotation suggests that Hofstede assumes culture to be fixed, exogenous and hardly changeable, the last two quotations clearly allow for an endogenous culture, as assumed by the culture as preference approach.

In the preceding pages we have discussed the forces of value change over time. It could be that over time values change whereas at the same time the differences in values between groups remain relatively stable. Vinken *et al.* (2004: 21) call this phenomenon 'relative cultural stability'.

Conclusion

In this chapter we have briefly sketched developments that have led to an increased awareness of the possible relevance of intangible factors such as norms, beliefs and institutions for explaining economic phenomena. Within economic science this interest was generated by discontent with the results of the neoclassical economic approach, which relies heavily on the view of economics as economizing. Moreover, mainstream economics disregards the context within which decisions are made. More or less simultaneously with the increasing discontent with economic theory, economic developments also hinted at the relevance of other factors than those suggested by existing theory. The high levels of growth in a group of East Asian countries, and the transition of previously centrally planned economies to market economies suggested that values and attitudes are of relevance too. The fall of the Iron Curtain also opened mentally the possibility of investigating the differences between various market economies.

Culture has entered economics in at least three ways: as a residual explanation, as determining constraints and as preferences. The first way is uninteresting since it just ascribes the unexplained part to factors not yet considered. Culture is one of these variables. No theoretical arguments are used. The other two approaches – culture as constraints and culture as preferences – contain more elements for successful theoretical and empirical explanations of economic performance of countries over time and across countries. Moreover, by far the majority of the studies on culture and economics belong to one or both of these two approaches. The rest of this book considers applications of these two approaches in various subfields of economics using a variety of methods. In this way we hope to get answers to such questions as: how and when is culture important?, how can and is culture proxied?, is there evidence of a particular causal ordering?

Before discussing the results of studies on culture and various economic phenomena, Chapter 4 considers some methodological issues with respect to the study of culture and the methods used in recent studies on culture and economics.

Chapter 4

Methods and methodology of culture and economics

The previous chapter has reported an increasing interest in the relation between culture and economic phenomena during the past decades. In the rest of this book we give an overview of various economic topics for which a relationship with culture has been investigated. In this way we also provide an overview of the various approaches used. Before doing that, this chapter describes the methods used in these studies and discusses their pros and cons.

The literature on economics and culture discussed in this book aims to establish a link between culture and economic phenomena; institutions, governance and results. Conceptually, such a research programme consists of two phases. The first one consists of developing measures or proxies of cultural, institutional and economic phenomena. One could label this the measurement-phase. The second phase is devoted to establishing a relation between culture and economics. Often researchers will follow the two phases mentioned above by first deriving or collecting measures and thereafter establishing and testing hypotheses about the relationship between the cultural and economic phenomena at hand. However, the steps need not be taken sequentially. Some researchers apply the two phases implicitly or in an iterative way. The upper part of Figure 4.1 summarizes methods used for measuring cultural and economic phenomena. We make a distinction between obtrusive and natural (unobtrusive) methods. Under obtrusive methods subjects are not operating within their natural environment, but are taken aside to participate in an experiment, filling out a questionnaire or answering the questions in an interview. The artificial character of an obtrusive method's setting might easily lead to biased observations.

The bottom part of Figure 4.1 summarizes the methods used for testing the relation between culture and economic objects. Here the distinction between qualitative (essay, narrative, description) and quantitative (mostly regression analysis) is relevant.

The set-up of this chapter follows the logic of the two step procedure in that we first discuss methods for measuring culture and institutions and thereafter the ways that have been used for establishing relations between

Phase 1 Sources and methods for measuring cultural and economic phenomena

	Obtrusive	Unobtrusive (natural)
Words	Interviews Questionnaires	Content analysis of speeches documents, laws Physical objects
Deeds	Experiments • laboratory • field	Direct observation Hardware techniques; camera, videos Statistics

Phase 2 Establishing the relationship between culture and economy

Narratives, essays, (thick) description

Statistical and econometric methods
- cross-country regressions
- epistemological approach

Adapted from Exhibit 1.2 in Hofstede (2001: 17) and Kellehear (2001: 5).

Figure 4.1 Methods for studying the relation between culture and economic phenomena

the two areas. Before this discussion, the next section is devoted to essential methodological considerations to be taken into account when doing cultural studies.

Methodological considerations

In every study on culture researchers have to decide on issues such as: the definition of culture, whether one emphasizes the universal character or the cultural specific elements, the units to be studied, the method to be used. If experiments or surveys are used, then one also has to decide on the characteristics of the individuals to be included in the experiments and the sampling, the translation of questions and documents, etc. Here we briefly touch upon those aspects we regard as most relevant for this book. A more in-depth treatment of these methodological topics can be found in publications on comparative cultural research (Adler 1983, Van de Vijver and Leung 1997, Punnett and Shenkar 2004, Usunier 1998, Marschan-Piekkari and Welch 2004) and the methodological chapters in cultural studies (e.g. Hofstede 2001: Ch. 1, House *et al.* 2004: Chs 6–11).

As has been discussed at length in Chapter 1, many definitions of culture are in use. Studies on the influence of culture in economics and management often use Hofstede's or an equivalent definition of culture. Hofstede defines culture as 'the collective programming of the mind that distinguishes the members of one group or category of people from another' (Hofstede 2001: 9). A similar definition is used in the GLOBE project, where culture is defined as 'shared motives, values, beliefs, identities, and interpretations or meanings of significant events that result from common experiences of members of collectives that are transmitted across generations' (House *et al.* 2004: 15). These definitions concentrate on differences in values or meanings and thus exclude elements, such as customs and law, which are part of broader definitions (see Chapter 1). Hofstede (2001: 11) explicitly refers to the latter when he presents his onion diagram in which values are the core of a culture and rituals, heroes and symbols are its practices represented as the outer peels of the onion.[1] Essentially, researchers estimate the various values and then relate these to items such as laws, income per capita, wealth distributions, etc.

Various concepts of values are in use. Rokeach (1973: 5) defines a value and a value system as follows:

> a *value* is an enduring belief that a specific mode of conduct or end-date of existence is personally or socially preferable to an opposite or converse mode of conduct or end-state of existence. A *value system* is an enduring organization of beliefs concerning preferable modes of conduct or end-states of existence along a continuum of relative importance.

He provides various categorizations of values.

The difference between values as the desired and as the desirable plays an important role in the discussion between researchers who have derived cultural dimensions for a large set of countries, in particular Hofstede and the GLOBE-team. Hofstede (2001: 6, 7, especially Exhibit 1.3) presents various associated distinctions between values as desired and as desirable. Values as the desired refer to what people actually desire, are closer to deeds than values as the desirable, give the intensity of a value and are measured in terms as: important, attractive and successful. Values as the desirable refer to what people think they ought to desire, are stated in words, give the direction of a value and are measured by terms as good, right, ought and should. The majority of the questions in Hofstede's questionnaire refer to values as the desired and those in Schwartz's questionnaire to the desirable (De Mooij 2004: 39). Schwartz (1994: 88) regards values as 'the desirable goals . . . that serve as guiding principles in people's lives.' The GLOBE project makes a similar distinction by asking respondents' judgement of the present situation (As IS questions or practices) and the preferred situation (Should Be questions also labelled Values). The As Is questions, Should Be questions can be regarded as measuring values as the desired, respectively the desirable.

Culture refers to values as these are common to a group. This group can be small, a family, of intermediate size, an organization or an occupation, or as large as a society. In many cross-cultural studies society is identified by nation. Of course subgroups can be distinguished within larger groups.

The culture of a company's Finance Department is expected to differ from that of its Commercial Department. Likewise, within one nation different cultures can be observed based on differences in ethnic origin, religion, and social class (see Hofstede and Hofstede 2005: 34, 35). Particularly, the practice of equating society with nation has met with severe criticism (see especially McSweeny 2002).[2] Many empirical researchers are well aware of the limits of using a national concept of culture, but argue that although not optimal, nations are the only units available for comparison and are better than nothing (Hofstede 2001: 73). In addition, the nation seems to be the relevant unit when studying differences in nationwide concepts, such as laws, inflation, etc. The institutional fabric is set within national boundaries, so that the nation is the most appropriate unit of analysis (Redding 2005: 131, 132). Furthermore, empirical research using individual responses find a strong national influence. For example, a study on interpersonal trust reports a similar score for Catholics and Protestants living in the same society (Inglehart and Baker 2000: 35). Differences in trust are reported between different countries, suggesting that 'shared historical experiences of given nations, not individual personality, is crucial.' (ibid: 35). In conclusion, the nation seems to be the appropriate level in cases where one studies (differences in) nationwide phenomena. In other cases it seems to be the only available or empirically best proxy of the unit to be distinguished.

Since the culture of a group is constituted by the values and behaviour of its members, one can easily confuse the different levels. The ecological fallacy applies when one uses the reasoning and results of the ecological (higher) level to a lower level, mostly an individual. For example, a high correlation between the percentage of blacks in a region and the percentage of illiterates is interpreted as individual blacks are unable to learn reading and writing. The reverse ecological fallacy refers to practices that apply reasoning, valid at the individual (or more generally, lower) level, to that of a society as a whole. The root of this fallacy is a research design which treats cultures as individuals; societies as king size individuals (Hofstede 2001: 17). Hofstede *et al.* (1990)[3] found a clear difference between national culture and organizational culture. At the national level culture refers mostly to values, whereas at the organizational level it is associated with practices. These difference in contents of culture between society and organization are ascribed to the fact that people enter a society by birth and their values are predominantly formed during childhood, so when they are a member of a particular society. The members of an organization enter the latter at the time they are adults and their values have already been formed (Hofstede 2001: 394). Preferably multilevel techniques are used in cases where data from different levels (individual, organization and nation, for example) are available. In this manner the differences of culture itself and of its functions for each level can be studied A good example in this respect is House *et al.* (2004), who use hierarchical linear modelling for explaining the individuals' perception from both organizational and societal level cultural dimensions.[4] Other examples incorporating different levels in the same analysis are Earley (1993) and the classical studies mentioned in Hofstede (2001: 17).

In comparative cultural research one can investigate the differences or the similarities between cultures. In anthropology and cross-cultural psychology emic and etic refer to studies of the unique, respectively general aspects of culture.[5] Individual country studies are inclined to stress the uniqueness of a national culture. Historical events, religion and climate are often considered to have led to a particular culture. Cross-national comparative studies have a tendency to highlight similarities, which arise from the fact that all groups of human beings have to find a solution for similar problems; such as the hierarchy in the system and the division of tasks between the genders.

Cultures can be characterized by typologies or by dimensions. A typology consists of some ideal types, each of them easy to imagine. This ideal type describes all relevant aspects of a culture or economy. Often it describes a particular country so that one can easily understand the ideal type. For example, Germany is a typical bank-based country. In realty, however, countries are hybrids and it is often difficult to classify a particular country as a member of an ideal type. A dimension refers to a particular cultural feature, on which each country obtains a score. Each country is then characterized by a unique combination of scores on the various dimensions. An interpretation of each combination is more difficult than that of ideal types. The scores on the different dimensions can be used for further research. Hofstede (2001: 28) recommends typologies for teaching purposes and dimensions for research. Hampden-Turner and Trompenaars (2000) use typologies to illustrate the extreme positions of a dimension. The dimensions are obtained by factor analysis of cross-country scores on respondents' answers to different questions. These questions can be derived from a theory specifically formulated for finding cultural dimensions (House *et al.* and Schwartz), or are formulated for other reasons (such as work attitudes; Hofstede).

In comparative research sampling issues arise at two levels: the countries or cultures to be compared and the number and type of persons to be selected for interviews, questionnaires and experiments. A reasonable number of countries/cultures should be included in the analysis to arrive at valid conclusions and to test alternative hypotheses with respect to differences and similarities between countries. Hofstede (2001: 17) recommends using data from at least 10 to 15 societies in order to derive reliable results for these ecological dimensions. A study containing just a few countries should be regarded as a pilot study (Adler 1983: 38). It can also serve as an in-depth analysis of the mechanisms responsible for the results found in more general studies. On the other hand enlarging the sample to as many countries as possible might blur the results. Large differences in physical conditions and level of economic development might preclude a reasonable comparison between societies (Temple 1999, Roe 2000: 53, Bloningen and Wang 2005, and Chapter 5 of this book). Consequently, the selection of countries should be aligned as much as possible to the object of the study. If individuals are interviewed or involved in experiments, one also has to decide on the number and type of persons to be considered. In general the larger national samples are the better. Many researchers define a threshold which the number of individuals in the sample should exceed in order to derive reliable conclusions.[6] Another issue concerns the selection of respondents; should they constitute a representative or a matched sample? A representative sample reflects the trend in a particular society. Hence the results of such samples are influenced by national characteristics such as the environmental conditions, its state of development, specialization in particular industries, etc. These characteristics bias the results if one is interested in the differences in values between cultures: do values differ if persons operate in equivalent circumstances? Answering these types of questions requires matched samples, whereby the matching is based on theoretical grounds.

Researchers are part of a culture or cultures too. Hence, they risk viewing other cultures from their own perspective and regarding their own culture as dominant. Various measures can be taken to avoid biases resulting from such ethnocentrism. Preferably members of the research teams come from the different cultures to be investigated. Questions in questionnaires are derived from these cultures instead of being overly biased towards one culture. Alternatively, one could also test the robustness of a study by means of a replication containing a specific cultural bias. Examples are the Asian and African replication of Hofstede's study (see Chinese Culture Connection 1987 and Noorderhaven and Tidjani 2001, respectively). Care should be taken that the language used in every version of a questionnaire refers to equivalent concepts across cultures. Back-translation can be used to achieve equivalent translations. According to this procedure, a text is translated and then back-translated into the original language by different persons. Preferably more than one person is involved in back-translation and differences between translations are discussed, after which a decision is made. Ideally one would also check whether the language used has any influence on the results.

Some studies indicate that language can have an influence on both attitudes and actual behaviour. For Hong Kong/Chinese, Bond and Yang (1982) and Kemmelmeier and Cheng (2004) found that the language used (Chinese or English) influenced the answers in a questionnaire on self-construal scales. In Kemmelmeier and Cheng's study only women's self-construal were influenced by the language used, suggesting that women are responsive to their social environment. For students from seven countries Harzing and Maznevski (2002) found an impact from the language used (English or native language) on the responses to questions referring to culture and job characteristics. No effect was found on the answers to questions referring to neutral items. Not only attitudes but behaviour can be influenced by language, as has been observed by Akkerman *et al.* (2007). In Prisoner's Dilemma games Dutch students were found to behave less cooperatively when English instead of Dutch was used as an instruction language. This influence was strongest for participants who have had an active exposure to the Anglophone culture.

Methods used for measuring cultures

Obtrusive measures

Surveys

The majority of studies on cultural influences on economic phenomena make use of surveys in order to obtain a measure of culture or cultural beliefs. In survey studies respondents from different countries or ethnic groups fill out a questionnaire. In case information is collected for N individuals in n cultures, Leung and Bond (1989) have distinguished four multilevel analyses. A *pancultural* analysis, which pools data from all N individuals together regardless of the culture they belong to; a *within-culture* analysis, which is limited to the individuals within each of the n cultures; an *ecological* analysis, which is performed on aggregate measures of the variables for each of the n cultures (usually the means), and finally an *individual* analysis performed on the pooled data for the N individuals after elimination of the culture-level effects. Many studies on cultural influences are of the ecological type.

The size of the surveys can differ substantially. Some surveys are relatively small. Only one or a few countries are included and the number of respondents is also relatively small. Often these data are collected for studying a particular subject. Examples are Weber and Hsee (1998) and Sakwa (2006). In Weber and Hsee the survey is conducted with Chinese, American, Polish and German students with a sample size of 85, 86, 81 and 31, respectively. They found that on average the Chinese students were more risk-seeking than their American counterparts, whereas the Polish and German students were midway. Sakwa collected data for slightly more than 350 Roman Catholic students from four universities in Nairobi. He explores whether Biblical concepts of poverty correspond with the ideas of these students. Studies using such small samples for only one or a few countries, should be considered exploratory or 'only an opening chapter in cross-cultural differences' (Weber and Hsee 1998: 1216). Larger samples, containing both more countries and more respondents per country, are needed to derive convincing and robust conclusions. Luckily by now these large samples are available.

Two groups of large samples can be distinguished; representative samples and matched samples. In representative samples respondents are selected to stand for the population of the society concerned. Examples of representative samples are the World Value Survey, The European Value Survey, the European Social Survey and the Eurobarometer. Since, these samples reflect a country's demographical pattern, differences between countries with respect to the average of the answers on an item need not necessarily reflect differences in attitudes, but can possibly be ascribed to differences in demography: the average age of the population, gender composition, general occupation, etc. Matched samples are designed to circumvent the problems of representative samples. In a matched sample, the selection of respondents is such that respondents in different countries are equivalent to each other. Preferably this equivalence is a functional and not a literal equivalence (Adler 1983: 41). In this way the differences in the average scores between countries are more likely to be due to differences in opinion, regardless of personal factors such as occupation, age and gender. Examples of large matched samples are Hofstede (1980, 2001), Hoppe's survey, Schwartz (1992, 1994) and the GLOBE project (House *et al.* 2004). Hofstede's respondents are employees from one high-technology firm, IBM. These employees are likely to have more interest in technology and other modern items than the general population. This bias is expected to be larger for developing than for developed countries (Schwartz 1994: 91). In addition, the sample size was much smaller in the developing than in the developed countries. Hoppe's respondents are alumni of the Salzburg Seminar, a conference centre in Austria that received leaders in politics, business, labour, art and education. Since these respondents have on average a higher educational level, one often refers to Hoppe's elite. Schwartz (1992) deliberately chooses two types of matched samples; schoolteachers (grades 3–12) and university students. The GLOBE project uses middle managers in three selected industries: financial services, food processing and telecommunications (House *et al.* 2004: 19, 20).

One can use one or a few single answers or generate cultural dimensions, which are constructed using the answers to various questions. The trust variable used in many studies on economic growth is the best known example of a cultural variable derived from the answers to a single question. It is the average of the answers given on the question 'Generally speaking, would you say that most people can be trusted or that you can't be too careful in dealing with people?' (Inglehart 1997: 299). The trust question is part of the World Values Survey. Another less known example of a single item used is the Relative Unemployment Aversion index constructed by Van Lelyveld (1999) for a set of European countries. This index is generated from the answers to the question: 'Do you think the <insert nationality> government should give higher priority to reducing inflation or higher priority to reducing unemployment?'. The answers are recorded on a scale running from 1 ('A lot higher priority on reducing inflation') to 5 ('A lot higher priority on reducing unemployment'). The national index is the average score of the respondents in the country concerned. The Relative Unemployment Aversion is an estimation of the unemployment/inflation trade-off in the objective function of the Barro-Gordon model. This last example nicely illustrates that the mean of the answers on a single question can be used as an estimate of a particular parameter in a model. This presupposes that one single question can summarize the parameter's contents. A parameter reflecting a trade-off can be measured by a question which explicitly asks the respondents for the trade-off concerned.[7] Many other parameters cannot be derived in such a straightforward way: then more than one question or other techniques have to be employed. In many instances one does not possess an analytical model but wants to measure multifaceted concepts. Then a single question certainly will not suffice and cultural dimensions seem to be more appropriate.

Cultural dimensions are derived from the answers to various questions. Hofstede was the first author to derive cultural dimensions. Other well-known authors who did so are Schwartz, Trompenaars, Inglehart and the contributors to the GLOBE-project. These dimensions are considered to cover all elements of a culture. All societies are assumed to face similar problems and to differ in the way solutions are found. Schwartz (1992: 4), for example, lists 'three universal requirements to which individuals and societies must be responsive: needs of individuals as biological organisms; requisites of coordinated social action, and survival and welfare needs of groups.' An additional assumption is that the prevailing value emphasis in a society can be derived by averaging the answers of the individual respondents. Individual values are considered as partly a product of shared culture and partly as a result of unique individual experiences. The average is a proxy of the common part of the values (culture) and the individual variations around this average as the results of individual experiences (Schwartz 1994: 92). The GLOBE-team has corrected the individual scores for response bias. These corrected individual scores are then aggregated to the society level.[8] The range of these corrected scales is not equal to that of the original scale. For example, if the original scale was a 7-point rating scale, the corrected one can have negative values. Therefore, in a regression analysis the corrected scales were used to predict the uncorrected scales. The predicted values of these regressions are translated back at the original 7-point scale, and thus can be interpreted by referring to the adjectives anchoring the original response scale. Finally, the differences between the uncorrected and the regression-predicted scales were transformed into studentized residuals in order to find outliers. Description of the cultural dimensions derived by Hofstede,

Schwartz, Inglehart, Trompenaars and the GLOBE project are given in Appendix 1, Various Cultural Dimensions.

Cultural dimensions are constituted from the answers on several questions. Often factor analysis is used for reducing the original dataset. Several tests can be used for checking the validity of the dimensions thus obtained (see e.g. Hofstede 2001: 65–73). One test, which also enhances the interpretation of the dimensions, investigates the correlations between the dimensions obtained and 1) measures from other studies on cultural attitudes, and 2) economic, political and cultural characteristics of the cultures concerned. This procedure is followed in Hofstede (1980, 2001) and House *et al.* (2004). Variables used by Hofstede are among others: GDP per capita, economic growth in the past and in the future, latitude, and population characters such as the country's size, growth and population density. Hofstede (2001) also summarizes many studies that have found any relation between any of his dimensions and some economic or political variable. Smith (2006) and House *et al.* (2004) have criticized the use of GDP per capita as an explanatory variable for cultural attitudes. This procedure implicitly assumes a causal relation from wealth to culture, which in their view need not be valid. Smith (2006: 919) suggests that researchers report the results both with wealth partialled out and without it partialled out. House *et al.* (2004: Ch. 7) investigate the correlation between their scales and variables representing the economic, human, and political conditions in countries. Moreover, Wave 2 and Wave 3 of the World Values Survey and content analysis of the countries' culturgrams are used for validating the scales (House *et al.* 2004: Ch. 9).

These survey data provide information on the opinions of the respondents. Whether these opinions will result in actual behaviour as well as the mechanisms by which this will occur are unclear. Experiments can help to understand these mechanisms at the microlevel.[9]

Experiments

During past decades experiments have become important instruments for economic research. The majority of these experiments consist of a game that is played by the participants, mostly students. The researcher can control many conditions, so that in principle the experiments can be set up in such a way that they give insight into behavioural mechanisms. Some frequently used experiments are briefly described in Appendix 2, Some Experiments. The experiments have given insight into the (in)validity of behavioural assumptions underlying mainstream economic models; in games people are more cooperating and pro-social than is assumed in economic theories. Systematic differences in outcomes have been ascribed to differences in culture (see for example, Henrich 2000, Henrich *et al.* 2006, and Roth *et al.* 1991).

As with surveys, laboratory experiments are obtrusive so that one can question the generalizability of the results found. A survey of typical findings of games used for measuring social preferences is provided in Levitt and List (2007: Table 1). Several features of the experiments mean that experimental results might deliver a biased view on the real world.[10] First, the subjects of an experiment are keenly aware that their behaviour is monitored, recorded and scrutinized. As a result the relationship between the subject and the investigator can easily become similar to that of superior–subordinate. This scrutiny can and will lead to behaviour that is more in accordance with social norms than it would be in a real setting. Second, in a laboratory the identity of the subjects' decisions is known to the investigator. This lack of anonymity can lead to pro-social behaviour not found in a real setting. Third, the results can be influenced by the amount of money subjects can earn in the experiment. One would expect that financial considerations would become more important when the stakes are increasing. The literature finds only partial support for this thesis (Levitt and List 2007: 164). Fourth, the participants in experiments differ in a systematic way from the actors in a real world setting. Often participants are students, who voluntary participate in the experiment. Some studies find that their behaviour significantly differs from other groups (such as CEOs). Furthermore, in an experiment restrictions are introduced on the available choices and on the number of times one can make a choice. For example, in an experiment participants are obliged to make a choice that is often framed as giving money to another participant. In a real world setting one can sometimes avoid making a decision, or one can select a non-pecuniary reward, such as volunteering time. Finally, the context of an experiment matters for its result. Relevant aspects are features under control of the experimenter, such as the phrasing of the setting, the words used 'partners' versus 'opponents', and the language used (Akkerman *et al.* 2007), and contextual aspects not under the investigator's control. The latter part of the context consists of the subject's past experiences and internalized social norms. These differences in context form the basis for using laboratory experiments to investigate differences in behaviour due to differences in culture. One compares the behaviour of respondents in laboratory experiments who are almost identical in every aspect except for the culture from which the participants come.

In a natural field experiment the researcher intervenes in the natural environment of the subjects.[11] Field experiments can be considered a meeting ground between the laboratory experiments and the quantitative regressions analysis (Harrison and List 2004: 1009). Various types of field experiments can be distinguished, differing on whether participants are selected, obtain a participation fee, and thus are or are not aware of the fact that they are participating in an experiment. Harrison and List (2004) present a taxonomy of field experiments and discuss various methodological issues of these experiments, where they compare these experiments with laboratory experiments. The probability of measurement bias is much smaller when subjects are not aware of the fact that they are part of an experiment. Their reaction can be assumed to reflect natural reactions. In these cases experiments can be considered unobtrusive. Since the experimenter influences the subjects' environment (although the latter is not aware of this) others (Kellehear 2001, for example) consider all experiments to be obtrusive.

Unobtrusive methods

The obtrusive methods for measuring beliefs and behaviour influence the response by the subjects. Natural or unobtrusive observations are observations for which the measurement activity as such does not influence the behaviour of agents. This does not imply that the researcher does not have any influence on the reported measure. Depending on the activities' nature, the translation of activities into quantitative or qualitative measures will be influenced by the researcher's choices. Unobtrusive methods include the use of: texts and audio-visual records; physical subjects such as vases; settings and traces; simple observations; hardware techniques such as camera and video, and statistics collected by statistical bureaus. Note that (as, for example, Hofstede) I consider statistics as unobtrusive, although these figures are collected by means of questionnaires so that the respondents are well aware of the recording of their activities. In general, they are obliged by law to fill out the forms. In some cases, for example providing information for tax collection, respondents can get punished by a fine if they provide false information. This illustrates that there can be an incentive to misreport.

Unobtrusive methods have several advantages.[12] First, they study actual instead of reported behaviour. Second, the measures are usually safe both for the researchers and the subjects. Third, since the methods do not disrupt others, they are easily repeatable; hence, other researchers can recheck the findings and investigate the reliability of the measures. Fourth, the observations can be discreet and non-involving. Moreover, access is not a problem and inexpensive. Finally, since the unobtrusive measures are non-disruptive, inexpensive, accessible and safe, they are ideal for longitudinal study designs. This enables researchers to develop measures that are consistent over time.

Disadvantages are attached to unobtrusive measures too. First of all, the observations might be distorted because the records are not intended to give an unbiased view. Texts such as firms' annual reports and leaders' public speeches are good examples in this respect. For managers and leaders these documents are instruments for selling their policy. Consequently, these official documents will contain a tendency to emphasize the authors' success and wise decisions. Failures are easily ascribed to unfavourable external conditions. Examples of the latter are firms' managers complaining about unfair levels of exchange rates and foreign economic policy. This bias can be circumvented by selecting texts that are written by independent persons, who have no direct interest in a prejudiced view. Statistics might be biased because the reporters want to hide some information. Income can be underreported in order to reduce tax payments. Social pressure can lead to underreporting of the causes of, death, for example, death by suicide or death due to a certain disease (HIV/AIDS, for example). Second, researchers are outsiders so that their view can differ from that of insiders. Moreover, an individual researcher's subjective view can bias the results. Each researcher has his or her own interests, experiences, and cultural upbringing which can colour his or her observations. Methods aimed at mitigating this observation bias are the use of a clear written guideline for selecting the words and phrases, ranking by several researchers and an extensive discussion between the researchers in order to make sure that there is consensus about the concepts. Third, common sources of error can result from the fact that only particular sources are easily or regularly recorded. Annual reports are readily available and thus used more often than notes, emails and other internal documents, which might be more informative. Furthermore, unobtrusive methods have a limited range of application. Unlike interviews, unobtrusive measures can not be attuned to the situation and research questions at hand. Finally, unobtrusive methods are indirect in the sense that they require a theory that relates the material (text, etc.) to the subjects' intention or belief.

Content analysis

Content analysis of speeches and documents can be qualitative and quantitative. A qualitative analysis searches texts in order to find wordings which could indicate a change in contents or importance. Good examples are studies that look for changes in speeches of political leaders in order to find out whether there is a change in policy or in argumentation of an otherwise unchanged policy. Often this technique is used for studying the developments in a particular country or in a small set of countries. Examples of studies that use this technique for investigating the relation between culture and economic development are Kok Hwa's (1997) study of Singapore, and Maseland's (2006a) study of the Philippines and Malaysia.

A quantitative content analysis consists of deriving quantitative measures from documents or other historical material. Often the quantitative measure is the frequency by which a word or a group of words with similar meaning are used in texts, such as (annual) reports, speeches, stories and descriptive texts of countries.[13] Nowadays, this method is frequently used for obtaining quantitative measures of central bankers' communication. These measures are derived from the regularly organized press conference by the central bank's president (Rosa and Verga 2007, Berger *et al.* 2006), and from the editorial of the central bank's official bulletin (Heinemann and Ulrich

2005), or from irregular statements as these were reported by news services such as Bloomberg and Reuters (Jansen and De Haan 2007). Within the field of economics and culture, content analysis is used for validating dimensions obtained by surveys (GLOBE project) and for deriving a cultural variable. The GLOBE team read the text of culturgrams of the countries in order to find both words and phrases which explicitly or implicitly refer to the cultural dimensions derived. Thereafter these phrases were independently coded by two researchers and the resulting indices correlated with the cultural dimensions.[14]

In his book on the achieving society, McClelland (1961) relies on various studies using different techniques – interviews, questionnaires, experiments and content analysis – to measure the need for Achievement (*n* Achievement). The content analysis in this study uses texts, figures, and patterns on vases as the source for deriving scores on *n* Achievement. The texts are, folk tales from various preliterate cultures; the texts of classical writers and poets from Ancient Greece; four types of literature – fiction, verse, short stories or tales, and history – from Spain in the Late Middle Ages; drama accounts of sea voyages and street ballads from the fifteenth to the nineteenth centuries in England; American reading textbooks for the period 1800–1950; and children's stories for two periods (around 1925 and around 1950) from 21 countries geographically situated outside of the tropics. McClelland also reports two content analyses using designs on vases. The first one is a study in which vases from Ancient Greece are scored on the shape of figures and on the use of space (ibid: 124–126). The second is a study of Pre-Incan Peru in which the shape characteristics of funeral urns from there are scored (ibid: 152–154).

The stories selected should represent the attitude of as many persons as possible, the material from different countries and time periods should be written as nearly as possible for the same purpose, the literature should be chosen for its imaginativeness rather than realism, and the number of lines of each sample should be the same (McClelland 1961: 110–113). In case the last criterion is not met, one can correct statistically for the texts' differences in size. After the texts have been selected one has to formulate the criteria to be used for scoring the texts. Preferably two or more persons score the texts independently. These scores form the basis for calculating an indicator representing the cultural aspect one wants to measure: need for Achievement in McClelland's case.

Although the researchers' measurement activity does not influence the texts' content, this does not imply that an unbiased measure of agent's intentions and activities is obtained by analyzing texts.

Quantifying culture and institutions by official statistics

Many of the direct observations used in investigations of the relation between culture and economics are taken from official statistics, collected by national and international statistical offices. A great deal of these statistics are obtained by questionnaires developed by these offices and filled out by firms and non-profit organizations. We do not discuss in further detail these data, since they are used in many studies on social issues and there is no element to it, which is of particular interest for our subject. In this section we discuss those direct observations that are used in studies on economics and culture, and which deserve some attention because their appropriateness for measuring the concept they are supposed to represent has been questioned. Two types of variables are described, those used as a proxy for culture and some used as a measure of institutional fabric.

Besides the cultural dimensions and answers to single questions discussed in the section on surveys, culture is also represented by measures of primary language and dominant religion. Both dummy variables and frequencies are used (e.g. Stulz and Willamson 2003). In the case of dummy variables, a country is assigned a 1 if the largest fraction practices the religion or language concerned and a zero if not. Another measure of culture is the fraction of the population belonging to a certain religion, ethnicity, or speaking a particular language.

A common feature of the use of these proxies is the assumption that belonging to the same religion or speaking the same language leads to a common attitude with respect to economic issues. Empirical research, however, reveals that neither shared religion nor shared language will necessarily lead to common views. Within the great religions there are various denominations (see e.g. Hofstede 2001: 176, 177, 327–331) with quite different views on worldly affairs. Moreover, even small denominations can show a large diversity in opinion on the preferable economic organization. Iannaccone (1992), for example, reports that among the evangelical Christians in the USA the ideal economic system ranges from very pro free markets and capitalism to a flat rejection of capitalism in favour of socialism (see also Chapter 7). Using the same language facilitates the communication between the inhabitants of two countries, and thus might, but need not, lead to a common set of beliefs, since language, as such, certainly does not imply a certain belief. Empirical research shows that using the same language and having the same religion does not necessarily imply belonging to the same culture and vice versa. The culture of Dutch-speaking Belgium is very different from that of the Dutch in The Netherlands, whereas it is quite similar to that of French-speaking Belgium (Hofstede 1980: 229).[15]

Indicators of institutional arrangements are often derived by experts' interpretations of laws. Examples in the financial sector are La Porta *et al.* (1997a, 1997b, 1998b, 1999, 2000), Demirgüç-Kunt and Levine (2001) and Barth *et al.* (2006); for central bank independence (Cukierman 1992); for wage coordination and wage centralization (Kenworthy 2001); for labour markets regulations (Botero *et al.* 2004), and for the degree of consensus (Schneider and Wagner 2001). Since these phenomena are less well defined, some consider it impossible to approximate or measure them, although in general one regards the measurement of formal institutions less problematic than that of values. Forder (1998, 1999) even regards the measurement of institutions impossible because of, in his view, the high level of subjectivity in measuring them. Of course, he is right that the measurement of these institutions contains a certain degree of subjectivity. The latter can be reduced, however, when researchers publish a protocol in which they clearly describe the different categories they distinguish and the characteristics an institution should adhere to in order to be classified as belonging to a particular category. The subjectivity can be reduced even further, when two or more researchers independently score the institutions using the same protocol. The final classification is based on the scores by different researchers and discussion of the cases where researchers disagree. In this way the present method delivers less subjective scores of the institution than any other method we can think of. One should keep in mind that more qualitative methods (including case studies) often implicitly assume that institutions have certain characteristics. These assumptions are made explicit here.

Methods for testing relations

In principle two research designs for studying the relation between economics and culture are in use: the hypothetico-deductive design and ethnographic-inductive design (Kellehear 2001: Ch. 2). The first design consists of formulating a theory from which hypotheses are derived, after which these hypotheses are tested for a particular case or group of cases. The results found can induce the researcher to accept, reject or change the theory used. This procedure moves from the general idea or theory to the particular case. It is theory driven; the theoretical literature is taken as the starting point and hypotheses to be tested in the empirical part of the research are derived from theory. A typical sequence of activities is the following: reading the literature; formulating the theoretical model and the hypotheses; selecting the appropriate method for testing the hypotheses; describing the results found and discussing and explaining the results. The research provides an outsider's view of the subject and emphasizes the general applicability of a theory, maybe with some amendments reflecting the context. Essentially, the society is studied from an outsider's point of view (an etic approach).

The ethnographic-inductive design tries to understand the social system from the insiders' point of view (an emic viewpoint). It studies social life and from there it tries to explain the development of social processes. Hence, it takes the particular situation as a starting point and from that derives more general conclusions for theory. The theory is grounded in actual changes in society, hence the term 'grounded theory' is sometimes used. In principle, the theoretical perspectives of the ethnographic-inductive approach are opposite to that of the hypothetico-deductive design. The first claims to start from observations, whereas the second one starts from theory. In practice, a research programme set up according to the ethnographic-inductive design also starts by reading the literature on the subject under investigation and thereafter observes the society. A typical sequence of activities is reading the literature, collecting information by participation and observation and recording the activities (including discussions, etc.) in the society, and describing the theoretical implications of these observations. In this process attention is also paid to the position of the researcher, where he or she was and how he or she went about understanding the findings.

Within economics researchers use the hypothetico-deductive design, in anthropology the ethnographic-inductive design is widely accepted, whereas within sociology both approaches are used, but by different groups. Unfortunately, communication and exchange of ideas between the two groups are rare. Several researchers of each of the two approaches show hostile attitudes with respect to the other approach. Often this has led to an unfruitful *Methoden Streit* (see Chapter 2). The rest of this chapter is devoted to some methods used in the literature on economics, business and culture, in particular the cross-society regressions which are widely used nowadays.

Descriptive analysis

The descriptive method is traditionally used in studies on differences between countries and communities with respect to attitudes and economic organization. It consists of a 'thick' description of the societies or communities concerned. In fact all elements of Figure 4.2 are dealt with, although the borderlines between the different elements are often unclear. The information used comes from various sources: (a) written texts by politicians, academia, newspapers, novelists, etc., (b) interviews of key persons, (c) statistics and (d) observations by researchers themselves. The latter is necessary because written texts can often give a one-sided view of reality or its understanding is incomplete if not augmented by their own observations. Alatas (2002: 115), for example, argues that 'many pro-Asian values arguments are based on textual instead of concrete studies of values and societies'. An advantage of these descriptive studies is that in principle they can give a very detailed picture of the case and disentangle all causal relations. Moreover, different views on the subject can be given. Maseland (2006a), for example, tells three stories of Mahathir's successful attempt to enhance economic development in Malaysia. The researcher has much freedom with respect to collecting and interpreting information. He or she will arrange data and events in such an order that these prove his (her) position, whereas it is difficult for the reader to judge whether this opinion is correct or the most relevant one. This easily leads to a very subjective view. Maseland's procedure of telling three stories for the same event, can be regarded as a manner for diminishing the subjectivity of the study.

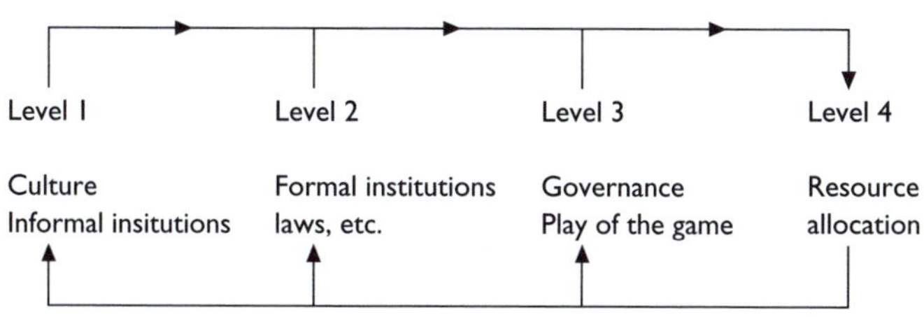

Figure 4.2 Theoretical framework

The analytical narrative, proposed in Bates *et al.* (1998), can be another solution to this subjectivity problem. The analytical narrative combines data and theory. It uses the analytical tools that are commonly employed in economics and political science with the narrative form, which is more commonly employed in history. As a narrative this method pays close attention to stories, accounts and context. It is analytical in that it extracts explicit and formal lines of reasoning which facilitates both exposition and explanation. The formal models can be models constructed by the authors for analyzing the current problem, models provided by others or a formal line of reasoning. The models serve to seek the essence of the stories and processes leading to the outcomes. The analytical character of the narrative facilitates a critical assessment of the analysis. Do the assumptions fit the facts? Do the conclusions follow from the premises? Do the implications of the model (broadly defined above) find confirmation in the data? How well does the theory stand up when compared to alternative explanations? Is the reasoning general? Can it be applied in different situations? Of course these or similar questions can guide the assessment of any method. This procedure does not necessarily lead to a cultural explanation. For example, Greif in his contribution in Bates *et al.* (1998) consciously chooses a political-economic rather than a cultural explanation for the cooperation between families in Genoa. The political-economic explanation can account for periods of cooperation and discords, which a cultural account can not. In Greif (1994), however, he chooses a cultural explanation for the differences in economic performance between the Maghribi and Genoese traders. Here the Maghribi stand for a collectivist society and the Genoese for an individualist society. Cultural beliefs coordinate cooperation and influence equilibrium selection and institutions. An analytical narrative thus can, but need not, lead to a cultural explanation.

Regression analysis

Disadvantages of descriptive studies are often regarded to be the subjectivity of the result, due to the way the author organizes the material and the fact that the research is often restricted to a few cases only. Consequently, it remains unclear whether and to what extent the results can be generalized. Regression analysis offers a possibility of including many observations in the analysis and thus drawing more generally valid conclusions. As mentioned above, the vast majority of quantitative cultural studies use ecological regressions: countries serve as the units of analysis. These regressions can show peculiarities resulting from among others, the small number of observations (Shalev 2007). A minority take the individual respondent as the unit of analysis. These respondents can come from different broader units (firms or societies), which warrants a multilevel analysis. Here we briefly discuss some of the main issues to be taken into account when employing cross-country regressions.

Cross-country regressions

After measures of cultural dimensions and formal institutions are obtained, the next step in the research strategy consists of formulating hypotheses. Since the concept of culture is vaguer than economic phenomena one should take care that the conclusions are not just based on correlations but are underpinned by valid theoretical considerations. We therefore recommend starting on the right-hand side of Figure 4.2 and deriving from the existing literature the main characteristics of the economic phenomenon concerned. In this way one finds the essential characteristics of the performance of and formal institutions which are conducive for each type of economic system. Thereafter, these characteristics of the economic systems (Levels 3 and 4 in Figure 4.2) and those of the formal institutions conducive to them (Level 2) are related to aspects of culture (Level 1). This last step is highly facilitated by extensive descriptions of the characteristics of the cultural dimensions. In this sense an advantage of Hofstede's dimensions is that for each dimension a wide range of phenomena associated with it are available. These associations greatly enhance the finding of relations between the cultural dimensions and the formal institutions and economic performance.

Measures of cultural dimensions and economic institutions are often available for one period only, so that the resulting relations are cross-country regressions of the type

$$Y = \alpha C + \beta X + \varepsilon \qquad (1)$$

where Y is the economic or institutional variable to be explained, C the matrix containing cultural variables and X a matrix containing other explanatory variables, and ε the disturbance term. By estimating these relations one supposes that on average the influence of culture on Y is the same in these countries. At least two conditions should be met in order for this hypothesis to hold: (i) the countries should be comparable and (ii) the estimated coefficients should not be influenced unduly by one or two observations.

The number of countries included in the regressions can be restricted in order to increase the comparability of the countries and to ensure that the content of a variable is the same across countries (see also Temple 1999). One can, for example, have doubts about the equivalence of meaning across countries of a particular dimension (see Chapter 5). Another reason can be that some institutional arrangements are not available in all countries. Pension systems, for example, are not known in many developing countries so that a distinction between funded and unfunded pensions systems does not make any sense. On the other hand, the number of countries should be large enough, so that the degrees of freedom allow a regression analysis and the variance in each variable is not reduced unduly. A regression analysis based on six (Jaggi and Low 2000) or seven (Zarzeski 1996) countries cannot deliver any significant and reliable result with respect to the influence of national culture because of too few observations; the variance of the individual variables is too low to allow a reasonably accurate estimation. Similarly, with about twenty observations the number of explanatory variables is also restricted to just a few (see e.g. Shalev 2007: 277).

The results of the cross-country regressions are vulnerable to influential observations: countries for which the characteristics are that far away from the general pattern that they have a determining influence on the results of the regressions. In particular in small samples, these outliers can drive the results. Hence, one should always perform tests on the possibility of influential observations. Scatter plots form a simple method for detecting possible outliers. More sophisticated techniques analyze the residuals of the regression and deliver measures for the relative influence of an individual observation on the fit (see e.g. Fox 1991). In case an observation is regarded as an influential one, one can decide to remove it from the sample or include it in the analysis but attach a lower weight to it. An advantage of the latter procedure is that the information provided by this observation is not lost. The procedure in Welsch (1980) is an example of such a bounded influence estimator. An alternative approach starts with the notion that each country is a unique case which can inform the researchers about the regularities between the few countries observed. Then graphs and tables can be used for investigating the relation between the factors considered (Shalev 2007).

Although one has carefully selected the number of countries and correctly taken care of influential observations, often the residuals are heteroskedastic. This means that there is still a systematic pattern in the residuals, for example, a clustering of large residuals for countries from a particular continent or a relation with GDP per capita. This heteroskedasticity reduces the precision of the estimates. White (1980) has developed a general procedure that delivers consistent estimates without the necessity to specify the type of heteroskedasticity. Unfortunately this procedure is only reliable in large samples of more than 500 observations. Small sample variants are presented in MacKinnon and White (1985). But still often the sample size is so small that visual inspection of graphs and tables will deliver better information about the structure in the dataset and the reason for a particular form of heteroskedasticity.

Another concern regards causality. Almost always, the cultural dimensions and or the institutions are observed for one period only. Consequently, the regression analysis cannot investigate the dynamics of the relationship. This, however, does not preclude the possibility of studying the causality between the variables. In order to be able to do that three necessary and sufficient conditions should be fulfilled: (i) association: two variables should be empirically correlated, (ii) time order: the cause should precede the effect in time, and (iii) non-spuriousness: the empirical correlation between the two variables is not due to variation in a third variable that is itself the cause of the variation in both variables. In addition, identifying mechanisms through which the effect operates considerably strengthens the case for causality.

Two of these conditions require special attention: time order and non-spuriousness. Time order is relevant in two ways. First, some economic phenomena, for instance some regulations and some patterns in financial systems, emerged before the 1960s, when the dimensions were measured. Can we explain such phenomena by cultural variables measured later in time? To do this, we must show that cultural variables are very stable. Second, in some cases the scores are based on surveys that were organized some decades ago. The survey that forms the basis of Hofstede's dimensions, for example, was held at the end of the 1960s and the beginning of 1970s.

Most sociologists agree that populations of nations hold deeply rooted values that change very slowly. The question, however, is whether cultural dimensions reflect such deep-rooted values. Hofstede (2001) presents an overview of the relation between his cultural dimensions and those found in studies by others. This group of other studies consists of replications of Hofstede's method on other populations, as well as studies employing different questionnaires. From this review Hofstede concludes that his dimensions are still valid and that the differences between countries remain. A similar result is found for the two cultural dimensions characterizing the European Values Surveys. An analysis of the three waves (1981, 1990, 1999) of this survey reveals that the period effects (differences between the three waves) are very small, whereas cohort effects (differences between people of different age) are much more important. Moreover, the latter remain more or less constant between the three waves (see Hagenaars *et al.* 2003). Similarly, Inglehart and Baker (2000: 34, 38) report a persistent influence of a society's historical–cultural history on the two cultural dimensions Inglehart (1997) derived from the World Values Survey. Hence, these dimensions can be used to represent culture for a more recent period than the beginning of the 1970s. The more so in studies that focus on the differences between countries, because research on changes in values reveals that if any change occurs, the cross-country patterns are unaffected.

If culture changes only slowly, then in all likelihood cultural dimensions and the independent variables are determined simultaneously: the adjustment process is so slow that they interact with each other. Such an interaction is even more likely since theoretically, culture, economic institutions and economic performance are assumed to influence each other (see Figure 4.2). Consequently, the cultural dimension in regression (1) is correlated with the disturbance term of this equation, so that the Ordinary Least Squares estimator is no longer unbiased and consistent (see e.g. Verbeek 2004: 130). Instrumental variables are often used to obtain unbiased and consistent estimates of the effect of culture. Instrumental variables are variables that are (a) exogenous to the endogenous variable and hence have no correlation with the disturbance term and (b) are highly correlated with the explanatory variable: the cultural dimensions in our case. The estimation procedure consists of two steps. In the first step the endogenous regressor (cultural dimension) is regressed on the instrumental variables. In the second step the fitted values of the first regression are used as explanatory variables in the original relation. In this way one obtains an estimate of the influence of the exogenous component of the cultural dimensions on the issue at hand. The quality of this Instrumental Variables (IV) estimator depends on the correlation between the instrumental variables and the endogenous regressor(s). Weak correlation between the two can lead to a severely biased estimate, so that the selection of appropriate instrumental variables is critical for the result. One can use the first step regression for investigating the influence of the instruments on the regressor. If the instrumental variable has an insignificant influence in this regression, one should not put much confidence in the results of the IV estimation.[16] Hofstede found that some of his cultural dimensions are related to exogenous variables such as latitude and the size of the country, so that these variables can serve as instrumental variables.

Another issue which requires special attention is non-spuriousness. This, of course, is related to testing rival hypotheses. It should be used together with Occam's razor, meaning that simpler explanations are preferable. This implies that if biological, economic, or technological factors are sufficient to explain a given phenomenon; cultural explanations should not be invoked. At the same time, we should not stop at explanations by political, institutional and regulatory factors, even if these explanations are good. Conceptually, political and regulatory factors are dependent on the more basic factor culture (see Figure 4.2). These are also reasons to perform robustness tests. Once a basic relation is derived, additional variables are added to the relation in order to check the robustness of the relation found. In those cases where the number of countries and hence the degrees of freedom are low, one has to add one variable at a time to the basic relation (see, for example, Black 2006, De Jong 2002, and Chapter 5). The result can be regarded as robust if all or a particular fraction of the estimated coefficients of the variable concerned do not change sign and remain statistically significant. This extreme bounds analysis has been developed by Leamer (1983) and used in, among others, Levine and Renelt (1992) and Sala-i-Martin (1997).

Multilevel analysis

Until now we have assumed that the variables in relation (1) all refer to the same (national) level. In some studies the dependent variable is a characteristic of a lower level than the national one: individual firms (Hope 2003, De Jong and Semenov 2006b) or individual respondents (Hooghe *et al.* 2006, Guiso *et al.* 2003). In all likelihood, the observations in the same country will be influenced by factors particular to that country, so that the within country correlation of the observations will be higher than the correlation across countries. In case the firms' (respondents') characteristics are explained by features at the firm (individual) level, one can take the common influences into account by adding a dummy variable for the country the observation belongs to. This fixed effects estimation technique is used in Guiso *et al.* (2003). The estimation procedure becomes more complicated if the set of explanatory factors is extended with variables at higher levels (state, industry or country). The number of independent observations at the higher level is smaller than at the lower level, introducing an explicit form of correlation between a set of explanatory variables. The Ordinary Least Squares (OLS) estimates do not take these interdependencies into account and thus lead to standard errors that are much too small, and results that are spuriously reported as 'significant'. A multilevel estimation technique has to be used in order to adequately take the consequences of these interdependencies into account (see Hox 2002 for an introduction to this technique). Unfortunately, only De Jong and Semenov (2006b) apply a multilevel technique, whereas Hope (2003), Jaggi and Low (2000) and Zarzeski (1996) do not. Consequently, one can doubt the significance of the results reported in the last three studies.

Panel regressions

In some cases observations from different periods are available. Then one is able to estimate the relationship for both the time frame and across countries. As such, the increased number of observations opens the possibility to investigate more rigorously the relation under investigation. However, care should be taken to allow for the different nature of the time-series and cross-section aspect of the data. Autocorrelation is an important issue in time-series analysis, whereas heteroskedasticity is an important issue for the cross-section part. One should carefully distinguish these two features of the dataset when estimating the relations. Moreover, the explanatory factors relevant in the time domain can substantially differ from those in the cross-section domain. Take for example unemployment. In the time domain, unemployment in the previous period and the phase of the business cycle are reasonable explanatory factors, whereas explanatory factors for cross-country differences are more likely to be differences in labour market institutions and culture.

Concluding remarks

In this chapter we have reviewed and assessed methods currently used for measuring culture and institutions and for investigating relations between culture and economic phenomena. Before the exposition of these methods we have discussed various methodological considerations that have to be taken into account when doing research in this field. The intention of this chapter is to make readers aware of the various methods available and the pros and cons attached to each. It definitely is not intended to be a brief introduction into methods of cultural analysis. For these methods we refer to textbooks (for example, Van de Vijver and Leung 1997, Punnett and Shenkar 2004, Usunier 1998, Marschan-Piekkari and Welch 2004). We hope this chapter provides the reader with enough background material to understand and judge the various studies to be discussed in the rest of this book.

Various methods have been described briefly. As these descriptions may have made clear we do not regard one method to be superior. Whichever method one uses, the researcher should ask him or herself, whether the particular method is suitable for investigating the problem at hand. Often one has to conclude that one method can only provide a limited explanation. Cross-country regressions, for example, are a good instrument for finding systematic patterns within a group of countries. Only if reliable data for several years are available, can regressions shed light on causality issues. Cultural dimensions and other measures of national culture are measured only once, so that such an investigation is not possible. Then supplementing the regressions with a study into the history of the issues is very useful. Such a use of more than one approach simultaneously is often called triangulation (see e.g. Hofstede 2001: 5). It is derived from the way one can measure distance to a point where one cannot go. Then one measures the distance to two points to which one can go and calculates from these two base points the distance to the third point. The more different the base points are, the more accurate the estimated distance. Similarly, the use of two quite different methods can deliver much information and understanding. In the next chapters when possible we will pay attention to the results of studies using different methods in order to illustrate the different insights obtained by applying various methods.

Chapter 5

Culture and cross-country differences in institutions

In Chapter 3 we described three ways by which culture has entered economics during recent decades: culture as a source of preferences; culture as a source of constraints; and culture as a deviation from the model. The last approach ascribes the unexplained part to culture, lacks any theoretical underpinning, and is therefore not considered explicitly in this book. The other two approaches differ with respect to the assumption as to whether culture can change quickly or not and whether the influence of cultural factors dominates (constrain) the rest of the societies' structure. Both approaches assume that values influence (and are influenced by) a society's institutions and the results (economic growth, etc.) obtained. Many empirical studies make use of large datasets on cultural dimensions and values (Hofstede, Schwartz, and World Value Survey) for studying relations between culture and economic phenomena.

Intergenerational transmission has been argued to be the most important way by which individuals form their values during the first twenty years of their life (see Chapter 3). Parents and teachers are the dominant figures in a child's life and hence play an important role in the formation of values. Consequently, adults migrating from one country to another will take the dominant values of their country of origin with them. In the host country they will raise their children according to the standards of the country of origin. Thus, preferences and behaviour of second generation immigrants will partly reflect the attitudes typical for the parents' country of origin. The epistemological approach tests this relationship.

The chapter starts with a discussion of this epistemological approach. It uses data on the behaviour of immigrants and their children to investigate whether this behaviour is systematically related to the behaviour of the individuals' country of origin. In this manner it tests the intergenerational transmission and the existence of different value patterns between host countries and countries of origin. However, it can not explain why one society differs from another, how and in which way values play a significant role in this respect, and the dynamic process by which these values and the relationship with institutions will change over time. Cross-country studies which explicitly relate a measure of (national) values to economic institutions are discussed in the rest of this chapter. We summarize research on the role of values in the design of financial systems, labour market arrangements, and policies to open the economy to foreign influences. Thereafter, these results are used for investigating whether the resulting system of institutional arrangements is a coherent one: are the institutions of each subsystem complementary to those of the other subsystems and are they correlated with the same set of values? In the mean time we use this literature review to draw attention to two other issues: the selection of countries in the sample and the possibility of a changing pattern between culture and institutions over time. In this way we hope to make the reader aware of the circumstances under which culture is and is not a plausible explanatory factor.

Epistemological approach

Intergenerational transmission has been argued to be an important if not the most important way by which values are formed (Chapter 3). Later in life society as a whole influences an individual's values and practices. Parents are the dominant educators during the first years of life, which are so crucial for the formation of values. Consequently, if culture in the sense of norms and values has any influence on economic activity, then one would expect a relation between the values formed during childhood and individuals' economic behaviour. More specifically, one would expect a relation between the values taught by the parents and the behaviour of their adult children. Distinguishing between parents' influences and those of society proves to be impossible if parents and children stay their entire lives in the same country. If they move from one country to another, however, differences in values of the country of origin and of the host country should be reflected in differences in behaviour between the immigrants and their children compared to the inhabitants of the host countries. This reasoning forms the basis of the epistemological approach, which relates the behaviour of (second generation) immigrants to the values of the country of origin.

Studies using the epistemological approach have investigated savings behaviour, female labour force participation, living arrangements, and the level of trust. In order to investigate whether cultural effects partly explain differences in saving rates, Carroll *et al.* (1994) study the savings behaviour of immigrants into Canada from countries with different savings rates. They distinguish immigrants from four areas: North and Western Europe (including the United States), South and East Europe, China and Southeast Asia, and other Asian countries. The national savings rate of the Southeast Asian countries is significantly higher than that of the other regions. The regression analysis of savings by immigrants into Canada does not single out the Southeast Asians as having different savings behaviour. Their main result is that the savings pattern of immigrants is not influenced by the area of origin and if there are any cultural differences, 'the point estimates suggest that Southeast Asians have a higher marginal propensity to consume (lower propensity to save) than other groups – precisely the opposite of the findings in the aggregate data' (Carrol *et al.* 1994: 698). Due to limitations of the dataset, Caroll and co-authors use dummies for the different areas of origin. Moreover, they analyze the behaviour of first generation immigrants, who have been exposed to the institutions of their countries of origin, so that it is unclear whether their behaviour results from intergenerational teaching or from the institutional structure in the countries they come from.

Studies relating the behaviour of second-generation immigrants to the behaviour of the corresponding issues in their parents' country of origin form a more direct test of the intergenerational transmission of values and attitudes. In a series of papers Fernández and co-authors perform such tests, when they relate labour force participation (LFP)[1] of second-generation American women to the culture of the women's country of ancestry. These women are born and raised in the USA and hence face the same institutions as their contemporaries whose parents are from the USA. They might differ in their cultural heritage during their childhood, but their parents have raised them according to values of the parents' country of origin. In order to test this hypothesis Fernández and Fogli (2007) explain these women's labour force participation by proxies of the culture of their parents' country of origin. From the 1970 census they study married women who are 30–40 years old, born in the USA and whose fathers were from outside the USA.[2] The fathers' country of origin is considered the women's country of ancestry. The labour force participation of these women in 1970 is related to the labour force participation in 1950 in their father's country of origin. This cultural factor proves to have a significant influence on the women's labour force participation, both in partial regressions and when one controls for the influence of the woman's education and her husband's education and income. As a robustness check, Fernández and Fogli include the influence of parents' education, ethnic human capital measured by the average years of education in 1940 of the immigrants from these countries, and the quality of education in the country of origin. The main results are robust to the inclusion of these factors.

In order to investigate whether wife's or husband's culture dominates the wife's labour force participation, Fernández and Fogli include cultural proxies for both spouses, where each spouse's culture is represented by the respective father's country of origin. Female labour force participation is positively and significantly influenced by the woman's and husband's culture. Surprisingly, the husband's cultural proxy dominates in size and significance when both cultural proxies are included in one regression. Finally, clustering of ethnic groups in the United States of America enhances the impact of culture on a woman's work outcome.

Giuliano (2007) applies the epistemological approach for explaining differences in behaviour in the countries of origin. At the beginning of the twenty-first century well over half of 18–33 year olds live with their parents in Mediterranean European countries. For other Western European countries less than 30 per cent of young adults stay at home. In 1970 the fraction living at home was low and similar across these countries. These cross-country differences can be explained by, among other things, unfavourable economic conditions, poor employment opportunities, and rise in parents' income. Giuliano (2007) argues that cultural differences play a role too. In Southern Europe the norm has always been to leave for marriage, whereas in Northern Europe the norm has always been the independence of the generations. Due to the sexual revolution of the 1970s, in all countries young adults postpone their marriage decisions. In the Southern European countries this implies that they stay at home until their marriage. In other European countries the young adults leave their parents' home anyway and the postponement of their marriage does not significantly influence this decision. Since cultural norms, economic conditions, and institutions all are country specific, a cross-country analysis of these European countries cannot properly identify the cultural effect. Guiliano therefore tests her hypotheses by means of data on the living arrangements of second-generation immigrants in the USA. If cultural norms are persistent then living arrangements of immigrants should parallel their counterparts in the home country (measured by the father's country of origin). The impact of economic conditions can be isolated because these immigrants all face the same labour market conditions and institutions. Dummy variables representing the country of origin and the fraction of 18–33 year olds living with their parents in the European country of origin are used to represent the cultural norms. Regressions with each of these proxies of cultural norms show a significant and positive coefficient for the decision of second generation young adults in the USA to stay at home. Each regression also contains a set of controls, such as age, sex, education, etc. As in Fernández and Fogli's study an effect of clustering of ethnic groups is present. A systematic relation is found 'between large increases in the stay-at-home rates of second generation Southern Europeans from 1970–2000 and higher concentrations of second generation Southern Europeans' (Giuliano 2007: 941). This effect is not observed for second generation immigrants from Western and Northern European countries.

Guiso *et al.* (2006) find that in the USA, the level of trust is systematically related to the respondents' country-of-origin. Moreover, the level of trust of second generation immigrants is positively correlated with the current level of trust in the corresponding country of origin.

Cultural dimensions and cross-country differences

The results of the studies belonging to the epistemological approach reveal evidence supporting the view that values play a role in one's economic decision making, and that these values are formed by the teaching and deeds of parents. These studies are able to explain differences in behaviour between minorities (second generation immigrants) and other inhabitants of a society by means of the differences in values. Hence, they can explain why and in which way (ethnic) minorities in a society behave differently from the majority. However, since these studies focus on minorities, they are not able to explain why the dominant view in one country differs from that in others and in which way these differences can explain differences in national institutions and national performance.

In this section we review studies aimed at explaining these cross-country differences by means of proxies for national preferences, such as the cultural dimensions, as these have been developed by Hofstede and Schwartz, and answers to questions included in the World Values Survey and European Values Survey (see Appendix 1 Various cultural dimensions for a description of these dimensions and questionnaires). A dimension measures an aspect of a country's culture relative to that of other cultures. It groups together a number of phenomena in a society that were empirically found to occur in combinations (Hofstede and Hofstede 2005: 24). Often the data from which each cultural dimension is derived have been collected only once. Consequently, an analysis of cultural and institutional change can not be performed, Moreover, the country scores on the dimensions 'do not provide absolute country positions, but only their positions relative to the other countries in the set' (Hofstede 2001: 36). The scores on the dimensions are related to indices representing formal institutions (Level 2 in Figure 5.1) or systems of governance (Level 3 in Figure 5.1), and variables measuring economic activity (Level 4). This figure is similar to Figure 3.2, except for level 0, which is left out. The reason is that this level is never explicitly used in any of the studies to be discussed.

As has been discussed extensively in Chapter 1, many definitions of culture have been proposed and used in the literature. This multitude of definitions reflects the fact that culture is a vague concept. Small wonder, studies incorporating culture or related concepts into economic analysis often are criticized as being vague, too particular, or drawing conclusions from some correlations without a rigorous theoretical underpinning. As described in Chapter 4, we, therefore, suggest starting the theoretical analysis on the right-hand side of Figure 5.1 and deriving from the existing literature the main characteristics of the economic phenomenon concerned. In this way one finds the essential characteristics of the systems' performance and of the formal institutions conducive for each type of system. In the next step, the characteristics of the economic systems (Levels 3 and 4 in Figure 5.1)

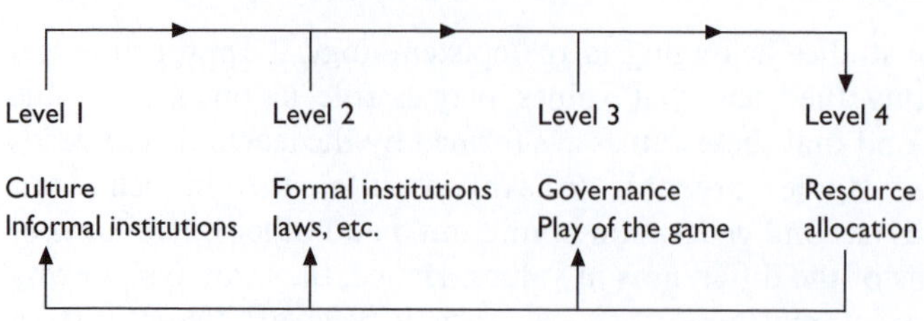

Figure 5.1 Theoretical framework

and those of the formal institutions conducive to them (Level 2) are related to aspects of culture (Level 1). For many economic phenomena, consensus exists with respect to its main characteristics and consequences and the type of laws contributing to its performance. The use of these theories as the guiding principles in deriving the relations between culture (as preferences) and economic activity preserves one from an impressionistic and theoretically unfounded analysis.

In the rest of this section we will discuss studies of cultural dimensions' influence on particular sectors of the economy. Sectors considered are: the financial system and corporate governance, labour market regulations, and regulation with respect to the openness of the economy. The review of the studies on financial systems and systems of corporate governance will also be used to illustrate the usefulness of a rigorous investigation of economic theory for deriving hypotheses about the relationship between values, institutions and economic performance, and for the selection of the countries included in the analysis. Both these studies and the study on the openness of economies shed light on the circumstance under which culture is relevant for explaining cross-country differences.

Financial systems and corporate governance

Financial systems are often classified as being either bank-based or market-based (Allen and Gale 2000, Demirgüç-Kunt and Levine 2001: esp. Ch. 3). In a bank-based system intermediaries (often banks) play an important role in providing external finance to companies. In the archetypal bank-based system, external finance is provided by bank loans. Banks are among the major owners of the company (or at least have a large stake in its supervisory board), and the banking sector itself is highly concentrated. Germany is often regarded as the best representative of bank-based systems. In a market-based system, external finance is provided by financial markets. Companies issue shares and bonds, which are traded on financial markets. The role of banks is to act as broker and advisor to non-financial firms. Firms' ownership is dispersed and competition between banks is high. The USA is regarded as the best representative of markets-based systems.

The various consequences of these differences in institutional set-up are often presented as trade-offs. Here we take the set of trade-offs provided by Allen and Gale (2000: Ch. 1) as the framework for discussing the pros and cons of each system. Added to this framework are the (mostly legal) issues suggested by others as relevant for distinguishing between types of financial systems. The trade-offs considered by Allen and Gale are: competition versus insurance, efficiency versus stability, public information but free riding versus private information and no free riding, and external control versus autonomy.

Financial markets need a certain amount of depth to work in an orderly fashion; that is, large volumes of trade and a large number of intermediary agents. Röell (1996) finds that institutional investors and pension funds in particular are critical of providing funds to be invested in financial markets. Consequently, financial markets are well developed in countries with funded pension systems and underdeveloped in countries where the state by means of pay-as-you-go systems plays a significant role in the provision of pensions. Under these conditions competitive financial markets can flourish and are (ex post) more efficient than systems based on large financial institutions. The draw-back of financial markets is, however, that markets are incomplete. Setting up markets is hampered by fixed costs for creating markets, asymmetric information, moral hazard, etc. Consequently, markets cannot offer insurance against many types of risk. Moreover, prices on markets can fluctuate for reasons unrelated to the fundamentals of the assets traded. A financial intermediary is in a much better position to provide custom-built risk-sharing and risk-smoothing financial instruments. These risk-reducing activities of intermediaries can be provided because of a long-lasting relationships between the institute and its client. Increased competition can undermine this long-term relationship and hence the insurance provided by it.

This brings us to the tension between the competitiveness of financial markets and a dispersed banking sector on the one hand and the stability of financial systems based on a few large institutions on the other. High competition between institutions can lead to risk-taking activities and undermine profit margins, and thus can give rise to bankruptcy. Also large markets that provide liquidity to individual banks in normal circumstances, may, in times of crisis, be a disadvantage if they force banks to sell assets at fire-sale prices. The result is often worse than when the banks' assets were not traded on the markets. Similarly, many small banks are more prone to financial contagion than a few large institutions. Hence, competition associated with market-based systems can undermine stability, which is associated with bank-based systems.

The way information is provided differs a lot between market-based and bank-based systems. In a market-based system, the ownership of firms is dispersed and owners and creditors operate at arms length. Consequently, no individual shareholder has the means or the incentive to scrutinize the firms' activities and management, and makes decisions based on publicly provided information and the prices of the firms' assets on markets. Moreover, in order to treat each shareholder equally, firms' management is prohibited from distributing information to (a group of) particular investors. Mandatory disclosure rules aim at ensuring that all information is made public. Rules on insider trading are there to prevent the misuse of private information. In an institution-based system with underdeveloped financial markets, ownership is often concentrated and important shareholders are members of the company's (supervisory) board. These close ties between management, shareholders and creditors form a good channel for obtaining information. Hence, regulation is more lax with respect to providing and using information on a firm's performance. Moreover, the large stake of a person, family or bank in a company forms an incentive to take greater efforts to acquire information about the firm.

The closeness of the relationship between management and owners is also important for the way management is corrected. Under an archetypal market-based system, shareholders do not have any relationship with the firm's managers. Hence, managers can operate quite independently as long as no signs of mismanagement are perceived. Regulation is in place to protect minority shareholders against the misuse of power by managers and dominant shareholders. Moreover, judicial decisions are the source of law and legal judgements can be based on the principles of equity, and do not necessarily have to be based on legislation. In this way judges can punish corporate insiders who have found a way to expropriate outsiders (minority shareholders) that is not explicitly forbidden by law. Furthermore, where judicial decisions are the source of law, one judicial decision punishing the actions of outsiders not forbidden by law becomes a precedent that is likely to be followed by all judges. Allowing multiple sources of law, and allowing each judge a large degree of deviation from legislation results in much less certain and predictable outcomes than judgements made through strict applications of the legislation that is established by one authority and is based on a coherent legal doctrine (Damaska 1986). In cases of mismanagement shareholders may sell their shares, the firm's stock price may decline and a competitor or investor may make a hostile takeover. The latter occurs at a higher frequency and is a more acceptable way of correcting management than in a bank-based system. In a bank-based system, important shareholders have a direct say in the decision making of the company. Often strategic decisions are made by consensus. Hence, control is much more direct due to the close ties between (dominant) owners and managers. Regulation does protect the minority shareholders less than in a market-based system.

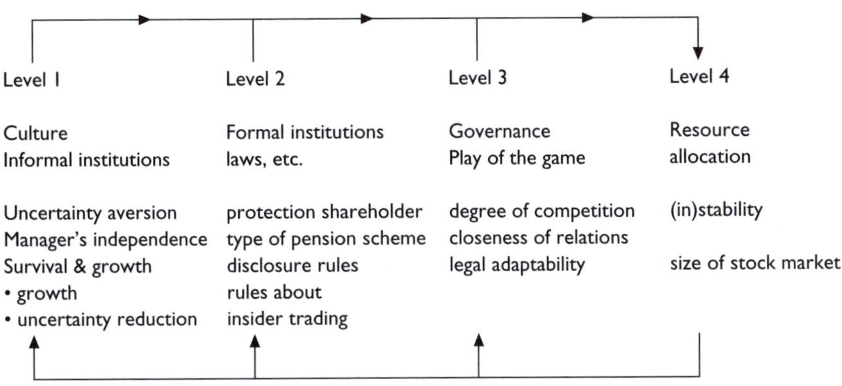

Figure 5.2 Theoretical framework of financial systems

The trade-offs between market-based and bank-based financial systems (and every intermediate system) and the related legal and institutional aspects refer to issues with respect to the performance of a financial system, its governance and its formal institutions. The most important aspects of each of these levels are summarized in Figure 5.2 (the three columns at the right hand side).

The next step (see also Chapter 4) identifies the cultural dimensions associated with the characteristics listed in the three columns at the right hand side of Figure 5.2. The instability of systems with dominant stock markets is considered by all authors as an important, if not the most important, factor distinguishing financial systems from each other. Countries where financial markets instead of institutions play a dominant role are characterized by more fluctuations in wealth and consumption, and less intergenerational risk-sharing. Moreover, the associated legal adaptability also leads to higher levels of uncertainty. Consequently, Hofstede's Uncertainty Avoidance is expected to be negatively correlated with indicators of stock market activity and arrangements enhancing the existence of stock markets, such as formal institutions (protection of minority shareholders) and governance (legal adaptability). These hypotheses on the relationship between Uncertainty Avoidance and characteristics of financial systems have been tested by various authors for various groups of countries. All find significant coefficients with the theoretically expected signs. As a robustness-check, Kwok and Tadesse (2006) and De Jong and Semenov (2004) subsequently add another explanatory variable (such as GDP per capital and legal origin) to the relation. The coefficients of the cultural variables remain significant.

Within the group of studies using Hofstede's dimensions, De Jong and Semenov (2004) also derive relations between characteristics of financial systems and the other three original dimensions found by Hofstede.[3] They argue that a high degree of competition and a funded pension system (a minor role for the state) are compatible with a society that scores relatively highly on Masculinity. A masculine society is characterized by fighting out conflicts (competition) and a relatively low level of solidarity (no collective pension schemes).

With respect to Power Distance, De Jong and Semenov argue that the sign of the coefficient with stock market capitalization is ambiguous. A high score on Power Distance means that unequal distribution of power and wealth are accepted by members of the society. Since a stock market is a mechanism by which each individual can acquire wealth and a well-functioning stock market necessitates regulation that curbs the power of dominant shareholders, one expects a negative relationship between Power Distance and the prominence of financial markets. On the other hand, in high-Power Distance societies the relations on the firm level are full of conflicts and close relationships prove hard to establish. Consequently, financial markets could prove to be the only way of attracting external finance.

Finally, Individualism is associated with a relatively large role for funded pension systems and stock markets. De Jong and Semenov, however, note that in some collectivistic countries in-groups can be formed by a few dozen people at most (Taiwan) and in others the in-group can consist of thousands of people (Japan). Hence, in some collectivist countries the relationship of firms with stakeholders will be closer under the influence of collectivism, whereas this will not hold for other societies. The extent to which it would be the case is not reflected in available cultural indicators. Hence they decide to control for it by concentrating on individualist countries, which essentially means excluding the Asian countries from a set of industrial countries.[4]

In order to investigate the sensitiveness of the results to the countries selected, De Jong and Semenov present estimates for a group of Western countries and a group of non-Western countries. Within the group of Western, individualistic countries, Uncertainty Avoidance, Masculinity and Power Distance all show a significant relation with stock market performance (see Table 5.1, column 1). For Uncertainty Avoidance and Masculinity the coefficient has the theoretically expected sign. On theoretical grounds no unambiguously signed coefficient for Power Distance was expected. De Jong and Semenov found a negative sign between Power Distance and stock market capitalization, indicating that due to the inability to establish close relationships at the firm level, in high Power Distance countries, firms have to rely on stock markets for external financing. For a group of 25 non-Western countries from all over the world, only Uncertainty Avoidance proved to have any significant influence (Table 5.1, columns 3 and 4). Estimating the relations for the entire sample shows that Uncertainty Avoidance and Masculinity are the significant cultural variables (Table 5.1, column 5). Augmenting the equation with control variables suggest that Masculinity is

Table 5.1 Stock market capitalization and cultural dimensions

	Western countries		*Non-Western countries*		*Entire sample*	
	1	2	3	4	5	6
Intercept	51.733***	−49.207	93.997**	−211.843***	74.889***	−64.759*
	(3.72)	(−0.11)	(2.39)	(−4.01)	(4.13)	(−1.69)
UA score	−1.425***	−1.358***	−0.883*	−1.476***	−0.954***	−0.320*
	(−7.10)	(−3.93)	(−1.90)	(−5.50)	(−4.20)	(−1.88)
MAS score	0.578**	0.558**			0.551**	0.606**
	(2.68)	(2.56)			(2.03)	(2.63)
PDI score	1.176***	1.159***				
	(5.90)	(4.36)				
GDP per capita		10.098		47.106***		12.725***
		(0.24)		(6.02)		(3.38)
Legal justification				−61.031***		−51.808***
				(−4.74)		(−3.18)
Growth						4.380***
						(3.20)
Adjusted R^2	.48	.44	.17	.79	.30	.56
Number of observations	17	17	25	24	45	45

Dependent variable is stock market capitalization as a percentage of GDP, average for 1985–1996. White heteroskedasticity consistent *t*-statistics are in parentheses. The superscripts *, **, *** indicate a significance level of 10, 5 and 1 percent respectively.

Source: De Jong and Semenov (2004).

more important (both more statistically significant and a larger size of the coefficient) than Uncertainty Avoidance (Table 5.1, column 6).

A similar difference in results between two groups of countries is reported in Licht *et al.* (2005). They find Uncertainty Avoidance, Individualism and Power Distance to significantly influence the degree of protection of shareholders' rights in groups of countries, excluding Asian countries with common law. Extending the sample with these countries leads to insignificant results for Individualism and Power Distance. Once again Uncertainty Avoidance remains significant. These results indicate that the choice of the countries included in the analysis can be of great importance. Within a restricted group of countries the cultural dimensions signify some nuances between otherwise (stage of development, etc.) similar countries. Within a large group of quite different countries, the nuances are swept away and only the dominant influences are found.

In cross-country studies the appropriate selection of countries is a well-known issue; in particular, the difference between developed and developing countries appears to be relevant. More economically developed countries possess institutions (such as pensions systems, welfare arrangements) which are not available in developing countries. The latter have not arrived economically at a point where their economies demand large firms (Roe 2000: 539), and thus lack legal arrangements needed for attracting external finance. Many arrangements are informal. The social safety net is provided by the (extended) family instead of official measures. Consequently, the influence of some institutions in developed countries is quite different from that in developing countries. For advanced countries Carlin and Mayer (2003), for example, find a higher growth rate and a higher level of expenditure on Research and Development in industries in countries with a dispersed banking systems. By contrast, in low income countries concentrated banking is associated with high growth rates. Similarly, for his cultural dimensions Hofstede reports different relationships for developed versus developing countries. Uncertainty Avoidance, for example, correlated negatively with the Index of Economic Freedom for a group of 26 wealthy countries, whereas no correlation was found for a sample of 27 poorer countries (Hofstede 2001: 174). For all countries included in Hofstede's sample, Individualism is primarily correlated with Power Distance; for the 22 wealthiest countries the correlation is with Uncertainty Avoidance. These results illustrate the different relations between a group of wealthy, affluent societies and the rest of the world. The affluent societies can in many respects be 'regarded as a distinct social type' (Scheuch 1996: 68). Consequently, 'comparisons that include both types of countries produces differences that are hard to interpret – if they make sense at all' (ibid: 68). Great differences in physical environment make cross-cultural analysis meaningless (Van Raaij 1987: 698).

One of the few studies using Schwarz's dimensions (Licht *et al.* 2005) finds a negative relation between shareholders' rights and Schwartz's dimension of Harmony. This is the expected sign since in countries scoring high on Harmony head-on confrontations are avoided, 'so it should discourage embodying economic interests in strict legal form and zealously enforcing them in court' (Licht *et al.* 2005: 236).

Licht *et al.* (2005) and Stulz and Williamson (2003) pay attention to the relation between culture and creditors' rights. Using Pearson correlations, Licht *et al.* find that creditors' rights are negatively correlated with Harmony, and positively with Embeddedness, Hierarchy and Uncertainty Avoidance. Excluding the Asian countries with common law, results in a significant negative correlation for Harmony and Power Distance only. Stulz and Williamson use common language and dominant religion as proxies for culture.[5] They find a negative relation between protecting creditors' rights and Catholicism as the dominant religion and Spanish as the dominant language.

Labour markets and welfare systems

Labour market relations and regulation differ quite a lot between OECD-countries. These differences refer to formal regulation, governance as well as practices with respect to flexible contracts and the treatment of women. Formal regulation differs among others with respect to legislation about working time, flexible contracts, minimum wages, and the number of months' notice required before termination of a labour contract. Two aspects of the governance of labour markets are important: the degree of centralization of wage bargaining and the degree of corporatism. The relationship between culture and aspects of the performance of labour markets are studied for the position of women, the use of performance related contracts, flexible employment practices, and labour mobility. The influence of culture has been studied by means of regression analysis and case studies. The regression analyses mostly used Hofstede's indices of cultural dimensions.

Regulation

Labour market regulation differs between OECD-countries in the degree employees are legally protected against decisions by employers. Regulations can be in place for, among others, fixed-term and flexible contracts, minimum wages, the number of months' notice required before termination of employment of workers, and the number of months of salary pay given to workers as severance pay upon dismissal. These regulations provide certainty for the individual employee, constrain market forces and aim at protecting the rights of the weak party. Consequently one would expect labour market regulations to be more restrictive in countries that score high on Uncertainty Avoidance and Femininity and low on Power Distance. Femininity is associated with a sceptical view with respect to markets, which are associated with fighting-out problems, and a positive attitude towards the weak. High scores on Power Distance correspond to less concern with the feeble. All OECD-countries score relatively high on Individualism, so that it is unlikely to find any correlation with Individualism within this group of countries. If there is any relationship then we expect to find a negative one between Individualism and labour market protection, since Individualism is positively associated with a pro-market attitude. The empirical results listed in Table 5.2 confirm the expected positive relationship between labour market protection and Uncertainty Avoidance and Femininity. No relationship is found for Individualism and only one with the correct sign for Power Distance.

Governance of labour markets

Differences in governance structures of labour markets between OECD-countries are intensively studied. Two aspects are distinguished: the degree of centralization of wage bargaining and the degree of corporatism. Bargaining can be at the level of the firm, the industry or the nation. Corporatism is a type of social organization that is intermediary between capitalism and

Table 5.2 Culture and formal labour market institutions in OECD-countries

Dependent variable	*N*	*MAS*	*UAI*	*PDI*	*IDV*
Employment rigidities					
Labour standards (log)	18	–	+		
Employment protection	20	–	+		
Notice 1956–84	15	–	+	–	
Severance 1956–1984	17	–	+		
Treatment unemployed					
Max duration u/e benefit	16	–			
Active labour market program	20	–			

Meaning of symbols.
N number of observations (countries), MAS masculinity, UAI uncertainty avoiding index, PDI power Distance Index, and IDV individualism.

Source: Black (1999).

socialism. Organizations representing economic activities (mostly labour federations and employers' associations) and the government cooperate and coordinate across occupations and industries. Key elements of corporatism are: 'large, almost monopolistic organized interest groups; overt, explicit interaction with the government; coordination of actions within the organized interest groups across large segments of the economy' (Teulings and Hartog 1998: 27). So, corporatism includes a high degree of centralization and adds interaction and coordination with and through the government. This tripartite cooperation is more likely if i) the parties trust each other, ii) value freedom to act, spontaneity and flexibility less and appreciate predictability and certainty, iii) seek to avoid competition and conflict, and iv) discount the future less.

Cultural dimensions are related to each of these attitudes. Values will crucially influence how far agents trust each other in the beginning, and how easy it is to form trust in their interaction. Collectivist societies are more supportive to formation of 'naïve' trust within a collectivity, but may be less supportive to trust non-members of collectivities. The question is whether a collectivity is formed at the given level (be it firm, religious group, or the society as a whole). We would expect that people in more feminine societies will a priori expect other members of their societies to have empathy and relationship orientation rather than ego orientation, and thus will trust them more. This trust, however, can be broken at the first violation and is not the same as a 'naïve' trust within a collectivity. A process of cooperation may greatly facilitate the formation of experience-based trust. People in societies with higher Uncertainty Avoidance are likely to be less trustful because trust implies acceptance of some ambiguity (giving it into other's hands) and a potential loss of control. Finally, societies with large

Power Distance parties with unequal power perceive each other as being 'of a different kind', different from each other in all important respects, alien to each other; these attitudes are not conducive to formation of mutual trust. Flexibility, spontaneity and freedom to act will be appreciated less in countries that score high on Uncertainty Avoidance and Collectivism. Moreover inhabitants of Uncertainty Avoiding societies dislike ambiguity and unpredictability. Consensus seeking is an important characteristic of feminine societies. Consequently, one would like to avoid conflict and competition. Such an attitude is also found in high UA-countries. In sum, corporatism is expected to be positively associated with Femininity and Collectivism, and negatively with Power Distance. The sign of Uncertainty Avoidance is ambiguous; high Uncertainty Avoidance corresponds with low trust and hence negatively influences cooperation, whereas its correspondence with aversion to ambiguity and unpredictability suggests a positive relationship. The results of studies using regression analysis for determining the relationship between cultural values and the degree of centralization and cooperation in labour markets reveal that both centralization of wage bargaining and the degree of cooperation between trade unions and employers associations are negatively related to Power Distance and Masculinity and positively to Uncertainty Avoidance (the results listed in Table 5.3).

Semenov (2000) compares classifications of industrial relations with groupings of scores on Hofstede's cultural dimensions. The classifications of industrial relations are for 16 industrialized countries during the period 1945–1990 and are obtained from Crouch (1993). Following Crouch, Semenov argues that the manner in which bargaining relations are organized will correspond with the mode of formation and implementation of economic policy. Centralized wage bargaining is expected to be more frequent in countries where a relatively few people from various political and functional interest organizations engage in a large number of transactions in different policy areas. In these countries actors treat a particular exchange as one of a multitude of exchanges over a prolonged period of time; while in other countries each exchange is treated as one-off. Centralized bargaining took place for most of the period in rather feminist countries (Semenov 2000: 235). Centralized wage bargaining almost never took place in countries with relatively large Power Distance or masculine small-PD, low-UA countries. Countries where the intensity of centralized bargaining changes over time are culturally relatively diverse. Coordination of bargaining and cooperation is found in countries with small Power Distance in combination with i) high uncertainty avoidance or ii) low uncertainty avoidance and low masculinity (Semenov 2000: Table 6.13). In general, large Power Distance is associated with contestation.

According to Semenov's results both high and low levels of Uncertainty Avoidance can lead to coordination and cooperation. A further analysis, using Therborn's classification of peaceful industrial relations sheds light on

Table 5.3 Culture and governance arrangements of labour markets in OECD-countries

Dependent variable	*N*	*MAS*	*UAI*	*PDI*	*IDV*	*source*
Collective bargaining						
• extension	19		+			Black (2005)
• coverage	19		+[a]	–[a]	+	Black (2005)
Bargaining						
• coordination	19	+		–	–	Black (2005)
• centralization	19	–				Black (2005)
Employer coordination	20	–		–		
Trade union coordination	20	–	+	–		
• Calmfors-Driffil (centralization)[a]	18	–	+	–		Black (2001a and 2001b)
• Calmfors & Driffil (corporation)[a]	16	–	+	–		Teulings & Hartog (1998)
• Lehmbruch (corporation)[a]	16	–		–		Teulings & Hartog (1998)
• Bruno & Sachs corporation	17	–	+	–		Black (2001a)
• JLN employern coord	20	–		–		Black (2001a)
• JLNtratdeunion coord	20	–	+	–		Black (2001a)
Collective bargaining	20	–	+	–	+	Black (2001b)

Symbols in heading, see note Table 5.2.
a: the indices on the degree of corporation by Calmfors and Driffil, Lehmbruch, and Bruno and Sachs are based on ranking, which implies that a high number in the index refers to a low degree of corporatism, which is opposite to the other indices used for trade union coordination. We have reversed signs in order to make their interpretation similar to those of the other variables.

this ambiguous sign of Uncertainty Avoidance. Therborn (1992) finds that in post-war history the level of industrial conflicts has been low in countries with both high and low levels of centralized wage bargaining. He argues that a relatively peaceful industrial order can be organized in two fundamentally different ways. One way is institutionalization of consensus and partnership with formalized decision-making bodies and extensive legal backup. This form is found in Austria, Germany and Switzerland. The other way is institutionalization of conflict, which is characteristic of the Scandinavian countries. Trade unions and employers' organization are not social partners but autonomous organizations whose rights of industrial conflict are untouchable. Semenov (2000: Table 6.14) finds institutionalization of consensus in countries scoring high on Uncertainty Avoidance and low on Power Distance, and institutionalization of conflict in low-UA feminine countries.

Table 5.4 Culture and labour market performance in OECD-countries

Dependent variable	N	*MAS*	*UAI*	*PDI*	*IDV*
Earnings dispersion	18	+			–
Wage dispersion[a]	14–17	+			
Female activity rate	19	–			
Female % of labour force	19	–			
Self employment	18	–			
Part-time employment	19	–			
Temporary employment	19	–			
Flexible employment practices					
• part-time work	14			–	+
• temporary work	14				
• fixed-contract	14		+		–
• telework	14	–			
• shift work	14		+	+	–
• annual hours contract	14				
Labour mobility					
Average job tenure (log)	12				–
Job tenure <2 yrs	16				+
Job tenure <1 yr.	13				+
Employment/population	20				
Overall labour supply	20	+			
Unemployment (log)	20	–			

Symbols in heading, see note Table 5.2.
a. Wage dispersion: these signs hold for data from different source for different years (between brackets): United Nations (1983), International Labour Office (1975 and 1984), Bureau of Labor (1975 and 1986).
In many cases the regression also included one or two other explanatory variables.

Sources: Black (2001a) for earnings dispersion, wage dispersion, Raghuram *et al.* (2001) for all results on flexible employment practices, and Black (2001b) for the rest.

Performance of labour markets

Empirical research with respect to wage dispersion within OECD countries reveals that the score on Masculinity is by far the most important cultural factor (Table 5.4). The difference in pay between employees is higher in masculine societies. Moreover, in these countries the female labour market participation is less and there are fewer self-employed. Part-time employment and temporary employment are also less frequent in masculine societies. These results are based on multivariate regressions using country averages.

Raghuran *et al.* (2001) analyze the flexible employment practices within 14 European countries, using data collected from 4,876 firms in 15 separate industries/services within the private and the non-profit making sector of each country. All firms have 200 or more employees. The national means of each practice are correlated with the value indices of Hofstede and the extent to which the variances in national differences can be explained by each cultural dimension are calculated. These partial regressions deliver quite different results from those reported above. Masculinity, which dominated the previous outcome, is only statistically significantly correlated with telework (Table 5.4). It has the expected negative sign. Shift work and fixed-contracts are popular in Uncertainty Avoiding countries. Power Distance is negatively related to part-time work and positively to shift work. The latter and fixed contracts are negatively related to Individualism and positively with part-time work. Although the majority of these results are in accordance with the expected signs, one should keep in mind that these are partial correlations. Individualism, for example, is highly correlated with income per capita, so that the negative relationship between shift work and Individualism could reflect a negative relationship between income per capita and shift work.

Individualism is the only cultural factor explaining differences between national levels of labour mobility. The estimates (see Table 5.4) suggest that labour mobility is higher in countries that score high on Individualism.

The influence of culture on indicators of overall labour market performance (employment, overall labour supply and unemployment) is much less significant than those with respect to indicators of governance and regulation (compare the last rows of Table 5.4 with the results in Table 5.2 and 5.3). Employment relative to the population is unaffected by culture, whereas overall labour supply is found to be positively and unemployment to be negatively related to Masculinity. These results suggest that the less favourable protection of workers (Table 5.2) and lower degree of centralization and coordination of bargaining (Table 5.3) and higher dispersion of wages (Table 5.4, top rows) in high masculine societies induce people to search for a job and thus be employed. The latter are net effects of regulation and governance, so that some effects due to regulation can be cancelled out or reinforced by the effects of the governance system. Moreover, the relation between governance systems and employment can be nonlinear, as has been argued by Calmfors and Driffill (1988), who report a U-shaped relationship between centralization of wage bargaining and unemployment. Hence, it is difficult to derive theoretically correct signs of each of the cultural dimensions' influence on (un)employment.

A summary of the main effects reported above is provided in Figure 5.3. Since Individualism is found to be relevant for labour mobility only, it is not included in the figure. Masculinity appears to be the dominant cultural factor explaining differences between industrialized countries in labour market regulations, governance and performance. Uncertainty Avoidance appears to be of importance for regulation and governance, whereas Power Distance significantly influences the governance of labour markets only.

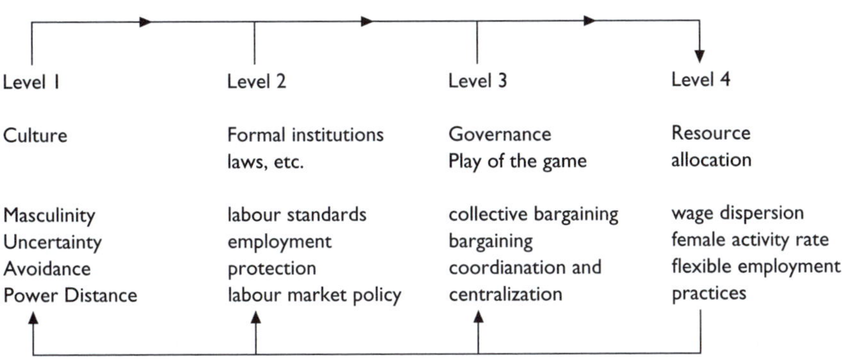

Figure 5.3 Theoretical framework of labour market

Welfare systems

Public spending on unemployment and active labour-market programmes constitute just one category of government expenditure on social programmes. Others are government expenditure on old-age, disability, health care, housing, and low-income households. Alesina and Glaeser (2004: 19) notice that these social expenditures are significantly higher in Europe (both continental Europe and the UK) than in the US. Economic explanations appear to contrast with the facts (unequal distribution of pre-tax income) or not robust (openness of the country). The most convincing explanations are the ethnic diversity of the US population versus the much more ethnical homogenous European countries and differences in political institutions. Analyzing the General Social Survey question on support for spending for the poor, Luttmer (2001) reports that the level of support for redistribution increases with the proximity to welfare recipients of one's own race and decreases with proximity of welfare recipients of another race.

Proportional representation, which dominates in Europe, is positively related to welfare spending. Proportional representation has been introduced in Europe by left parties, whereas in the United States conservative forces always have been able to stop efforts to reform the constitution and reduce the position of the wealthiest people. Reasons for these differences are the fact that after the Civil War, the United States of America never have fought a war on its own territory. Many great wars have been fought on European territory. After these wars the defeated army was demoralized, sympathetic to the demands by the working class and often in chaos. This helped left parties to cease power and change legislation, Moreover, within Europe the distance is much smaller between places of protest and the governmental centre than in the USA. Consequently, the American government and army were much less sympathetic to demands of the working poor.

These differences in social welfare spending appear to be supported by differences in public opinion about the poor. Within Europe, a large proportion of the public believes their income is determined by luck, so that the low level of living standard of the poor is not their fault. Americans are much less sympathetic to the poor. Moreover, the latter (including the poor) care much less about inequality (represented by left wing attitude) than the Europeans (Alesina *et al.* 2001: 242, 243). These differences in opinion could cause the differences in welfare spending.

Alesina and Glaeser argue in favour of the reverse causality and think

> that ideology is more of an effect of the political success of the right than a cause of that success, and that the root causes of right-wing political success are institutions and heterogeneity.
>
> The central view of this hypothesis is that ideology is created by political actors who use it to support their agendas.
>
> (Alesina and Glaeser 2004: 185)

For instance, the suggestion that the United States forms a country of unlimited possibilities, where the poor can easily escape poverty is not supported by the facts. Many studies do not find significant differences in social mobility between the USA and European countries and sometimes report that within European countries the poor have a greater chance of upward mobility. The image of the United States as the land of opportunity has been propagated by writers 'who had strong financial interests pushing them towards inducing immigrants to come from Europe.' (ibid: 199). Since in the USA the right-wing parties were almost always in power they were able to shape public opinion and similarly the government by leftist parties in Europe propagated the pro-poor and pro-redistribution attitude. Consequently, 'in neither case do these ideas reflect economic reality. Instead they are the legacy of the political success of different groups' (ibid: 216). Hence both are good examples of 'politicized culture': a purposefully created view on the developments and values of the nation. This phenomenon is dealt with more extensively in the section Politicized culture of Chapter 6.

The changing influence of culture

In the section on financial systems we have seen that the selection of the countries used in the analysis can affect the results with respect to the influence of cultural dimensions on economic institutions. In a sample of many countries, only the dominant cultural variable appeared to be relevant. Smaller samples leave more room for discovering nuances between countries. In a study on the openness of economies De Jong *et al.* (2006) find that within a given sample of countries, the influence of culture can also change depending on the time period considered. In their study, openness does not refer to the relative size of international flows but to policy measures. So a more open economy is one where regulation allows for free international trade flows, capital flows and the country is a member of international organizations (such as the International Monetary Fund). An advantage of this definition is that it refers to policy and is less influenced by factors out of control of policy makers.

Under similar circumstance countries follow different strategies. For example, up to the 1980s the United States, Canada and Germany were much more open than France and Japan, without a clear (economic) reason for it. Similarly, during financial crises countries' reactions can differ significantly. During currency crises within the European Monetary System, France was systematically much more inclined to use restrictions on capital flows than Germany and The Netherlands. During the Asian crises some East Asian countries installed capital controls for curbing capital outflow, while others refrained from installing such market-unfriendly measures. In all these cases economic theory is unable to explain the differences between policy measures taken by the national authorities.

In order to see whether culture can be helpful in explaining these differences, De Jong and co-authors summarize the pros and cons found in the literature of allowing international transactions in goods, services and capital.[6] The standard economic arguments in favour of free international flows is that it will improve the efficient allocation of resources and hence welfare. More recent arguments are that an open economy will capture knowledge from international flows of goods and even more from foreign direct investments. Moreover, openness will increase domestic competition and the efficiency of domestic firms and institutions. Apart from these positive effects, three main categories of disadvantageous results are distinguished. First, the government might want to shield the economy against foreign influences; a more open economy is more vulnerable to fluctuations originating in foreign countries; relatively young industries have to be protected against foreign competitors and they want to remain independent. Second, left-wing governments have a preference for redistributing income and for direct control on the economy. In order to prevent capital outflow, they will install capital controls. Third, developed economies are often more open than developing ones.

These characteristics of a country's openness are related to Hofstede's four original dimensions. An individualistic country is expected to be more open because inhabitants of such a country more easily engage in (business) relationships with persons they do not know than agents from collectivist countries. The theoretically expected sign of the relationship between Masculinity and openness is ambiguous. A masculine society is more directed to competition and emphasizes economic growth, suggesting a positive sign. On the other hand in such a society inhabitants are resistant to immigrants and corruption is high, which would suggest a negative sign. A negative sign is also expected for Power Distance since scores on this dimension correlate with corruption. Finally, inhabitants of high Uncertainty Avoiding countries accept exogenous uncertainty less, are more resistant to immigrants and less prepared to live abroad, so that a negative relation with openness is expected.

The relations are estimated for a group of 53 countries for the years 1959, 1973, 1982, 1988 and 1997. In these estimated relations, Masculinity is never significant. As expected, Uncertainty Avoidance and Power Distance have a negative and Individualism a positive sign. These coefficients are only significant for the 1970s and 1980s. Adding GDP per capita to the relation in order to control for economic development, leaves the results for Uncertainty Avoidance unaffected. Individualism becomes insignificant (except for 1959 when it is negative) and Power Distance has only a significant positive coefficient in 1959 and 1983. The fact that most variables have a significant effect for the 1970s and 1980s is considered only as evidence for the hypothesis that cultural influences are most prominent in periods when the government's scope for choice is largest. During the 1950s this *room de manoeuvre* was restricted because of scarcity resulting from continental Europe's destroyed infrastructure. The scarce resources had to be used wisely, leaving no room for preference for other reasons. Due to, among other things, the success of the export-led growth in the Asian Tigers and the demise of centrally planned economies, in the 1990s the dominant view became that opening an economy is the best policy. Hence, no influence of culture could be found.

The coefficient of Power Distance became positive when GDP per capita was added to the relation. A further investigation into the relationship between Power Distance and GDP per capital revealed that in countries with a low level of GDP per capita there exists a positive relation between Power Distance and openness, whereas in the more developed countries no effect exists at all. This finding is in line with the idea that poor countries sometimes need authoritarian leadership in order to open up their economies and, in general, to realize important changes; an idea also found in a case study of Sri Lanka's trade liberalization (Ganeshamoorthy 2003). This result once again illustrates the importance of country selection as discussed in the section on financial systems and in Chapter 4.

Institutional complementarity

Hitherto, the relation between culture on the one hand and institutions of a particular type on the other has been studied. The diversity of capitalism literature, however, argues that one should not study a particular institution in isolation but investigate the consequences of an economy's entire set of institutions (Amable 2003, Hall and Soskice 2001). Institutions can be complementary 'if the presence (or efficiency) of one increases the returns from (or efficiency of) the other' (Hall and Soskice 2001: 17). In comparative economics this implies that in well-functioning economies, institutions in one sector will complement those in other sectors. Hall and Soskice distinguish liberal from coordinated market economies and expect that within one economy the institutions of all spheres will converge towards a particular degree of coordination. An important role for stock markets reflects market coordination in the financial sphere and thus is expected to be complemented by free labour markets with low employment protection (ibid: 19). Indeed, Hall and Gingerich (2004) find a strong tendency for institutions of different sectors to belong to the same type of coordination. Moreover, their estimates reveal higher rates of growth for countries in which the institutions of labour relations and corporate governance are complementary. Hence, the literature on varieties of capitalism presents evidence that institutions of different parts of the economy are complementary and that an economy in which all institutions reflect a similar type of coordination delivers higher rates of economic growth. From this result we expect that the same (set of) cultural variables is relevant for each of the different segments of an economy; deeply held beliefs should influence all aspects of life in a consistent way.

To our knowledge no study has been published yet, which systematically investigates the relation between culture and different sectors of an economy. Nevertheless, combining the results of various studies gives us an idea whether the same set of cultural variables are related to a set of complementary institutions. We consider institutions of the labour market, the financial sector, and the resulting type of production. Uncertainty Avoidance is singled out as the relevant cultural dimension. The overview of studies on industrial relations (Tables 5.2, 5.3 and 5.4) reveals that a low level of Uncertainty Avoidance is associated with a low level of employees protection, decentralized wage bargaining and individualized wages. According to Amable's types of social systems of innovation and production, these forms of labour markets are associated with market-based financial systems. From the discussion on the financial system, we know that Uncertainty Avoidance is the dominant cultural dimension for distinguishing market-based financial systems from bank-based systems; societies where financial markets are important are more risk accepting. So a low score on Uncertainty Avoidance is correlated with both decentralized labour markets and market-based financial systems.

Do decentralized labour markets and financial markets also lead to a production system characterized by a low level of Uncertainty Avoidance? Financial markets are in a better position than systems with a large role for intermediaries to finance very innovative products (Allen and Gale 2001: Ch. 13). The crucial factor is the great dispersal of opinion on the chances of success of fundamentally new products. Each individual investor himself decides upon the amount to be invested in products traded on financial markets. Consequently, those who are optimistic about an innovation's success rate will invest in it, whereas pessimists will not. Hence, chances are high that firms are able to attract money for investments in very innovative products or processes. An intermediary, however, will take the views of both optimists and pessimists into account, which results in a tendency to be conservative and to shy away from fundamentally new innovations (as opposed to incremental innovations). Consequently, we expect industries producing innovative products to be more important in countries scoring low on Uncertainty Avoidance: the attitude towards financial markets enables the financing of these industries.

Indeed some recent empirical studies (Rajan and Zingales 1998, Carlin and Mayer 2003, Svaleryd and Vlachos 2005) provide empirical evidence of a positive relationship between the importance of financial markets and the share of innovative sectors in an economy. For different manufacturing industries, Rajan and Zingales calculate the degree of dependence on external finance. A panel analysis for the 1980s with 41 countries and 28 sectors reveals that for sectors depending on external finance value added grows faster in countries with developed financial markets measured by stock market capitalization or accounting standards. Similarly, the number of new establishments in these sectors is also positively related to the accounting standards. These results suggest that 'financial development could indirectly influence growth by allowing ideas to develop and challenge existing ones' (Rajan and Zingales 1998: 579). This suggestion is confirmed by Carlin and Mayer (2003), who find that for advanced countries information disclosure (which is high in countries where financial markets are important), is associated with higher growth and expenses for R&D of equity financed and skill-intensive industries. Hence, their study provides some evidence of a link between financial systems and types of economic production in advanced countries. This idea of a country's comparative advantage resulting from the structure of its financial systems is confirmed by Svaleryd and Vlachos (2005: 135), who find that the 'countries with well functioning financial systems tend to specialize in industries highly dependent on external financing.' The size of the effect is unexpectedly large: differences in financial systems are more important explanatory factors of the pattern of specialization in a sample of OECD-countries than differences in human capital. Since financial markets and regulation enhancing the functioning of these markets is negatively related to Uncertainty Avoidance, we expect R&D and specialization patterns in R&D intensive industries to be negatively related to Uncertainty Avoidance too.

This hypothesis is confirmed by studies on the relation between innovation and culture, which find negative relationships between various innovation enhancing leadership styles and Uncertainty Avoidance (see, for example, Shane 1995, Shane *et al.* 1995, Shane and Venkataraman 1996). The more uncertainty-accepting the society a respondent comes from, the more he or she prefers the championing role of making it possible for the innovators to avoid being stymied by the organizational hierarchy; of persuading other organization members to support the innovation; of making it possible for organization members to gain autonomy from organizational rules and procedures, and of operating under loose monitoring systems (Shane 1995: 62–64). In this study individuals are used as observations, whereas Shane *et al.* (1995) employ national means. They find that 'the more uncertainty-accepting a society is, the more people in it prefer champions to overcome organizational inertia to innovation by violating organizational norms, rules and procedures' (Shane *et al.* 1995: 945). Shane and Venkataraman (1996) distinguish two strategies for getting support for innovation. The rational champion, who follows standard operating procedures and the renegade champion who violates the organizational norms to get their projects initiated and implemented. The latter uses his or her personal network of colleagues to support the innovation. Using the attitudes of managers from six organizations in 28 countries, they report a preference for the renegade strategy among managers from countries scoring low on Uncertainty Avoidance and high on Individualism. In a study of top management leadership styles and innovation in 12 European nations, Elenkov and Manev discover a negative relationship between Uncertainty Avoidance and both product/market innovation and organizational innovation (Elenkov and Manev 2005: 396).[7] A more detailed analysis of leadership factors shows that Uncertainty Avoidance is negatively related to inspirational motivation and intellectual stimulation (ibid: 397), both aspects of an innovative environment.

Similarly, consumers more easily adopt new products in countries that score low on Uncertainty Avoidance (Lynn and Gelb 1996, De Mooij 2004: 266–269). For 16 European countries, Lynn and Gelb construct a national indicator of innovativeness from the percentage of households in a nation owning a cordless telephone, a telephone answering machine, a home computer, a microwave, a compact disc player a video camera and a satellite dish. They find that this indicator of innovativeness is significantly related to purchasing power, Individualism and Uncertainty Avoidance. These two cultural dimensions are also found to correlate with the percentage of consumers buying new consumer packaged goods in a group of five European countries and the USA (by Steenkamp, cited in De Mooij 2004: 267). Innovators are able to cope with higher levels of uncertainty, and thus are found more often in societies that can more easily handle uncertainty.

Summarizing the results of various studies of different sectors of the economy are as pieces of a jigsaw puzzle fitting nicely together. In societies easily accepting uncertainty, a relatively high share of production consists of innovative products, and innovators make up a large part of consumers. Financial markets, which more easily finance innovative products than bank- or intermediary-based systems, are important and labour markets are decentralized and labour contracts individualized. Whether this uncertainty accepting attitude and associated institutions will lead to a higher level of income will be discussed in the next chapter.

Concluding remarks

This chapter has reviewed the epistemological approach and the research relating cross-country differences in institutions to differences in value patterns. The results of the epistemological approach validate the assumption underlying many of the economics and culture views that values are transmitted from one generation to another. Immigrants' children behave in a manner systematically related to the behaviour of the inhabitants in their ancestors' countries.

The epistemological approach cannot answer the question what has caused society-wide changes in values, institutions and performance and how these areas are related. Research using national cultural dimensions focuses on the relation between values, institutions and economic performance across countries. Note that since this research deals with differences across countries, it investigates the relative position of countries and not the evolution over time. So it could be that a common trend (globalization for example) influences values and institutions in a uniform way, leaving the relative positions of countries unaffected. Then, cross-country research will find a stable pattern between values, institutions and economic performance; the relative position of countries did not change.

The review of the literature on values and institutions taught us some lessons both with respect to the nature of this relationship as well as to the circumstances under which it is plausible that culture plays a role. For industrialized countries culture appears to be systematically related to the institutions of various sectors of the economy; the financial system, the labour market, the type of products produced and the government's policy with respect to opening the economy to foreign influences. Moreover, a systematic pattern emerged suggesting a structure in which institutions are complementary to each other and systematically related to one culture dimension; Hofstede's Uncertainty Avoidance Index. A society in which inhabitants accept uncertainty relatively easily is characterized by a market-based financial system, flexible labour markets, an open economy, and specializes in innovative products.

This chapter also contains some lessons on the way to perform research on the relation between culture and economics. Culture is a vague concept (see Chapter 1). Consequently, any analysis risks relating intuitively aspects of culture to economic variables or to be led by the results found. In order to prevent these practices, we recommend starting from economic theory and the characteristics of the economic subject at hand in order to derive hypotheses about relations between culture (values) and economic phenomena. So start from the right-hand side in Figure 5.1, and derive plausible relations from the theory which is available on the determining factors of the endogenous variable. Naturally, values will appear along economic and political factors explaining the phenomenon concerned. If these 'hard' variables (economic, biological, and technological) predict a variable better, cultural indexes are redundant (Hofstede 2001: 68). Such an application of Occam's razor, gives culture its rightful place in the list of explanatory variables instead of under- or over-valuing its role.

In this chapter we found that culture will play only a minor or even no role if physical circumstances dominate. Consequently, culture will only explain a small part of the differences in institutional structures between countries if the sample contains both highly developed and developing countries. Then the differences in development dominate. Similarly, culture is of no or minor importance if countries are faced with physical constraints resulting from, for example, war damage. The constraints can also be man-made in the sense that a common view exists on the best policy or institutional design. Examples of the latter are the fact that after 1990 export-led growth represented by an open economy was held as the best way to obtain growth and an independent central bank as the most effective way of containing inflation.

Chapter 6

Culture and economic performance

The previous chapter focused on the relation between values and institutional structure. It did not pay attention to the question whether these different structures would give rise to different rates of economic growth and different levels of economic income per capita. These issues are picked up in the present chapter, which focuses on the relation between values and economic performance, especially economic growth and the level of economic development measured by income per capita.

In addition to the subject of economic growth, this chapter deals with an important issue relevant to all research on culture and economics, namely endogeneity. As is illustrated by the arrows in Figures 3.2 and 5.1, culture, institutions, governance and economic performance influence each other. This raises questions with respect to the dynamics of this process and the most plausible direction of causality. In particular, do the factors leading to change originate from the box on culture (as is supposed by the adherents of the culture as constraints approach), or by the performance of institutions and the resulting level of economic development? In this chapter we discuss the way economists deal with endogeneity and relate that to the way researchers from related disciplines handle this issue. Moreover, we pay attention to the scarce literature on the dynamic process between values and economic performance.

The set-up of this chapter is as follows. In the next section we discuss the various phases of economic development from a pre-industrialized agrarian society to a post-modern service-oriented one and the values associated with each of these phases. These values are trends in the opinions of large groups. As the discussion of the welfare systems in Europe and the United Sates in the previous chapter already illustrated, political figures can have an overwhelming influence on the formation of opinions. A similar phenomenon can be observed during periods of economic and political change. We therefore devoted a section to these politicized cultures. Thereafter, the way economists deal with causality is described and related to the way researchers from related social sciences deal with this issue. Finally, the results on the relation between culture and economic growth and economic development are compared with those of the previous chapter on culture and institutions. The chapter ends with a concluding section.

Values and phases of economic development

The importance attached to particular values depends on the phase of economic development a country is in. Since Max Weber's '*The Protestant Ethic and the Spirit of Capitalism*', the relation between culture and economic growth has been widely studied. Voluminous historical writings (Landes 1999, Lal 1998), case studies (e.g. those collected in Harrison and Berger 2006) and econometric analyses deal with this subject. In this chapter we describe the main results of studies that did not use religion (which is considered in the next chapter) as a proxy for culture.

The three periods of a nation's economic development distinguished by Marini (2004) are used for schematically presenting the arguments and the results found. These periods are the period before economic growth takes off, the period when an economy grows from a low income level to a high one, and finally the period in which a country has attained a relatively high level of income per capita. Different attitudes correspond with each of these phases of economic development. A traditional economy is characterized by a low level of per capita income and a flat productivity curve. People are mainly concerned with the fight for survival. Since there is almost no increase in wealth, acquiring privileges is important to acquire a larger share of existing wealth. During the take-off phase of an economy technological and scientific knowledge is applied, the savings rate and the level of economic growth are high and economic achievements are regarded as important. Industrial production is relatively important during this phase, which is also known as the modernization phase. The post-modern stage starts when income per capita is at such a level that the masses do not have to worry about their basic needs. Then the relative importance switches to secondary goals such as self-expression and the quality of life, which previously were only the privilege of the upper classes. Services are important in these countries.

A confirmation of the hypothesis that each of these three phases corresponds with different attitudes is reported by Inglehart and Baker (2000). They use the percentage of the agricultural, industrial, and services sector in the economy as a measure of the economy's phase of development: traditional, take off, post-modern stage, respectively. When correlating these characteristics with the two cultural dimensions Inglehart derived from the World Value Survey (see the Appendix 1, Various cultural dimensions for a brief description of these dimensions), they find for the traditional/secular-rational dimension a negative correlation with the importance of the agricultural sector and a positive one with the percentage of the industrial sector. Hence, the transition from a traditional to an industrial society is associated with different scores on this dimension. The post-modern societies, represented by a high share of services in GDP, score high on the survival/self expression dimension (ibid: 38).

The concept of time and the orientation on the past instead of the future is an aspect of culture often found as characteristic of a traditional society. Before the industrialization of Germany, British and French travellers regarded the Germans as slow and never in a hurry. According to a French manufacturer they 'work as and when they please, and "just look for ways to get fired"' (Landes 1999: 281). Similarly, in 1915 an Australian management consultant told Japanese government officials 'to see your men at work made me feel that you are a very satisfied easy going race who reckons time is no object' (Chang 2008: 182). Nowadays comparable statements are made about Africans:

> The African, anchored in his ancestral culture, is so convinced that the past can only repeat itself that he worries only superficially about the future. However, without a dynamic perception of the future, there is no planning, no foresight, no scenario building; in other words, no policy to affect the course of time.
>
> (Etounga-Manguelle 2000: 69)

This quote is made by an African himself, indicating that the view of a lack of future orientation is not a prejudice of foreign observers but shared by domestic agents. Focus groups and survey studies reaffirm this. Members of a South-African focus group singled out the concept of time as an important difference between Africans and Americans (Bernstein 2006: 40). Similarly, a questionnaire with a deliberate African bias found a factor called Traditional Wisdom (Noorderhaven and Tidjani 2001). Items included in this factor are: it is important to show hospitality to strangers; wisdom is more important than knowledge; wisdom comes from experience and time, not from education; and it is better to discuss a decision than to impose a decision (ibid: 39). African countries score high on this factor. Moreover, this Traditional Wisdom is highly negative correlated with the cultural dimension Confucian work dynamism, which Hofstede later labelled Long-term orientation. The latter is associated with: thrift, sparing of resources, most important events in life occur in future (as opposite to in present), large share of additional income is saved (Hofstede 2001: 360), and has a high correlation with economic growth during the years 1965–95 (ibid: 367).

Two aspects of the culture associated with the take-off phase of an economy are often distinguished; one, achievement, is related to individuals' behaviour, the other (trust) to the way individuals cooperate. Aspects of the achievement dimension are: independence, thrift, determination and hard work. Economic growth and material goods are valued highly. Kunio (2006), for example, considers these aspects of the Japanese values system and the importance attached to investment in education as important explanatory factors for Japan's growth until the end of the 1980s. In order to sustain growth, markets should function properly. Market transactions are dominantly between non-relatives, who do not know each other or know each other for this particular transaction only. Consequently, mutual trust, supported by legal rights, is critical for markets to flourish. High levels of trust are supposed to reduce transaction costs and help individuals to solve collective action problems.

An index of achievement motivation is constructed by Granato *et al.* (1996). (see Appendix 3: Construction of cultural items from the World Values Survey). Achievement motivation is expected to be important for the transition from a traditional to an industrial society. The transition from an industrial to a post-industrial or post-modern society is tapped by the materialist/postmaterialist dimension. During this transition the emphasis on economic growth declines and that on protection of environment and quality of life increases. For a group of 25 countries Granato and co-authors find support for the hypothesis that besides economic factors (GDP per capita at the start of the sampling period and primary education) cultural factors influence economic growth per capita. In particular, achievement motivation enters the relations significantly.

Marini (2004) refines Granato *et al.*'s analysis in that he constructs a cultural variable for each of the three stages distinguished above. The traditional economy is associated with what Marini calls the limited good syndrome, which consists of obedience, religious faith, tolerance and good manners (see Appendix 3 Construction of cultural items for its construction). The take-off phase is characterized by achievement (independence, thrift, determination and hard work) and generalized trust represented by responsibility. The values associated with the post-materialist phase are imagination and unselfishness. Using the same countries and the same period as in Granato *et al.*'s study, he finds economic growth per capita is negatively correlated with the items of the limited good syndrome, positively with those of achievement and generalized trust and not with post-materialistic values (Marini 2004: 777). These results are based on partial correlations. For a multivariate regression analysis Marini constructs two cultural indices. The first one corresponds with the achievement motivation in Granato *et al.*'s study and the other is an extension of it in that it includes generalized trust (see Appendix 3: Construction of cultural items for details). Along with per capita GDP in 1960 and primary education in 1960, each of these two cultural indices significantly influences economic growth per capita.

The other aspect of culture associated with the take-off phase, trust, is found to significantly affect cross-country differences in annual growth in per capita income over the years 1980–92 (Knack and Keefer 1997). In these studies trust is measured as the percentage of respondents in each country that replied 'most people can be trusted' in the World Values Survey (see Appendix 1: Various cultural dimensions for the exact wording of this question). Knack and Keefer's sample consists of 29 market economies. Zak and Knack (2001) extend the dataset to 41 countries and once again find a positive and significant relation between trust and growth. Similar results are found by others (see Durlauf and Fafchamps 2004 for a review). Beugelsdijk *et al.* (2004) perform a robustness analysis with respect to the results found by Zak and Knack. One of these tests consists of applying an Extreme Bounds Analysis to the dataset.[1] From this analysis Beugelsdijk *et al.* conclude that in the original sample of Knack and Keefer trust is only significant in 4.5 per cent of the regressions. This percentage of significant coefficients increases if subsequently countries with lower levels of trusts are added to the sample. Hence, the significant results in Zak and Knack (2001) are due to the inclusion of less developed countries with low trusts. Beugelsdijk (2006) splits the sample in low-trust and high-trust countries, which more or less corresponds with a division between developing and developed countries. He finds that trust is only significant in the sample of low-trust countries. These results once again point at the importance of country selection (see also, Chapters 4 and 5). One should always ask oneself whether it makes sense to include such diverse countries in the same sample. Chances are high that in a very heterogeneous sample the differences can easily be explained by physical constraints resulting from the different stages of development instead of differences in culture.[2]

When a society passes the threshold where basic needs have been met, secondary needs such as self-expression and the quality of life become important. These post-materialist goals are emphasized after and because people have attained material security. Material and physical security are still valued highly, but the relative priority has switched towards the post-material values (Inglehart 1997: 35). Growth rates will be lower during this period than during the take-off phase. Kunio (2006: 94) notes that Japanese people no longer feel guilty about spending money on luxury items. Japan's low growth rate during the 1990s is partly ascribed to the low appreciation of individual goals by the Japanese. At that time the costs of production in Japan were so high that it was too costly to rely on traditional low innovative industries. Japan's type of production should move towards the IT-sector and in particular to the innovative part of it. The innovations needed in this type of industry rely heavily on hard-working individuals instead of groups. Innovation by individuals is stimulated by rewards depending on an individual's performance and individual-oriented values. The collectivistic values of the Japanese did not fit with these requirements (Kunio 2006: 95, 98). Consequently, cultural attitudes that are growth promoting during a particular period cease to be that at a later stage.[3]

As said before, Hofstede's cultural dimensions, Long-term orientation (LTO) is conceptually related to time orientation. Inhabitants in a country that scores high on LTO are more oriented towards future events than present events, and save a large share of income. Scores on LTO are highly correlated with growth. This relation holds for growth rates in the past (before the survey was organized) as well as those in the future (the years after the questionnaire was organized) and for all groups of countries distinguished: all countries, the poorer countries and the wealthier countries. The correlation between Long-term orientation and future economic growth is stronger than with past economic growth, from which he concludes that it 'speaks in favour of an arrow of causation from LTO to growth' (Hofstede 2001: 367). Of the other four cultural dimensions, Hofstede (2001: 366, 367) reports significant correlations for past economic growth only (1960–70) in the wealthier countries: Individualism (negative) and Power Distance and Uncertainty Avoidance (both positive). In a stepwise regression, only Individualism made a significant contribution. An analysis with Hofstede's original four cultural dimensions and those of the Chinese Value Survey also finds a positive influence of Long term orientation (then still called Confucian Dynamism) on economic growth (Franke *et al.* 1991).

Other cultural dimensions that are sometimes found to have significantly negative effects on growth are Individualism, Power Distance and Integration. The last dimension comes from the Chinese Value Survey. Higher scores on it reflect that respondents are more tolerant and harmonious. Hofstede considers culture as a necessary but not a sufficient condition for economic growth. A market and appropriate political conditions are in his view also necessary (Hofstede 2001: 368). The regression analysis reported so far with respect to Hofstede's dimensions, contain cultural variables only. Dieckmann (1996) develops an endogenous growth model, which includes cultural activity as a production factor. He is ambiguous whether the cultural input is an activity or refers to values. In an empirical analysis for 40 countries over the period 1960–90, he finds a negative relation between Uncertainty Avoidance and economic growth. Other significant variables in the regression are initial income, the investment share in GDP, tertiary education and the average government share in GDP.

High levels of economic growth are associated with the take-off phase, whereas high levels of GDP per capita are characteristic of the post-materialist period. Consequently, the cultural factors explaining economic growth need not be the same as those explaining the level of economic development measured by GDP per capita or a broader measure such as the Human Development Index (HDI). Regressions using Hofstede's four original cultural dimensions confirm this idea.[4] For a group of wealthy countries, Individualism is negatively correlated with cross-country differences in economic growth and positively with measures of GDP per capita (insignificantly) and human development (see Table 6.1, columns 1–3). In some regressions Uncertainty Avoidance influences cross-country differences in growth negatively in human development positively. These results

Table 6.1 Economic performance and Hofstede's cultural dimensions

Dep. var	*(1)*	*(2)*	*(3)*	*(4)*	*(5)*	*(6)*
Constant	30.693,731***	77,855***	9,038***	29,196	9,277	40,953***
	(9.356,564)	(0,681)	(1,700)	(5,279)***	(0,910)***	(3,914)
Power Distance		−0,022***	−0,002	0,115*	−0,033	0,088**
		(0,007)	(0,018)	(0,055)	(0,014)**	(0,041)
Individualism	41,233	0,115***	−0,051	−0.065		−0,066*
	(99,964)	(0,006)	(0,016)***	(0.050)		(0,037)
Masculinity	45,286	−0,016***	2,06E -7	0,126***	−0,027**	0,078**
	(89,240)	(0,005)	(0,012)	(0,041)	(0,012)	(0,030)
Uncertainty Avoidance	−134,394*	0,042***	−0,034***	−0,040	0,011	−0,046*
	(77,358)	(0,004)	(0,011)	(0,034)	(0,01)	(0,025)
Observations	24	24	24	22	22	22
R-squared	0,148	0,643	0,497	0,529	0,348	0,542
Adj. R-squared	0,026	0,638	0,397	0,424	0,246	0,440
F-statistic	1,212	132,613	4,949	5,046	3,388	5,326

Standard errors in parentheses
* significant at 10%; ** significant at 5%; *** significant at 1%
(1) = GDP per capita in constant 2000 US$
(2) = Human Development Index 1980
(3) = GDP growth (annual %)
(4) = GINI Index
(5) = Income share held by lowest 20%
(6) = Income share held by highest 20%

do not confirm those reported by Hofstede, who finds that the correlation between Individualism and GDP per capita is the strongest of Hofstede's five cultural dimensions (Hofstede 2001: 272). It holds for all countries and for 22 wealthier countries. For these two groups of countries Uncertainty Avoidance negatively correlates with GDP per capita.

Power Distance and Masculinity are the most important cultural dimensions for explaining income inequality across countries. The income distribution is more unequal when Power Distance and Masculinity are relatively high (Table 6.1, column 5). This result corresponds with the findings on wage dispersion reported in Chapter 5, Table 5.4. As a consequence, the share of the lowest (highest) 20 per cent of the population is relatively low (high) in these countries (Table 6.1, last two columns). Individualism and Uncertainty Avoidance tend to lead to a more equal income distribution, although their influence is much weaker than that of Power Distance and Masculinity.

Using regions within one or a few countries constitutes a much more homogenous sample than one consisting of countries at different levels of development. Hence, a sample of different regions from one or a few similar countries can solve the problems of heterogeneous datasets mentioned earlier.[5] An additional advantage of using regions is that the number of observations can still be quite large. Finally, using regional data can reveal the differences in cultures within one country. Studies using regional data are Beugelsdijk and Van Schaik (2005a, 2005b) and Tabellini (2005). Beugelsdijk and Van Schaik (2005b) construct a measure of social capital including generalized trust and (passive and active) group membership. They find a significant positive relation between this measure of social capital and the growth over 1950–98 of regional GDP per capita relative to the country mean. Disentangling the components of social capital reveals that this positive effect is due to the influence of group membership. In particular active membership is important for regional growth. Generalized trust is never significant (Beugelsdijk and Van Schaik 2005a).

In an interesting analysis,[6] Tabellini (2005) considers 69 regions in eight different European countries. In his view culture is determined by historical developments. As historical indicators he uses regional literacy rates at the end of the nineteenth century and indicators of political institutions in the period 1600–1850. He suggests that regions with higher illiteracy and worse political institutions in the past tend to have cultural traits today which hamper economic development. The indicators of culture are obtained from the 1990–91 and 1995–97 waves of the World Values Survey. Proxies for culture are: trust; the conviction that individual effort is likely to pay off; respect and tolerance for other people, and whether obedience is an important quality that children should learn. The first three variables are expected to have a positive and obedience a negative influence on both GDP per capita and economic growth.

Instrumental variables estimates are used to estimate the exogenous influence of culture on income per capita. First, culture is explained by the literacy rate at the end of the nineteenth century and the political institutions in previous centuries. The fitted values from these regressions are used in the regression for output per capita. Hence the estimated coefficient measures the effect of culture as far as this is represented by illiteracy and political institutions in previous centuries. Both these individual aspects of culture as well as their first principal component are significantly explained by illiteracy rates and political institutions in previous periods. In the second stage regressions, the coefficients of cultural variables are significant and have the expected signs when explaining the average of per capita output over the period 1995 to 2000.

In order to illustrate the procedure, Table 6.2 presents some of Tabelinni's 2SLS regressions.[7] The odd columns contain the first stage regression and the even ones the second stage regression. Beneath each coefficient two standard errors are presented. The first one is the standard deviation resulting from OLS, the second is corrected for clustering within countries. It takes into account that observations within a country often have a higher degree of correlation than those between countries (see the section on multilevel estimation in Chapter 4). The first column shows that the principle component of culture is significantly determined by the first principal component of institutions and literacy at the end of the nineteenth century. The fitted values of this regression are the observation of pc_culture of the regression presented in the second column. Average income per head in 1995–2000 is significantly explained by the urbanization rate in 1850 and the exogenous part of the principle component of institutions; the part explained by the exogenous variables in column 1. The columns 3 to 6 show the results for two individual aspects of culture, namely trust and obedience. The current value of trust is significantly determined by literacy rate in the past and the first principle of institutions (Table 6.2, column 3). The component of trust that can be explained by these historical facts has a significantly positive influence on income per capita in 1995–2000 (column 4). Similarly, obedience is explained by illiteracy in the past (column 5), and the fitted values of it explain income per capita (column 6). In this way Tabellini argues that historical facts (literacy and political institutions in the past) influence present culture and through culture economic performance in the twentieth century.

His claim that these past institutions influence 'economic performance *only* through culture' (Tabellini 2005: 26, italics added), seems to us to be too strong. It could equally be that past institutions have determined both present institutions as well as present values. In order to find out whether historical circumstances are more important for explaining culture or institutions, one should run regressions for proxies of both culture and institutions. The resulting regressions can then reveal information on the

Table 6.2 Culture and output: instrumental variables estimates, unweighted

Dep. variable	*(1)* *pc_culture*	*(2)* *yp9500*	*(3)* *trust*	*(4)* *yp9500*	*(5)* *obedience*	*(6)* *yp9500*
urb_rate1850	0.03	0.48	−0.09	0.91	−0.10	−0.10
	(0.16)	(0.22)**	(0.06)	(0.32)***	(0.06)	(0.48)
	(0.14)	(0.26)	(0.06)	(0.45)*	(0.05)*	(0.41)
pc_culture		1.07				
		(0.26)***				
		(0.34)**				
literacy	0.48		0.13		−0.14	
	(0.19)**		(0.07)*		(0.07)*	
	(0.18)**		0.08		(0.04)**	
pc_institutions	10.16		1.99		−1.32	
	(2.82)***		(1.13)*		(1.13)	
	(2.24)***		(0.72)**		(0.87)	
trust				4.83		
				(1.69)***		
				(1.44)**		
obedience						−5.66
						(2.19)***
						(1.61)***
Number of observations	67	67	67	67	67	67
Adj R-squared	0.76		0.63		0.76	
F statistics	13.55		4.47		3.35	
Chi^2 (1) p-value		0.18		0.59		0.96

Standard errors in parentheses (above: OLS; below: clustered, allowing for arbitrary correlations within countries).
* significant at 10%; ** significant at 5%; *** significant at 1%.
Country dummy variables and *school* are always included in the first and second stage regressions.
Estimation method: 2SLS. First stage in odd columns, second stage in even columns.
F statistics is F-test of the excluded instruments. Chi^2 (1) is the value of the Sargan statistic testing the over-identifying restriction.

Source, adapted from Tabellini (2005), Tables 9 and 10.

significance of each of the channels. Chances are high that both channels appear to be relevant.

Politicized culture

Up to now culture has been understood as a general trend to which the majority of the population adheres and which is understood as the people's ingrained attitudes towards different aspects of life. It is assumed to be formed by the common cultural and historical heritage. Except for the study by Alesina and Glaeser (2004) the formation of culture is understood as a neutral process in which no particular party plays a specific role. Some authors, however, emphasis that culture is not neutral but often consciously created by power-holders to justify their actions and privileged position. Hence, 'it would be naive to believe that culture is neutral: in virtually every society, it legitimates the established social order – partly because the dominant elite try to shape it to help perpetuate their rule.' (Inglehart 1997: 26). Regression analysis of survey data is insufficient to find the powers behind the process of cultural change. As Alesina and Glaeser claim, one has to augment the analysis with a historical study to find out which forces and groups have shaped the present view on society. Case studies can also be very helpful for finding the interests served by the dominant cultural pattern.

Some recent case studies have found what is called a politicized culture; a purposefully created view on the development and origins of a group (mostly nations) created by political leaders.[8] Examples of politicized cultures are the Asian and Islamic Values debate in Malaysia and the African renaissance under Mbeki in South Africa. In the early 1980s when Malaysia was in a recession, Mahathir, the then prime minister of Malaysia, launched the Look East campaign.[9] Japan and Korea figured in this campaign as models for economic growth. The Eastern work ethic, which was thought to be an important explanatory factor in these countries' success, was stressed as an example for the Malays. Later on, during the boom of the late 1980s and 1990s, the idea 'shifted towards the argument that such values already existed in Malaysia, . . . they were also present in Islam, and thus part of the Malaysian heritage' (Maseland 2006a: 167). At that time Mahathir organized an Islamization of public life, in which contents of Islam were promoted which are in accordance with economic reforms. The pursuit of knowledge, thrift, and hard work were argued to be basic Islamic values. Moreover, according to the official interpretation Islam was open to other religions. This view was summarized in Vision 2020, the ideological agenda of Mahathir's future formulated in 1991. Whereas in 1970 in his The Malaya Dilemma, Mahathir had characterized the Malaya culture as backward, in the 1990s he pointed at the economic success and capabilities of the Malaya, summarized in the slogan 'Malaysia Boleh!' (Malyasia can). This superiority was also expressed in the Petronas Twin Towers, the tallest building in the world. It consists of five towers, referring to the five pillars of Islam, and thus embodying the compatibility of modern Islam with economic progress.

The African Renaissance is the invented element of South African politicized culture.[10] It is promoted by President Thabo Mbeki and a small group of followers. Elements are the attack on African inferiority, and the promotion of African dignity. It shows pride in Africa's heritage but also in its capacity to modernize and take responsibility. African Renaissance 'enables its proponents to advocate economic reform and democratic governance . . . as aspects of an African renaissance and prerequisites for the continent to claim its rightful place in the world. Essentially, it saves face while promoting intrinsically Western ideas about change for the continent' (Bernstein 2006: 27). The African Renaissance can serve as a tool and set of beliefs for the leaders, it seems to have less impact in the South African people in general (ibid: 28).

The study by Alesina and Glaeser illustrates that in the modern Western countries, politicians also manage the public's view to get support for their own ideas and position. The idea of the United States of America being the country with unlimited possibilities was created by leaders, who had a (financial) interest in attracting immigrants to the USA.

Long chain

In Chapter 5 we found Uncertainty Avoidance as an important dimension explaining cross-country differences in institutions. Uncertainty accepting societies are characterized by an important role for financial markets, a low level of employees' protection, decentralized bargaining, a positive attitude towards innovation and foreign influences. In accordance with these findings, these countries appear to specialize in R&D intensive industries and to export relatively many R&D intensive products. All these characteristics are often considered to be pro-growth. If true, this would imply a higher rate of growth and a higher level of income per capita in countries scoring low on Uncertainty Avoidance than in those scoring high on this dimension.

An inspection of data on Uncertainty Avoidance and indicators of economic well being of 20 rich countries suggest that such a relation does not exist. Within this group of wealthy countries the scores on Uncertainty Avoidance range from 23 (Denmark) to 112 (Greece), which is almost the entire range of scores on Uncertainty Avoidance within a group of 74 countries and regions.[11] The results of some simple regressions confirm thus first impression. Uncertainty Avoidance has even a negative affect on cross-country differences in the level and annual growth of income per capita (Table 6.1, columns 2 and 4). Hence, values can be of importance for the way a society is organized, but need not necessarily affect the level of income per capita or the country's growth rate.

The theoretical framework set down in Chapter 3 can provide an explanation for this seemingly contradictary result. As this framework (see Figures 3.1 and 3.2) shows, values (by some also called informal institutions) are expected to be closely related to formal institutions, less to governance structures and even less to economic performance. Or starting the argument from the side of economic performance, one can argue that economic growth can be acquired in different ways: specialization in high-tech intensive industries or in more mature technology-intensive industries, in services, in the exploitation of natural resources, etc. Each of these ways of specialization can lead to the same level of average income per capita, whereas the societies' structures (values, institutions and governance) are quite different.

Germany and the USA can act as examples underscoring this argument. Both countries have a relatively high level of GDP per capita. Their score on Uncertainty Avoidance is quite different: that of Germany is high, whereas that of the USA is relatively low. In accordance with these scores on Uncertainty Avoidance the institutions of the financial sector and of the labour market are quite different, Germany being the archetype country of a bank-based system with coordinated bargaining and the USA as the counterpart of a financial markets-based system with decentralized bargaining. Moreover, the German industry is specialized in improving existing technology, whereas as the American industry is more characterized by fundamental innovations.

Both the example of Germany versus the USA and the various studies discussed in this and the previous chapter reveal that values can be related to institutions and governance, but need not in a consistent way lead to more wealth. This is likely to reflect that values and economic performance are both at the extremes of the chain from values, through institutions and governance, to performance.

Causality

As has been argued before, culture can influence institutions and economic performance, but the reverse causal relation can also be relevant. The culture is thought to reflect power distribution in and possibilities of a society. For example, the lack of planning in poor countries can be explained by the few devices these economies provide with which people can plan for the future (Chang 2008: 195). Culture (values) remains constant, as long as the conditions in which values are grounded remain fairly stable. Value structures may change rapidly, however, in response to major technological, economic, political, and security upheavals (Schwartz 1992: 47). A few studies have investigated the most likely causal direction by means of almost identical surveys organized for different years.

The interviews with IBM personnel, on which Hofstede bases his dimensions, were organized in 1967–69 and 1971–73. For the countries included in both surveys, Hofstede investigated the differences in results for these two waves, and found a clear increase in Individualism over the four years between these two surveys. He explains this by the strong correlation between Individualism and wealth (income per capita). In a step wise regressions wealth and latitude remained as significant variables. He interprets this as a causal relation from wealth toward individualism; 'poverty makes people depend on the support of their in-groups, but when a country's wealth increases its citizens get access to resources that allow them to "do their own thing"' (Hofstede 2001: 253). The questions composing the indices of

Power Distance and Uncertainty Avoidance did not shift together in time, so that these indices should not be used for longitudinal culture change (Hofstede 2001: 181). For Masculinity the longitudinal effect was weak. Moreover, in both waves older people were less masculine. In an aging society that implies a gradual shift towards more feminine values. This move is reinforced by the environmental problems threatening mankind. These problems will increase the conservation-consciousness of all people and thus lead to more feminine values (Hofstede 2001: 335). Of course a period of four years is so short that only very preliminary trends can be discovered. Observations covering a much longer period are needed for drawing more reliable conclusions.

Ideally, one would study the evolution of the economy and the pattern of dominating values during a lengthy period in order to find evidence of a causal relation. Allen *et al.* (2007), the European Values Survey and the World Values Survey to a great extent approach this ideal. Allen and co-authors study the changes in cultural values in nine East Asian and Pacific Island nations over a period of twenty years by repeating in 2002 the 1982 study of Ng *et al.* (1982). The 2002-samples of university students reproduce the 1982-samples as much as possible; the same number of males and females, the same universities, etc. (see Allen *et al.* 2007: 252). The same questionnaire as in 1982 is used. This questionnaire includes the questions from which Schwartz's seven dimensions can be derived. A discriminant analysis of the answers of the 2002-wave produced roughly the same first function as in 1982. The second function of 1982 was not found in the 2002 sample, so that Allen and co-authors only considered the first function: Dionysian versus Submission. The Dionysian pole refers to Mature love (sexual and spiritual) and exciting life (in the 1982-survey) and the Submission pole to Obedience, politeness and national security. During the last two decades of the twentieth century the nations became more polarized on this dimension: in 2002 Dionysian (Submission) values were higher in nations that scored already high on it in 1982. Moreover, the support for Dionysian values increased in countries with a high and fast-growing per capita income, whereas more support for Submission was found in slower growing economies. Support for the causal link from economic conditions to values is found in both samples.

As described in Chapter 3, values are formed during one's childhood. If correct, on a national level the correlation between the Dionysian versus Submission dimensions should be highest for the years of the respondents' childhood. This appears to be correct for both samples. Moreover, high levels of GDP per capita in 1982 correlate with a shift from Hierarchy towards Egalitarianism. This finding corresponds with Hofstede's assertion that an increase in wealth leads to a higher score on Individualism.

Evidence in favour of the effect of values on economic development is found too. High scores on Mastery versus Harmony in 1982 correlate positively and strongly with GDP growth during the subsequent two decades, indicating that Mastery values lead to economic growth. Finally, support for Inglehart's position that the causality changes over time is also available. On the one hand high scores on Mastery lead to high growth rates in subsequent decades. However, as economies grew during this period, 'nations increasingly rejected Mastery values. This . . . may support Inglehart's view that achievement motivation and related values improve a country's national economic development initially, but that the effect of a strong economy is a shift toward post-modern cultural values' (Allen *et al.* 2007: 262).

Inglehart's analysis is based on trends in the 1970–71, 1981 and 1990 waves of the World Values Survey. He finds support for both directions of causality. Economic growth has lead to such a high level of income per capita that the great masses do not have to care about their survival. This material security has led to a shift in priorities from attaining material wealth by economic growth (materialist values) to a good quality of life (post-material values). The post-material values are 'emphasized after people have attained material security, and because they have attained material security.' (Inglehart 1997: 35). Hence, economic development leads to value change. On the other hand, due to less emphasis on economic growth in post-materialist societies, economic growth is relatively low in these countries (ibid: 222). Then values shape performance.

As Inglehart's results and reasoning illustrate, values, institutions and economic performance are simultaneously determined. One can argue, as Inglehart does, that during some periods one direction of causality dominates the other. Many empirical analyses are, however, cross-country studies, which preclude analyzing the dynamic process. Even in cases where observations of values are obtained from more than one period, the number of observations in the time domain is too low to entangle empirically the direction of causality. Hence, the simultaneity problem remains. This problem is not specific for cultural studies but is present in all cross-country studies, including studies on the institutional differences between countries.

Many researchers in economics use Instrumental Variables (IV) Estimators in order to solve the simultaneity problem. Tabellini's study of cultural differences between regions in Europe, described in a previous section, is a very good example of the use of the Instrumental Variables procedure. In the first step of IV estimates, the cultural variable is regressed on exogenous variables. These exogenous variables should have a high correlation with the cultural variable, in order to explain the latter to a reasonable extent. In addition they should not be determined by the endogenous variable at hand. The adjustment process associated with the interaction between culture on the one hand and economic institutions and economic performance on the other is often regarded as being very slow and gradual. Consequently, one has to select historical events or arrangements relatively far in the past, such as the literacy rate at the end of the nineteenth century and the political institutions in previous centuries (Tabellini 2005), or settlers' mortality rate (Acemoglu *et al.* 2001). Other candidates for instrumental variables are the average temperature and altitude. In the second regression, the coefficients of the instrumental variables estimate the effect of the cultural variables as far as the latter is determined by these exogenous factors. For example, the effect of trust on per capita income as far as trust is significantly determined by the literacy rate at the end of the nineteenth century. Accordingly, the questions tackled by this estimation procedure are: to what extent influence historical or other external factors present values?, and second, what are the effects of the exogenous part of culture (values) on current economic institutions and economic performance?

Are these really the questions one would like to answer? Moreover, does not such a strategy implicitly assume a very static concept of culture? I tend to answer the first question in the negative and the second in the affirmative. Paradoxically, this procedure consolidates a static view on culture, whereas it starts with a dynamic concept. It is noteworthy that economists regard the IV-procedure as mandatory for a valid estimation procedure, whereas researchers from sociology do not use this or similar procedures. The latter apply regression analysis in order to see whether a statistically significant relation is present. No claim with respect to causality is brought forward. The most likely direction of causality is based on theory and/or the sequential order of the observations. In my view this procedure is to be preferred to the search for appropriate instrumental variables, which distracts the researchers' attention from the mechanism by which culture and other variables interact. These are the questions of interest.

Concluding remarks

This chapter has discussed the literature on economic growth and culture. For the industrialized countries the relation between economic development and cultural dimension was weak, much weaker than that between the institutional structure of various sectors and culture reported in the previous chapter. So it seems that for these countries culture can explain the differences in institutions but less often those in economic performance. Assuming that the theoretical structure as set out in Chapter 3 and represented by Figure 3.2 is correct, this result reflects the assumption that culture is more directly related to institutions than to economic performance; it is a long way from culture via institutions and governance to economic development. The finding that culture is much more important for explaining differences in institutions than differences in performance for this group of countries corresponds with Shleifer and Vishny's conclusion that different institutions of corporate governance can deliver good results, in the sense of economic development (see Shleifer and Vishny 1997).

Another issue concerns causality. Many surveys are organized for one period only or successive waves are so close to each other that one cannot claim any causal direction. The epistomological approach, dealt with in the previous chapter, circumvents the causality issue by relating second generation immigrants' behaviour to the behaviour of their generation in their parents' home country. In this way one can investigate whether values are transmitted from parents to children independent of the institutional structure they live in. The epistemological approach cannot answer the question – what has caused society-wide changes in values, institutions and performance and how are these three areas related? The route taken in cross-country studies using survey data is to apply the Instrumental Variables (IV) technique in order to disentangle causal relationships. This technique amounts to a search for exogenous, mostly historical, variables, which can serve as proxies for the cultural dimension. The IV method delivers consistent estimates of the coefficients of culture. In order to obtain these estimates it implicitly applies a static view on culture. Moreover, it does not answer the question: Have values been driving economic changes during recent decades or was the direction of causality reverse? For answering this question the researcher has to rely on theory and longitudinal analysis of values, institutions and economic performance. As Alesina and Glaeser (2004) illustrate, a historical (case) study of the phenomenon can also help to disentangle the underlying forces of the relation found. It is remarkable to note that the IV technique is widely used by economists but not by sociologists studying similar problems with similar techniques. The latter are well aware of the difficulties of causality and therefore, circumvent firm claims about the causal direction of the correlation found. In our view, the collection and investigation of longitudinal data as this is presented in Allen *et al.* (2007), is a much more promising way of dealing with the dynamics between culture and other elements of society than searching for appropriate instrumental variables.

Chapter 7

Religion as culture

In the previous chapters culture was represented by values in general. Many hold religion as an important, if not the most important, source of values. According to some (Inglehart 1997: 217, Williamson 2000: 596) the value system of most pre-industrial societies takes the form of religion. The religions' Holy Scripts and the explanations of these scripts are regarded as an important source of these values. Max Weber is well known as the social scientist who has pointed at the importance of religious values for economic growth. Since the mid 1990s there is an increasing awareness within development organizations for the role of culture and religion (as part of culture) for economic development. This awareness is noticeable in various reports by the World Bank and the activities of the World Faiths Development Dialogue. At the same time, in social sciences and in particular economics, the model of the rationally acting individual came under attack (see Chapter 3). As a consequence, other ways of explaining economic phenomena obtained increasing attention, such as evolutionary economics, behavioural economics, and economics and culture. In this literature culture is defined as the collective programming of the mind that distinguishes the members of one group (country or society) from another.[1] Religion, defined as a 'shared set of beliefs, activities and institutions premised upon faith in supernatural forces' (Iannaccone 1998: 1466), is then considered as part of culture. Since 11 September 2001 religion is on the agenda of many. Religion, and Islam in particular, forms an important issue in the political debate in countries all over the world. It has also drawn the attention of policy advisors. This increasing attention for the role of religion has inspired us to devote one entire chapter to religion as culture.

Religion and religious activities can influence society in two ways.[2] First, religious activities such as church attendance are a form of social activity and thus comparable to meetings of football clubs, tennis clubs, scouts, political parties, etc. These meetings can be instruments for establishing networks that could be of use for economic activities in the region and could also be helpful for establishing trading relations with partners from other countries who belong to the same religious group.[3] Such networks can

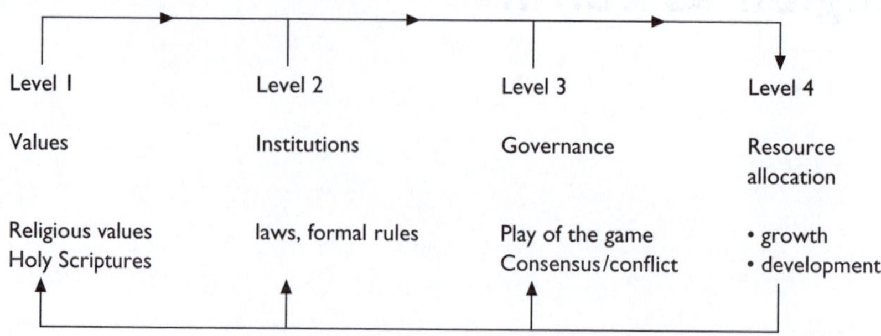

Source: Adapted from Williamson (2000), Figure 1 and De Jong (2002).

Figure 7.1 Religious values, institutions and growth

stimulate economic growth. Of course church attendance costs time, which cannot be spent on economic activities, so that a reduction of income could be the result. A second channel by which religion influences society is by the values taught by the adherents or most important leaders of the religion concerned.

In this chapter we focus on the latter channel and consider the role of religious values – if possible, religious rather than broad humanistic values – for explaining differences in institutions and in economic development.[4] Figure 7.1, which is a slightly revised version of Figure 3.2, presents the structure of the discussion. Compared to similar figures in previous chapters, the box of culture is filled with values and norms as these are taught and adhered to by members of a particular religion. Formal religions base their worldview on a Holy Script (Bible, Qur'an, etc.) and the exegesis by important scholars or (former) leaders. This chapter is also used to assess the adequacy of using broad concepts such as religion and language as representations of culture.

The set-up of the chapter is as follows. In the next section, we discuss some measures used in quantitative studies on religion and economics. Thereafter, we review studies on the relationship between religion and economic institutions and various forms of governance. Interest has been debated over centuries by adherents of many religions, a special subsection is devoted to this topic. Next, the relation between religious values and economic growth is discussed. This starts with the seminal study by Weber about Protestantism and Capitalism and critics of this study. Then recent quantitative studies and case studies of this relationship are discussed. One section deals with development, which is a broader concept than economic growth, and religion. The chapter concludes with a discussion of three issues: the assumption of the main religion's homogeneity, Islamic economics and identity, and causality.

Measures of religion

Obtrusive measures

According to the scheme developed in Chapter 4 we make a distinction between obtrusive and unobtrusive measures of religion. Surveys are the most prominently used obtrusive measures of religious values. Many large-scale surveys, such as the European Value Survey, the World Value Survey and the Eurobarometer, contain questions asking the respondents' attitude with respect to religious issues. Examples are: Do you believe in God? Do you believe in hell? Do you believe in heaven? Some researchers, Sakwa (2006) for example, formulate questions directed at specific issues: in Sakwa's case Biblical concepts of poverty (See Table 7.1). In both cases respondents are asked to indicate on a particular scale to which degree they agree or disagree with the statement concerned. Some answers can be coded dichotomously. For example, the answer on the questions: do you belong to this religion: yes/no?

The scores of the answers in these questionnaires can be used in two ways. First, one can use the individual scores in the regression equation. The estimated coefficient reflects the average influence of religious values and other variables on characteristics of persons (or households). In these micro-studies, the number of observations equals the number of individuals in the sample. In all likelihood, individuals from the same country are influenced by variables that are particular for that country. In order to take these common influences into account, in cross-country regressions a dummy variable for the country is included: so-called fixed effect estimates (see also the discussion on multilevel regression in Chapter 4). This method is used in, for example, Guiso *et al.* (2003). Micro-studies confined to respondents from one country only are Cuesta (2004), Sakwa (2006), and Sakwa *et al.* (2005). Cuesta uses the results of 3,000 households in Honduras, and the results in the studies by Sakwa are based on the answers of about 250 students from four universities in Nairobi. Table 7.1 contains an example of the type of questions used by Sakwa.

The scores of the questionnaires can also be used for macro-studies. Then for each country the average of the scores on a particular question is

Table 7.1 Example of questions used for measuring a Biblical concept of poverty

Defining statement: *Isaiah 58: 7–10 God blesses those who provide for the poor*
Items included in the questionnaire
3 God provides for the poor as we share our food with them.
11 God provides for the poor as we shelter them.
19 God relieves the poor as we show that we are on their side.
The respondents' answers were on a five points scale.

Source: Sakwa (2006: 31 and 32).

calculated first. These averages are included in a regression together with other variables at the country level, such as an index of the quality and nature of institutions. The independent variable is often economic growth or GDP per capita. In this way one studies the macro-effect of religion. Then the number of observations in the regression analysis equals the number of countries in the sample. This method is used in the work by Barro and McCleary and the studies that commented on the work by these two authors.

Unobtrusive measures

Examples of unobtrusive measures are the fraction of the population belonging to a particular religion and a dummy variable representing the dominant religion. The latter equals 1 if the largest part of the population belongs to the religion concerned. So, if in a country 35 per cent of the population is officially a member of the Roman Catholic Church and 30 per cent is Protestant, then the country is labelled as Roman Catholic. This example already illustrates the problems attached to the use of these dummy variables. A country is listed in a particular religious group just because a large minority belongs to this group. Moreover, no information is obtained with respect to the values that are associated with the membership of the religion concerned. It is implicitly assumed that all members of a particular broad religion hold the same values and attitudes, which does not need to be true. Whether this is a valid assumption will be discussed at the end of this chapter.

Religion and institutions

Economic and political *institutions of high quality* reduce transaction costs and hence enhance economic growth. Religious upbringing and active religious participation increase trust towards government institutions and reduce the willingness to break any sort of legal rule (Guiso *et al.* 2003: 249). La Porta *et al.* (1998) find that in countries with weak legal protection, other mechanisms are in place for protecting the rights of investors and owners. For example, poor investor protection in French-civil-law countries is associated with extremely concentrated ownership. In these France-civil-law countries Roman Catholicism is the dominant religion.

Another claim is that the *adaptability of institutions* is important for economic development. Kuran (2004b, 2007) nicely illustrates the importance and the historical evolution of adaptability of law for economic development. In his view the underdevelopment of the Middle East can be explained by the inheritance system as laid down in the Qur'an. The Qur'an contains only a few economic rules, one of which constitutes the inheritance system. Two-thirds of any estate is reserved for a list of extended relatives. The individual testamentary powers are limited to one-third of an estate. This inheritance system was meant to give everybody a reasonable share in the property and to limit the concentration of wealth. However, it also hindered the preservation of successful enterprises or other assets across generations. Asset owners could preserve their wealth by means of a *waqf*, which is a 'trust founded under Islamic law by a person for the provision of a designated service in perpetuity' Kuran (2004b: 75). The founder could appoint himself as the trustee or manager. Moreover, because a *waqf* was considered sacred, rulers were unlikely to confiscate the assets. Finally, the inheritance regulations could be avoided be appointing one child as the inheritor. In a changing economic environment the *waqf* system became too rigid. It kept resources locked into uses decided centuries earlier. Paradoxically, fundamental changes were also hindered by the flexibility of the judges.[5] Ambiguities in the founder's stipulations were exploited to modify the aims of *waqf*, and the latter were approved by a sympathetic judge. Consequently, the pressure for change was diminished. Essentially these were illegal practices and thus contributed to the prevalence of corruption. In sum, the fact that the Holy Scripture was quite explicit on a particular economic item, under changed economic circumstances lead to ways to circumvent the literal interpretation. This had unexpected side effects as the acceptance of corruption and in the end did not bring a fundamental solution for the new situation.

A related issue concerns the consequences of treating minorities differently.[6] In the Middle East the Pact of Umar, which dates from before the ninth century, allowed minorities in the Muslim world to use the courts of their own denomination for settling disputes between non-Muslims. Islamic law had to be applied in cases involving Muslims and in criminal acts. Until the eighteenth century, granting non-Muslims the possibility of using different legal systems lead to a convergence of the legal systems of Muslims, Jews and Christians. One reason was that Muslim courts were more powerful in enforcing their rules. Hence, non-Muslims sought the judgement of these courts. Another reason was that in some cases minorities made their laws analogous to those of Islam in order to prevent members going to Islamic courts to obtain a more favourable treatment (Kuran 2004c: 494). Consequently, this system of legal plurality did not favour one group over the others.

Matters changed in the eighteenth century when Europe became the dominant commercial power. Since non-Muslims in the Middle East could use both Islamic and foreign laws when trading with non-Muslims, they were the ideal trading partners of the European merchants, who wanted to accomplish deals under their own legal system. Moreover, European law allowed banking and insurance activities and had developed the legal figure of a corporation. Partners in a corporation share in the profit and losses of the corporation, which performs several activities over time. Islamic law acknowledges partnerships consisting of individuals for a particular transaction or activity. It does not allow partnerships for several activities over time. Due to the Pact of Umar, non-Muslim minorities could reap the benefits of the more efficient European legal system and the European request for trading under their own legal system. In this way local non-Muslims obtained a pivotal position in the trade between East and West. As a result, at the end of the nineteenth century the non-Muslim minorities dominated the commercial transactions with foreigners and banking and insurance activities. Their living standard was higher than that of the Muslim population. Trade between Muslims, who lived within Islamic countries, was dominated by Muslim merchants.

Religion and governance

Trust and cooperation are often found to be positively associated with economic growth. Following Knack and Keefer (1997), many studies have found a positive relationship between economic growth and trust (see Chapters 6 and 8). Mutual trust is then proxied by the score on the question 'Generally speaking, would you say that most people can be trusted, or that you can't be too careful in dealing with people?' The trust variable is the percentage of people responding that most can be trusted, after the don't knows have been deleted.[7] On the macrolevel, La Porta *et al.* (1997b) find a negative relation between a hierarchical religion such as Roman Catholicism and trust. On the microlevel Guiso *et al.* (2003) find that trust is affected mostly by religious participation; for all religions a higher attendance at religious services is associated with higher levels of trust. Religious upbringing has a negative effect on trust for Catholics, Muslims and Hindus, and no effect for the other religions. The sum of the two effects is positive for Christian religions and more so for Protestants. A more detailed analysis reveals that Catholics raised after Vatican II are more trusting of other people than Catholics raised before Vatican II (Guiso *et al.* 2003: 265). In Cuesta (2004) it is the Honduran Evangelists who trust people less than other religions and participate less in social control mechanisms. This finding is likely to be due to the fact that in Honduras the Protestants are a very small minority: 97 per cent of the population is Roman Catholic and only 3 per cent is Protestant (CIA Fact Book).

Freedom is often regarded as a source for wealth creation. Open borders and free movement of persons, along with an open mind for new ideas, is regarded as growth enhancing. A regression analysis for the period 1975–90 for 80 countries with growth rates of real per capita GDP finds that 'more economic freedom fosters economic growth, but that the level of freedom is not related to growth' (De Haan and Sturm 2000: 238). So for countries with a growth rate below their long-term level, more economic freedom will bring them more quickly to that level. The level of this steady state growth, however, is not affected by the degree of economic freedom.

In a recent study, Alon and Chase (2005) found that for a sample of 54 countries real per capita GDP (hence the level of income and not the growth rate as in De Haan and Sturm 2000) is always positively influenced by economic freedom and in three out of four cases also by religious freedom.[8] A totalitarian regime, on the other hand, tends to neglect opportunities offered. The results are even worse when totalitarianism is combined with cultural triumphalism (Landes 2006: 11). In China, for example, this combination led to a rejection of the strange and foreign and thus hampered the adoption of new ideas. The Chinese even forgot much of what they had once known. At the heart of this matter is a resistance to change and a fear for foreign influences. Landes mentions several factors explaining this attitude, among which is the disdain of Confucianism for scientific research (Landes 2006: 17). One can question the idea that the religion's attitude towards science has caused the low growth rates. It is well known that some pietic Protestants are also very hostile to scientific knowledge, but their religion is in general to be praised for pro-growth. In all likelihood in these cases, religion has been adopted to the prevailing dominant view or incentives resulting from the existing institutional structure (Kuran 2007). Guiso *et al.* (2003) find a negative relation between adherents of religions and tolerance. Only Buddhists are more tolerant. Catholics became more tolerant after Vatican II. The intolerance of a religion appears to increase when this religion is the dominant religion in the country.

Corruption is generally regarded as detrimental to economic growth,[9] although predictable corruption is found to be relatively harmless (Paldam 2001: 390). Unpredictable, large and lasting corruption is a serious problem. In a macro-study (countries are the units studied) Paldam (2001) reports two groups of religions that decrease perceived corruption as this is collected by Transparency International; Reform Christianity (Protestants and Anglicans) and Tribal religion. No significant result is found for the other religions; Catholics, Orthodox and Islam. Note that one reason for the Reformation (although almost 500 years ago) was to fight corruption by officials of the Catholic Church.

Many are of the view that growth goes with a *pro-market attitude*, which is reflected in a positive attitude with respect to income differences as incentives for individual efforts, private ownership of firms, competition, hard work and thrift. The relation between these pro-market values and religion appears to be complex and often not uniform. Guiso *et al.* (2003) analyse the World Values Survey and find that people raised religiously are less willing to trade off equality for incentives and are less in favour of private property. However, those who attend the sermons regularly hold the opposite view. Religious people also emphasis thrift, individual responsibility and that the market outcome is fair. The differences between religions are greatest in their position on the trade off between equality and incentives. Protestants and Hindus are more willing to trade off equality for incentives, while Jews and Muslims are less so. For the other religions the effect is insignificant. Protestants, Catholics and Hindus want more and Muslims want less private ownership. Interestingly, in Guiso *et al.* (2003) more than other religious groups (including Protestants) Catholics favour competition, thrift, and private ownership. This is somewhat at odds with Weber's claim. The respondents in Sakwa (2006) had difficulty with competitiveness. These Roman Catholic students recognized that the market motivates the poor towards improving their well being (Sakwa 2006: 64, 65). However, the path analysis did not find any relation between competitiveness and any of the four aims of poverty alleviation (Sakwa 2006: Table 7.1). A reason for this ambiguous attitude towards competitiveness could be that competition creates both losers and winners.

In traditional environments, where the majority of the active people are farmers or craftsmen, *trade* has often met opposition. The craftsman and farmer work for their living and seek sufficient food and material to support them. The merchant, however, aims at buying cheap and selling dear and thus obtains a profit which often is more than he needs for his livelihood (see e.g. Tawney 1962 [1926]: 35). That such an attitude is not limited to medieval or Biblical times but is a reflection of traditional societies is illustrated by the next story. After the fall of communism, Ascherson went in the beginning of the 1990s to a village in the Don delta, where he met a priest of the Russian Orthodox Church. This priest told him about new people, who do nothing beyond buying and selling. In his view to go on streets and sell vegetables which you have grown or a product of your craftsmanship is good, even natural. But these people 'buy an article in one place, and then may come here to sell it for a higher price. They do not work, they do not make anything! I have told my congregation that it is a wickedness, a sin, to make money out of what you have not produced.' (Ascherson 1995: 107). In the Middle Ages this problem of earning money without making anything was solved by regarding profit as a particular form of wages.

Freedom for women to occupy any job they like is favourable for growth. It is often argued that some religions and Islam in particular, stimulate a view that is hostile to *women's rights*. Gallup's World Poll does not confirm this popular image. Majorities of women in the Muslim countries surveyed, said that women deserve the same legal rights as men: the right to vote, to work at any job they are qualified for and to serve at the highest levels of government (Esposito and Mogahed 2007: 102). These results do not imply that Muslim women would like to be treated as Western women. They think that in the West men do not respect women. In their view the latter are too often indecently dressed and looked upon as sex symbols. The actual participation of women in education and formal work differs tremendously across Muslim countries. The percentage of women with post-secondary education varies from 8 per cent in Morocco to 52 per cent in Iran. The ratio of women to men enrolment in secondary education in

2001–2002 was even higher than 100 per cent in countries such as Jordan, Algeria, Kuwait, Indonesia and Malaysia. In other Islamic countries women's participation in basic education is still low: in Yemen women's literacy rate is only 28 per cent versus 70 per cent for men.

Within the Islamic world female labour market participation in 2000 varied from 9.3 per cent in sub-Sahara Africa to 38.3 per cent in Southeast Asia (Spierings *et al.* 2006: Table 1). Spierings *et al.* (2006) use a multivariate analysis for investigating the explanatory variables of female labour market participation in a group of countries in Africa, Asia and the Greater Middle East. The degree of urbanization positively influences female labour market participation (FLMP). Oil endowment increases urbanization and in that way indirectly supports FLMP. The degree of Islamism and formal and practical democracy do not affect FLMP. Practical democracy plays an important role for *relative* FLMP. Islamic countries with higher levels of practical democracy have higher relative FLMP. Practical democracy is positively related to high levels of GDP per capita and negatively to the degree of Islamism. Hence indirectly the degree of Islamism negatively affects the position of women on the labour market.

Religious teaching with respect to usury

Asking for interest has often been very debatable and is still regarded by some as unjust. Apart from Islamic economists, nowadays adherents of alternative local systems of exchange such as Local Exchange Trade System (LETS) also regard paying interest as inappropriate. In their view money should function as a means of exchange only, and certainly not as an investment vehicle.

The idea that asking for (a high rate of) interest is unjust can be found by writers in Biblical and later times. The Old Testament contains various texts (see Appendix 4 Some Biblical text on interest) which indicate that asking interest is prohibited, especially when the debtor is poor. Differences remain with respect to a stranger. According to Leviticus it does not make any difference whether the debtor is a brother or a stranger, whereas according to Deuteronomy 23: 20 it is allowed to lend upon usury to a stranger. The few texts on interest in the New Testament are more favourable about paying interest. Jesus even recommends putting money at a bank in order to obtain usury (Matthew 24: 27). So, within the Holy Scripture of the Christians we notice a development from a relatively hostile attitude to asking interest (at least in the case of the debtor who cannot afford to pay it) to a more favourable one. In all likelihood this change is in accordance with a change in the organization of economic life: a change from an agrarian economy to one with financial institutions such as banks.

In ancient Greece the male citizen was expected to provide sustenance for himself and his family, and devote the rest of his time to the well being of the community. Farming a small plot of land was a common way of providing the sustenance. Activities that were not aimed at managing the family farm and obtaining the necessary goods were held in low esteem. These activities included manufacturing, business, trade and investing money in order to obtain money. In particular the elite regarded these activities as of lesser value (Engen 2004). In accordance with this view, Aristotle in his Politika (book I, Chapter 10) argues that money is a means of exchange only. Its value always remains the same. Paying an interest implies a growth of the amount of money, which is against nature. Money (as a means of exchange) cannot bear fruit. This idea about the fruitlessness of money is found in arguments for banning interest in later centuries, within different religions, and by non-religious authors.[10]

Within the Middle Ages a similar pattern of losing the prohibition of asking usury can be found (see Tawney 1962 [1926]: 42–55). It was forbidden to ask interest for a loan. Arguments for an interest ban were the same as those mentioned above and the notion that present goods are more valuable than future goods. By borrowing money, one buys goods one otherwise would have obtained only in the future. Consequently, a borrower buys and a lender sells time. Time belongs to God and thus it is forbidden to sell God's assets. Practical considerations were also given for an interest ban (Tawney 1962 [1926]: 44). At that time providing credit was exceptional and some feared that allowing usury would stimulate the rich to lend money for interest and not invest in riskier activities such as providing credit to poor farmers. Hence, the latter would not have enough assets to cultivate the land so that all poor would die of the resulting famine. This argument illustrates that the object of the interest ban was not directed at loans provided by banks to merchants but was to protect the poor against the well-to-do money lenders, who could exploit them.

During the Middle Ages the restrictions on paying interest were lessened. Under various conditions a reward for providing a loan was allowed. The lender could obtain a reward for a partnership, ask compensation when the principal was not repaid on time, and for any loss that he incurred or any gain he had foregone. In modern terms the latter are opportunity costs and nowadays an argument for paying interest. What appeared to be essential was whether the lender bore risks. It was unlawful to obtain a fixed interest payment which had been set in advance. These restrictions were circumvented by a combination of transactions. For example, a landowner could sell land and obtain it back for a higher price, where the latter incorporated the rent. In the later Middle Ages these unnecessarily complicated transactions were replaced by direct loans carrying an interest payment (Samuelsson 1961: 89). At the end of the fifteenth century the Franciscans established funds for loans to the poor. In order to cover the administrative costs, they charged an interest on these loans. The opponents of these loans found it unjust to ask interest from those in need. The argument by its defenders was practical:

it is better to ask a low interest than to see the poor paying high interest to the professional money-lenders (Tawney 1962 [1926]: 90).

The reformers Luther and Calvin held quite different views on providing loans and asking an interest. These differences can be traced back to the economic environment in which each of them was living. Luther lived in south Germany, a rural area in which the peasants were suffering under the yoke of nouveaux richex from the town. The latter bought land and drove up rents. The peasants had to increase *corvées* and pay more money to these new landowners, and their common rights were curtailed. Luther accepted the existing social hierarchy, and thought that the most admirable life was that of a peasant, who in his view was least influenced by commercialization. Merchants and financiers represent commercialization of society and were opposed by him with the same passion as he fought the commercialization of religion. He did not come up with any proposals for changing the ban on interest. His theory of social life was in many respects 'more medieval than that held by many thinkers in the Middle Ages' (Tawney 1962 [1926]: 91). In my view this attitude can be explained by the facts as he saw them in South Germany.

Calvin, the other great Reformer, lived in Geneva the centre of commercial activity at that time. He and his followers accepted the need for capital, credit, and banking as an essential element of commerce and finance. Consequently, they regarded income from these types of activities as of equal respectability as that from labour. No longer are economic motives regarded as opposite to the life of the spirit, and the capitalist is not seen as one who has necessarily grown rich on the misfortune of others. Wealth as such is not bad, but its misuse for self-indulgence is. Calvin regarded interest as lawful and, provided that it was not too high, the borrower reaped as much advantage as the lender; the lender did not obtain excessive certainty and no one gained at the expense of his neighbour. Moreover, loans provided to the poor should be interest free (Tawney 1962 [1926]: 106). In Geneva, the Consistory, consisting of ministers and laymen, judged and punished offenders of the laws on interest and prices. Fines were to be paid by those who asked a higher interest or price than the maximum subscribed by law (ibid: 119). Although, Calvin made the payment of interest generally acceptable, he was not the first, as we already noticed above (see also Tawney 1962 [1926]: 107, Samuelsson 1961: 88–91).

Moreover, although asking interest was allowed, the Methodists disapproved of excessive credit operations. Credit was permissible where there was collateral in the form of goods. Borrowing and lending transactions for financing speculative activities were condemned. One should live a sober life and realize that it is good when one possesses sufficient assets for a decent living (see Samuelsson 1961: 35).

Nowadays, the interest ban forms an important if not the most distinguishing aspect of Islamic banking. The arguments are similar to those put forward during earlier periods. Paying a fixed interest is regarded as unfair because it places the risk entirely on the borrower. Other arguments are, interest is a reflection of the desire to accumulate wealth and of selfishness; interest turns people away from productive enterprises, and it enhances the redistribution of money from the poor to the wealthy (see Kuran 2004a: 8).

The financial instruments used by Islamic banks avoid that, at least on paper, the lender does not bear any risk. *Mudaraba* and *musbaraka* are two related and popular forms of finance. Under *mudaraba* investors entrust capital to an entrepreneur and obtain a prespecified share of the entrepreneur's profit and the principal in return. A *musbaraka* is a similar arrangement but now the entrepreneur adds some money to the amount given by the investors. By far the most popular financing instrument of Islamic banks is the *murabaha*. It works as follows: a producer or trader submits to the bank a list of goods he wants to buy; the bank buys the goods and then sends a bill to the costumer with a higher price for them than that at which the bank bought the goods, to be paid on some jointly agreed moment in the future. From the Islamic point of view it is essential that the bank becomes owner of the goods during a certain period. Another popular instrument is lease financing, some times called *ijara*. The bank rents an item to a costumer for a specified period of time at a rate that reflects the costs of the item and the time-value of the money. After this period the costumer can have the option of purchasing the item. Once again according to Islamic law this transaction is allowed because during the leasing period the bank bears losses from damage. In practice, however, the banks shift this risk onto others by requiring the user to put up collateral and pay for insuring the asset (Kuran 2004a: 10 and 11).

According to Kuran, Islamic banking is still a small share of the market. In his view this is due to inefficiency and the costs attached to asymmetric information. Inefficiency arises because often one has to sign two contracts, one for buying the item and one for selling it, instead of only one contract as is the case with conventional banking. Formulas on profit or risk sharing can only be adhered to if both parties possess all the relevant information. In practice the entrepreneur knows much more about the project than the financiers, so that the latter have to add costs for acquiring information in order to judge whether they obtain a fair share. In these cases a fixed interest rate saves these costs. These features make the products of Islamic banks more expensive than those of conventional banks. Since in almost all countries Islamic banks operate alongside conventional banks, only a tiny fraction of customers use products of Islamic banks. Moreover, due to the problems associated with asymmetric information Islamic banks sustain a relatively large share of the bad risks.

Within the Islamic world opinions differ with respect to the eligibility of asking interest. There are those who read from the Qu'ran that asking a fixed interest is forbidden, but others claim that such a statement is incorrect. According to a treatise published in 1988 by Süleyman Uludağ a ban on interest reflects a misreading of the Qu'ran; the Qu'ran does not forbid paying interest but it does prohibit asking an exorbitant interest (the usury in Judeo–Christian terminology). In 1989, a legal opinion (*fatw*) of the Egyptian mufti Muhammad Sayyid Tantawi, declared that interest-based instruments are not necessarily corrupt, because they may benefit everyone involved. Within the Islamic establishment this constitutes a minority position (Kuran 2004a: 16).

From this description on the development and motives of the interest ban, we draw two conclusions. First, the regulations were adjusted according to the economic conditions. Interest payment was forbidden in situations where providing credit was an exceptional transaction and interest payments would be too high a burden on the shoulders of the poor. In other circumstances, in particular when financial institutions exist and providing loans was part of the regular activities of a profession, various exceptions were allowed. The other conclusion is that the aim of the restrictions was often to protect the poor.[11]

Economic growth and religion

Weber and his critics

Without any doubt Max Weber's '*The Protestant Ethic and the Spirit of Capitalism*' is the initiator of the discussion on economic performance and religious values. From the very beginning this publication has met much resistance and criticism. In order to judge the validity of this criticism we briefly describe as clearly as possible the line of thought of Weber and the qualifications he makes himself.[12]

Weber starts in the Introduction by observing that at the beginning of the twentieth century the Western civilization stands out in various aspects: the stage of development of science and the form of capitalism. Capitalism in the sense of economic activities based on the expectation of profit (Weber 2001 [1930]: xxxii), is found in many parts of the world and throughout its entire history. The Western form of capitalism differs, however, from this general notion of capitalism in the following aspects (Weber 2001 [1930]: xxxiv–xxxv): the rational capitalistic organization of (formerly) free labour; separation of business from household; rational book-keeping. When explaining why this particular form of capitalism has developed in the West, one should recognize the importance of economic factors 'but at the same time the opposite correlation must not be left out of consideration' (Weber 2001 [1930]: xxxix).

In the following chapters he sets himself to consider this 'opposite correlation' as an explanation for economic development. He observes that at the time of writing his first essay, the German Catholics complained of their minor position compared to the Protestants. The latter were overrepresented in the higher levels of economic occupations: business leaders, capital owners, and commercially trained personnel. This fact does not imply any causality. It could be that religious affiliation is a result of economic conditions (ibid: 4). Weber notes that the majority of the wealthy towns went over to Protestantism in the sixteenth century. Why did that happen? It could be that Protestants (at least particular branches) developed an economic rationalism which cannot be observed among Catholics.

In his second essay '*The Spirit of Capitalism*', Weber argues that economic conditions are insufficient for explaining economic development. He provides evidence for this by discussing the possible consequences of low and high wages on the employees' effort. When piece-rates are used, increasing these rates would not necessarily lead to more working hours and thus higher levels of production. Although higher rates offer the opportunity of earning more, workers with a more traditional view could also choose in favour of working less for the same amount of money as before. On the other hand, low wages are not identical with cheap labour. Low wages could also indicate low productivity. Since both high and low wages do not necessarily lead to higher levels of production, another explanation seems to be relevant. Weber concludes 'Labour must, . . . be performed as if it were an absolute end in itself, a calling . . . such an attitude is by no means a product of nature. It . . . can only be the product of a long and arduous process of education' (Weber 2001 [1930]: 25).

This calling, that labour is an end in itself, can be found in pietistic denominations of Protestantism, sects such as the Mennonites and Quakers. It is not found in an important Protestant denomination such as Lutheranism. Within Calvinism the calling is related to the belief in predestination. According to this theory, from the beginning God has already decided who will be elected. One cannot arrive at the stage of the chosen by one's own efforts. Consequently, this belief in predestination can lead to fatalism. Weber, however, argues that it has led to an attitude of active self-control and a life of good works. At some time believers will want to know whether they are elected, and they regard good works and prosperity as signs of this election. Consequently, Calvinism requires active self-control and an entire life of good works whereas Catholicism asks simply for single good works. So the monastic virtue of self-control was transformed in a practical ideal of self-control in this world: 'every Christian had to be a monk all his life' (Weber 2001 [1930]: 74). Believers considered themselves as weapons in the hand of God and executors of His will. This attitude motivated them to suffer tremendous sacrifices which they would most likely never have accepted for just worldly reasons. Pietism is more emotional than Calvinism. But as in Calvinism, material success acquired by hard work is regarded as a sign of God's blessing. Often the opposite view is also held to be true, namely, that poverty and failure is regarded as a sign of a person's disbelief. This opinion is found more frequently in the USA than in Europe[13], and in particular in Protestant sects than in large Protestant denominations. For example, in the 1980s and 1990s the Pentecostals in Cameroon considered those who were unsuccessful in their enterprises to be unable to resist the temptations of the devil. They thought the devil let them suffer in their poverty, so that they would turn their backs on God and join him (Akoko 2007).

Wealth as such is considered a great danger. It can lead to 'relaxation in the security of possession, the enjoyment of wealth with the consequence of idleness and the temptations of the flesh, above all of distraction from the pursuit of the righteous life' (Weber 2001 [1930]: 104). On the other hand, it is a sign of blessing of one's work. Believers have to work because in the words of St Paul 'he who will not work shall not eat' holds for every individual. Unwillingness to work is then a symptom of a lack of grace. Labour as a calling is regarded as a means of attaining certainty of grace. This view legalized both the exploitation of labour and the employers' activities and accumulation of wealth, as long as wealth is used profitably and the wealthy lead a sober life.

In this way Weber showed how the belief of some Protestant sects was conducive to economic growth. This does not imply that Weber dismissed the possibility of reverse causality. At the end of his last essay he writes: 'it would also further be necessary to investigate how Protestant Asceticism was in turn influenced in its development and its character by the totality of social conditions, especially economic. . . . But it is, of course, not my aim to substitute for a one-sided materialistic an equally one-sided spiritualistic causal interpretation of culture and of history. Each is equally possible.' (Weber 2001 [1930]: 125).

Weber's hypothesis has been criticized on several aspects by various authors. Overviews of critics can be found in Samuelsson (1961: 8–24), Giddens (2001) and Fase (2005: 87–90). Others, Tawney (1962 [1926]) for example, start by being quite critical but end by being relatively mild and quite in favour of Weber's main hypotheses.[14] First, one critique concerns the empirical evidence of Weber's hypothesis. According to Samuelsson (1961: 137–150) the data in Webers's first essay do not even indicate a correlation between Protestantism and economic prosperity or the overrepresentation of Protestants in schools of higher education. When demographical conditions are taken into account the probability of Protestant children attending a school of higher education is similar to that of Catholic children. Moreover, the facts do not support Weber's thesis when applied to periods of economic prosperity in various countries and regions. In some prosperous regions like Belgium and the city of Amsterdam, the majority of the population was Catholic. In addition, especially the ascetic forms of Protestantism, which Weber holds responsible for pro-growth attitudes, attract relatively many poor people. Second, another form of criticism points at Weber's neglect of changes within the Roman Catholic doctrine on issues like usury, and other pro-capitalist attitudes (Samuelsson 1961, and the previous section of this chapter). Third, his characterization of Protestantism and interpretation of calling, and the effect of predestination are incorrect according to some (see e.g. Samuelsson). Fourth, the forms of capitalism in the centuries before the period of reformation were not that different from that of the time of the Reformation (Samuelsson 1961: 67). Finally, and most important for our discussion, the causality is opposite to the one proposed by Weber: 'it was economic activity that engendered religious change, not religion that transformed economic life' (Samuelsson 1961: 24). At the end of this chapter we devote an entire section to the issue of causality and there we also discuss the criticism on Weber's supposed view on causality.

Some case studies

In a recent comparative case study Maseland (2006b) deals with the role of culture in (the perception of) economic development in the Philippines and Malaysia during the 1980s and 1990s. The Philippines are considered a failure (both by themselves and outsiders), whereas Malaysia is regarded as a success story. Within the Philippines the general feeling is that the revolution still has to be finished and change has to occur in a dramatic, radical and abrupt way. This image refers to the first Philippine Revolution of 1896, when the leader against the Spanish colonizer, Rizal, was sentenced to death and executed. In the end, the revolution failed and the Philippines were handed over to America. This episode in the Philippine history has often been translated in a religious metaphor.

> 'Here was a man [Rizal, EdJ], widely perceived to be the saviour of the country, returning to the capital after years of absence, only to be arrested and executed by foreign oppressors pressured by clergy, a fate undergone without protest. Rizal's choice to walk the route from his prison cell to the place where he would be executed further supports the analogy.'
>
> (Maseland 2006b: 9)

The image is, of course, that of Christ being crucified by the Romans. In the 1980s this symbolic meaning of the martyrdom of Rizal/Christ was carried over to Beningo Aquino, who was killed when he returned to the Philippines. On the basis of this symbolism his widow, Cory Aquino, and the People Power Revolution could dethrone Marcos (the Pontius Pilate of that time) in 1986.

In Malaysia there is a more gradual movement towards change and the leaders present changes as a continuation of traditional Malaysian values.

Once again as far as possible religion, Islam in this case, is used as an instrument in this process. From the beginning of the 1980s Prime Minister Mahathir started an Islamization of Malaysia. This Islamization served two goals. It sought to increase the role of Islam in public life and in addition, it wanted to increase official control over the interpretation of Islam, and disseminate a 'true, progressive version' (Maseland 2006a: 168). An Islamic Centre and an Islamic bank were established. The latter had to collect the Malaysian savings and to propagate an interpretation of Islam that was thought compatible with economic development. In sum, Mahathir sought to promote a 'highly Protestant form of Islam' (Lee and Ackerman 1997: 36). Finally, the official interpretation of Islam stressed openness towards other religions and the Islamic character of these religions. In de-emphasising the specific Islamic nature of values the government could 'increase the role of Islam in public life, without upsetting the fragile ethnic harmony' (Maseland 2006a: 170).

Some quantitative studies

In a series of papers Barro and McCleary use some answers in the World Values Survey on the respondents' view of afterlife, in particular their answer to the question whether they believe in hell and/or believe in heaven. The average of the respondents' answers in a country is used in a regression with, as the dependent variable, the average growth rates of real per capita GDP over a decade: 1965–75 1975–85, and 1985–95. Apart from the two variables belief in hell and belief in heaven, the relation contains various control variables, such as monthly church attendance and the share of seven types of religion in the country. Belief in hell appears to positively contribute to economic growth (Barro and McCleary 2003: 773). Often the coefficient of belief in heaven is insignificant. Church attendance has a very significant negative impact on economic growth, indicating that the time spent in church goes at the expense of time for economic activity. Similar results are found in McCleary and Barro (2006).

Durlauf *et al.* (2005) criticize the studies by Barro and McCleary on several grounds. Here I confine myself to the more specific ones and leave the general remarks for the assessment section. Durlauf *et al.* re-estimate the Barro and McCleary relations and include as control variables the traditional Solow variables and three measures of other 'fundamental' theories of economic growth. The traditional Solow variables[15] are population growth, real investments (including government) to real GDP, average years of secondary schooling in the total population over age 25, and real per capita GDP for the initial year of the sample. The variables resulting from other growth theories refer to a country's climate and geographical isolation, its economic and political institutions and the degree of fractionalization in the society. In Durlauf *et al.*'s analysis none of the religiosity variables is significant at the 5 per cent level in any of the specifications used. Contrary to Barro and McCleary's result, it is belief in heaven that is sometimes marginally significant (10 per cent level).

Mangeloja (2005) combines the belief in hell and church attendance variables into one composed variable named religious production efficiency. This variable is high in Japan and Finland, due to the fact that in these countries church attendance is low. A panel regression for 8 OECD-countries over the period 1971–2001 does not give a significant result for this composed factor. Belief in hell appears to be very weakly significant. Time series regressions for the individual countries led to a significant coefficient for the religious efficiency variable for Finland only. A disadvantage of this study is that it pretends to have 30 years of independent observations in the time dimension. The data of the religious variables are, however, from four waves of the World Values Surveys only, which can never lead to 30 independent observations.

Noland (2005) uses the share of the population adhering to a particular religion as an independent variable in regressions of total factor growth and of real per capita income growth. Cross-country regressions are performed for samples of 34 to 76 countries. Moreover, within-country regressions are applied. Religious affiliation is often found to be significantly related to these measures of economic performance. However, no particular religion is found to be pro-growth. Since some commentators have claimed that Islam is anti-growth, additional within-country regressions are run for India, Malaysia and Ghana. In most cases the coefficient of the Muslim population share is significant and positive. It is only negative for the within-country regressions of Malaysia. For that case, however, other religions also have a negative coefficient. Moreover, in Malaysia ethnicity and religion are highly correlated, so that it is difficult to distinguish ethnical and religious influences from each other.

The countries included in the studies by Barro and McClearly are both industrialized and developing countries. There are also some studies that exclusively focus on determinants of the growth rates in former colonies. Grier (1997) finds that for the period 1961–90 the average growth rate of GDP is higher in former British colonies than in former French and Spanish colonies. Adding the growth rate of Protestant adherents from 1970–80 to the relation reveals a strong positive relation between GDP growth and the growth of Protestant adherents. However, the difference between the three types of countries remains. Similarly, in relations of GDP per capita the level of Protestantism in previous years slightly closes the gap between the income levels in former French and British colonies. These results indicate that Protestantism is positively related to growth.

Some papers belonging to the macro-studies, explain income per capita in the different states of the USA. A good example is Heath *et al.* (1995), where the average of income per capita in a state is explained by among other things the percentage of the state's population that is, respectively, Jewish,

Roman Catholic, fundamentalist Protestant, and non-fundamentalist Protestant. They find a negative and significant influence of the percentage of Roman Catholics and of fundamentalist Protestants. The percentage of Jewish people in the population has a positive influence in 1971 and 1980 and no influence in 1952. They ascribe this change in influence of the Jewish population to the influx of Eastern European Jews during World War II. These immigrants arrived with little or no wealth but achieved economic prosperity after a few decades.

Some studies use a *broader concept of economic development* than income per capita or factor productivity and include non-material items in the concept of development. To a certain extent there is an overlap with studies that take account of intermediary transmission mechanisms in that both pay attention to the same or similar items. Education, for example, can be regarded as worthwhile because it enhances economic growth, or it can be regarded as a valuable asset in itself. Here we discuss those studies that do not explicitly relate education and other items to economic growth and thus broaden the concept of development beyond economic growth.

Unsatisfied Basic Needs (UBNs) act as the proxy for development in Cuesta (2004). UBNs relate to a lack of drinkable water and electricity, and having earth floor in the household residence. The empirical results are based on the results of a questionnaire among about 3,000 households in Honduras. Religion (measured by belonging to a particular faith) does not have any influence on the unsatisfied basic needs (Cuesta 2004: Table 4). It should be noted that these results are likely to be biased since the majority of Hondurans are Roman Catholic, so that the variable religious affiliation does not vary enough to find any significant relation.

Sakwa (2006) and Sakwa *et al.* (2005) use a theoretical framework similar to that of Figure 7.1 for studying the relationship between poverty alleviation and culture in particular biblical conceptions of poverty. The two intermediary stages are the view on state–society relations and the means of poverty alleviation. The empirical results are based on a sample of 357 Roman Catholic students of four universities in Nairobi. It appeared that these respondents saw as major elements of poverty alleviation (alleviation ends): insurance (healthy environment, health care, social security and employment), education, income and assets (land in the case of Kenya). The respondents' view on God's claiming (God wants to be worshipped by extending kindness to the poor) influenced all four elements of poverty alleviation. God's sanctioning (God delivers the poor from the hands of the evil) and His active/passive acts each influenced three items, whereas God's provision (God blesses those who provide for the poor) only correlates with insurance.[16]

Assessment of quantitative studies

The studies discussed in the previous sections found mixed results with respect to the relation between religious values and religious affiliation and economic growth (or development). Barro and McClearly report that belief in hell is important for economic growth. A sensitivity and robustness analysis by Durlauf *et al.* (2005) does not find a significant relationship between economic growth and belief in hell and only a very marginally significant effect of belief in heaven on economic growth. Moreover, Barro and McClearly do not argue why among all possible views on supernatural forces, the thoughts about afterlife are the most plausible candidates for a relation with economic growth. Sakwa (2006) and Sakwa *et al.* (2005) derive biblical concepts of poverty from texts from the Old Testament. The selection of these Biblical verses is guided by the Sunday Missal of the Catholic Church, which has Biblical readings organized on a three-year cycle. These concepts are not related to the issues of afterlife distinguished by Barro and McClearly. Hence, no common view exists on the religious concepts that are most likely for influencing economic development.

This lack of a systematic relation is reaffirmed by a list of the ten most successful and the ten most failing nations as this is provided by Cuesta (2004: 6). Here success and failure are measured by the percentage annual GDP growth per worker over the period 1960–1980. The dominant religions in the ten most successful countries are Buddhism (5) Indigenous belief (1) Confucianism (2) Islam (1), Catholicism (1), Christianity (1), and Orthodox (1). In the failing states these religions are Christianity (4), Indigenous beliefs (2), Islam (1), and Catholicism (3). So, almost all major religions are the dominant religions in both successful and failing countries. The only systematic pattern is that successful states are former British colonies or were never a European colony.

The relation between religion and religious values on the one hand and economic growth on the other is not robust. Similarly, the relation between a particular religion and factors determining growth, summarized under the headings institutions and governance, is weak. Often the borderline is within a religion. Paldam (2001) finds that Protestants, Anglicans and Tribal religion are associated with low perceived corruption. Hence, in this case, the borderline is within Christianity. Moreover, a survey of many Muslims in various countries reveals that the great majority of these Muslims embrace values that are also found important in the Western world where Christianity is the dominant religion (Esposito and Moghahed 2007). This raises doubts about the implicit assumption of each religion representing a more or less homogenous worldview different from that of other religions; the topic of our next section.

Are major religions homogenous?

Many studies implicitly assume that religions are homogenous entities and that the major differences are between the various religions. This is especially true for those who proxy religion by the respondents answer to 'To which religion do you belong?', and studies that use shares of the population belonging to a particular religion and dummy variables for the dominant religion in a country. This assumption of the homogeneity of religions is highly questionable.

First, the main religions (Christianity, Islam, Hindu, etc.) contain many sects and sub-denominations. In the literature the distinction is often made between two important sub-denominations within Christianity, namely Protestants and Roman Catholics, and not forgetting the various (Greek, Russian, etc.) orthodox denominations. In the analyses the main differences in results are often obtained by separating the Protestants from the others (see e.g. Paldam 2001). Hence, the relevant and significant dividing line is *within* Christianity and not between the main religions. Similarly, within Islam opinions differ widely with respect to the economic order most compatible with the Qu'ran's teaching. Whereas some argue in favour of an interest ban, others regard such a ban as a misreading of the Qu'ran (see the Section Religious teaching with respect to usury). Views are also divided on the merits of markets. Some are in favour of the market and see private wealth accumulation as a prerequisite for economic growth. Others reject private ownership and would like the government to redistribute wealth and income, in a kind of centrally planned, communist system (Kuran 2004a: 67). According to Kuran (2004a: 119) within Islam opposing views can be found on many issues. These opinions will be determined by personal experience, so that the meaning of the Sharia 'can drastically vary from one person to another' (Esposito and Mogahed 2007: 54). Consequently, the political, economic and religious features of societies assumed to belong to the same religion can differ substantially. Esposito and Mogahed (2007: 4, 154) point at the differences between Islamic countries. The literature on diversity of capitalism focuses primarily on countries in which the majority of the population belongs to Christianity.

Second, even subgroups such as Protestants are often quite heterogeneous. The seminal study by Max Weber illustrates this point very nicely. Weber does not refer to the broad group of Protestants, but has a select group in mind, namely the pietistic dominations such as Quakers. Moreover, Iannaccone (1992) reports that the view of the leaders of evangelical Christians in the USA ranges from very pro free markets and capitalism to a flat rejection of capitalism in favour of socialism. This diversity in opinion is also found in survey data of faculty members of seminars and theological schools from Christian denominations and of white Protestants in the General Social Surveys of 1987, 1988 and 1989. These survey data reveal that a conservative view on moral issues like sex, drugs and gambling does not lead to a particular view on economics. The difference between Evangelical Fundamentalists and other Protestants on economic items is minimal (see Iannaccone 1992: 353, 354).

The diversity within a religion is also (indirectly) reported by Inglehart and Baker (2000: 36). They note that

> although historically Catholic and Protestant or Islamic societies show distinctive values, the differences between Catholics and Protestants or Muslims within given societies are relatively small. In Germany, for example, the basic values of German Catholics resemble those of German Protestants more than they resemble Catholics in other countries.

Similarly, the basic values of Muslim and Hindu inhabitants of the same country are much closer than those of Muslims or Hindus living in different countries. Hence, the shared historical experience of a given nation dominates the influence from religion. In consequence, one could conclude that there are at least as many variants within each religion as there are nations.

Islamic economics and identity

Although Islam is an old religion, Islamic economics is relatively new (Kuran 2004a: Ch. 4). It originated in the 1930s in India, when the movement for independence from the British colonizers got momentum. An increasing number of Muslims came to fear that the Hindus would dominate the independent republic of India and would discriminate against Muslims. Some asked for their own independent state to be ruled by Muslims. Others resisted the idea of an independent state and argued for a cultural instead of a political independence. The most important leader of this movement for cultural independence was Sayyid Abdul-Ala Mawdudi, who lived from 1903 to 1979 and was the founder of Jamaat-i Islam (Party of Islam).

In his view Muslims form a brotherhood which is entrusted with a comprehensive system of life to offer the world (Kuran 2004a: 84). They have to live faithfully according to the rules of Islam and do not need a national homeland. In his eyes the problem was that many Muslims relegated faith to the private sphere and did not integrate it into their daily activities. The limited adherence to the Islamic rules posed a greater danger to Indian Muslims than the transfer of political power into the hands of Hindus. In every domain of their daily life Muslims had to adhere to the rules of Islam. Consequently, economics would also fall within the purview of religion. In his view many of the Muslims paid too little attention to religion because they were educated at Western universities and tried to refashion Islam into the image of irreligious Western nationalism. Due to the Western influence Muslims regarded the West as superior to the Muslim world and forgot about their own achievements. Moreover, they judged Islam by Western standards instead of judging the West by Islamic principles. So the aim of Mawdudi was to make Muslims aware of their common values. In accordance with this, he did not pay attention to the differences religions it corresponds with Geertz's concept of religion as a ' and a model *for*. Religion (and culture) as a model *of* reality is a mbols that corresponds with the (economic) structure of society, ɔw chart is a representation of a physical phenomenon. Religion ure as a model *for* society serves as a guide by which a society e organized, much like a plan by which a house is build (Geertz 5).

ng the development over the centuries of religious views on a r economic issue allows us to understand the interaction between lopment of the economy and that of values in a manner that was ible in Chapter 6. In the section on usury we already described action between the development of financial instruments (such as ıd the theological view on asking interest. Even within the Bible s a more positive view on asking interest by authors of the New ıt than those of the Old Testament, a change in view which can be l by the more prominent role of loans during the time the New ıt was written. In this section we discuss the causality issue as it the fore in the discussion between Weber and his critics, historical f Islam, and the making of the Biblical book Deuteronomy. A brief of the scientific results of the making of a Holy Script can, in our lp in understanding the causality issue. As will become clear, are high that these texts, which by some are considered to reflect ill, are themselves influenced by forces similar to those shaping exts and views in the present.

regard Max Weber as the scientist who claims that religious values economic performance. A closer reading of his Protestant Ethic, reveals that he too was aware of the possibility of a reverse causal- ıdy in the beginning of his book, when discussing The Problem, he at the dominant position of Protestants in industry can partly be to historical circumstances 'in which religious affiliation is not a cause onomic conditions, but to a certain extent appears to be a result of 'eber 2001 [1930]: 4). At the end of his study he writes:

> ould also further be necessary to investigate how Protestant ticism was in turn influenced in its development and its character e totality of social conditions, especially economic . . . But it is, of se, not my aim to substitute for a one-sided materialistic an equally sided spiritualistic causal interpretation of culture and of history. is equally possible.
>
> (Weber 2001 [1930]: 125)

one can rightly claim that, although he studied the influence of reli- conomic performance, Weber did not disregard the reverse causal

between various groups within the Islamic w
among Muslims.

Mawdudi referred to the history of Islam,
sal Muslim *umma* or community, which is
to traditional principles of solidarity. In pa
'Golden Age', which consists of the 39 ye
of the Prophet Mohammad over the origin
'rightly guided' four caliphs who succeeded h
According to Mawdudi this period was a t
the earlier period. The Golden Age was in
justice, cooperation and self-sacrifice (Kuran

Referring to tradition and the intention
also prove an effective way of changing cur
Pakistan the advocates of women's rights cha
laws to Islamic principles instead of arguing
In the end, in 2006 Pakistan's parliament an
Women's Protection Bill (Esposito and M
the human rights organization TARGET, tr
female genital mutilation by arguing that it is
(Esposito and Mogahed 2007: 117). Therefo
will likely be most effective if promoted with

Nowadays, some authors present Islami
between capitalism and communism (Kuran
almost identical to that of many European
Way. Both groups claim to maintain the effi
in a humanitarian way: without harsh comp

As this history of Islamic economics illust
an important aspect of the identity of themse
to. The need for emphasizing an identity tha
is felt most urgently when the members of the
group or other groups. Since identity refer
also have consequences for the economic stru
impact of these attempts to restore medieval
(Islamic banking has only a tiny share of t
energy of economists who could have been bett
social problems (Kuran 2007: 22). This fact
associated with ideology; often the preferen
dominates that of solving actual social prob
communism are perfect examples in this res

Causality

The issue of causality and thus the endogenous
been discussed in Chapter 6. Here we pick

study c
model
set of s
like a f
and cu
should
1969: 6

Study
particu
the dev
not pos
the inte
loans)
one fin
Testam
explain
Testam
comes t
studies
overvie
view, h
chances
God's
secular

Many
influenc
howeve
ity. Alr
writes t
ascribed
of the e
them' (

it
Asc
by
cou
one
Eac

Henc
gion on
relation

The differences between Protestant groups can also be related to economic circumstances. From the discussion on usury we conclude that the more favourable view of the Calvinists on asking interest can be ascribed to the fact that the Calvinist denomination was located in centres of finance and commerce. The Calvinist theologian adapted 'as sympathetic a position as possible, towards wealth and economic activity' (Samuelsson 1961: 29) in order to win the merchants and business people. In a similar but less directive manner, Tawney (1962 [1926]: 104) notes that one could expect that representatives of faith with their headquarters in centres of commerce addressed their teaching to 'classes engaged in trade and industry, who formed the most modern and progressive elements in the life of the age'. Hence, Calvinist teaching started from the recognition of the necessity of capital, credit, banking and large-scale commerce and finance. The Lutherans, on the other hand, were living in rural areas and suffered under the yoke of the urban new rich. Hence, they held a less favourable opinion on paying interest.

Studies dealing with politicized culture, point at the political manipulation of (religious) opinions and thus at religious values as the dependent variable instead of an independent one. An example is Malaysia, where the leadership used (manipulated) Islam in such a way that it would fit with their political goals (see Chapter 6 and Maseland 2006a). In a similar mood, Alatas (2002: 117) argues that the Asian values and Protestant work ethics is an *ex post facto* rationalization of economic success in Southeast Asia and that the ethic and religious arguments seem to have followed rather than preceded economic growth in this part of the world.

The idea that a culture is a reflection of the existing institutions and economic circumstances can be found in other authors too. At the end of his study on economic change in world history, Jones concludes 'We find the reasons for suppressed growth not in the absence of desire or effort but in grasping by rulers and governments . . . as well as in their failure to create institutions conducive to change' (Jones 1988: 189). With respect to Islam this opinion can be found in Kuran (2007) and Rodinson (1980 [1966]). Kuran argues that Islamic laws, in particular the inheritance system and the *waqf* have reduced economic progress in the countries concerned. These institutions limit the growth of the civil society and have led to widespread apathy and complacence. Rodinson's book reveals a Marxist view on economic development and the influence of Islam on economic growth. In accordance with Marx's position he argues in favour of economic circumstances influencing perceptions. In his view Islam and Muslims are flexible enough to change their attitudes when time comes. The Muslims have to 'fight against reactionary interpretations of Islam wrapped in the folds of the banner of religion, tradition and traditional morality' (Rodinson 1980 [1966]: 233).

Until now we have assumed that religious texts are given and implicitly that these texts represent the view of God or the god of the religion concerned: a divine opinion without any trace of human influence. Research on the making of religious texts learns quite a different lesson. In many cases researchers are able to trace the influence of particular (groups of) persons and their interests in the texts of Holy Scriptures. Van der Toorn (2007: especially Ch. 6), for instance, argues that at least four editions preceded the version of Deuteronomy as it is presently included in the Old Testament. All four editions wanted to bring a slightly different message, which at times clearly served the interests of a particular group. The possibility of rewriting the text came naturally. Every 40 years or so the scroll on which the book was written grew threadbare and had to be replaced by a new one. This occasion of rewriting the scroll was used to make the text reflect ideas and insights that had developed over time. Priests associated with the Hebrew temple rewrote the scroll.

The first edition is the Covenant Edition because it is framed as a treaty (Van der Toorn 2007: 153). The reason for writing it as a treaty has to do with the religious reform implemented under King Josiah. The main objective of this reform was to centralize the Hebrew religion in the temple of Jerusalem. This reform was based on a covenant with the leadership of Israel, on which occasion the king read the scroll that was found in the temple (2 Kings 23: 1–3). The first edition of Deuteronomy presents itself as the text of that 'scroll of covenant'. To legitimize the measures taken by the king, the scribe of the Covenant Edition of Deuteronomy invented the notion of a previous covenant concluded in the land of Moab when Israel was about to enter the Promised Land (Deut. 28: 69), to serve as a historical precedent for the covenant of Josiah with the people. This does not imply, according to Van der Toorn (2007: 154), that the scribe of the Covenant Edition was simply producing a license for the king's reform plans. Close inspection of Deuteronomy reveals that the text is written after the reform. 'What the Covenant Edition contains, then, is a theological reflection on the reform, and an *aggiornamento* of existing law in light of the reform' (Van der Toorn 2007: 154).

The second edition is the Thora Edition. Thora means teaching, ruling, and law. It introduces an oral revelation as complement to the two stone tablets Moses received on Mount Horeb. This oral explanation is introduced to insert new material in the text. This version stresses the importance of the priests (the scribes' superiors). The priests constitute the highest court of law and where formerly the king had been supreme judge, the priests now take his place. The primary concern of the editor is to make sure that the monarch should be subservient to the Levitical priests. The Thora Edition also redefines the role of the prophets, who are turned into extensions of the priests, who possess the Thora.

In the third version, the History Edition, the text is rewritten so that it might serve as the basis of a larger historical work. The author of this version praises national history and sees his own time as lacking the greatness of the past. The fourth version, which is called the Wisdom Edition, is full of optimism about the possibility of a conversion of Israel followed by a return of the exiles. This note of optimism is lacking in previous editions of Deuteronomy; it most likely means that the editor lives in the time after the Exile. Moreover, in this edition faithfulness to the Thora is not built on the ground of authority (God says so) but on that of experience and the virtue of the teaching.

Several themes we encountered in previous sections are also present in this story about the making of the Biblical book Deuteronomy: political culture, reference to a great past, and several indications that the texts are written after the facts have materialized. The last feature indicates that causality runs from the facts to the opinion and view on the (ideal) world order. This is in accordance with the function of religion as a means of coming to terms with the events, not to change them. This notion of making the world acceptable is also found in Geertz (1969: 658), who describes the religious problem of suffering as 'not how to avoid suffering but how to suffer, how to make of physical pain, personal loss, . . . something bearable, supportable – something, as we say sufferable'. So the history of the making of Deuteronomy and the function of religion as making the events bearable, creating structure in the chaotic world, all affirm a view of religion, culture, as a reflection not a source of development.

Concluding remarks

In this chapter we have discussed religion as a source of values (culture) and its relation with economic institutions and economic performance. Several conclusions can be drawn from this discussion. Some of these correspond with those derived in Chapters 5 and 6. Religions and values derived from religion sometimes have a relationship with economic institutions and governance. A systematic relation between a particular religion and economic performance is not found. An explanation for this result is the long-chain argument given in the previous chapter.

In some cases the teaching and interpretation of a religion is manipulated by rulers in order to obtain a favourable view on their policy. Such a politicized culture was also noticed in Chapter 6. There are indications that some texts of Holy Scripts are also influenced by political forces at the time of writing the text. In other cases writers refer to a glorious past.

A number of conclusions explicitly refer to religion or the way religion is approximated in empirical studies. First, the frequent practice of (implicitly) regarding religions as homogenous is invalid. Many denominations can be distinguished within the main religions. Moreover, even when within a denomination a common view exists with respect to the ethical issues, chances are high that opinions differ widely on the preferable organization of economic life. Consequently, the use of dummies or the share of a population belonging to a particular religion does not reveal much if anything. In our view this also invalidates the procedure of using religion as an instrumental variable as is promoted in for example Guiso *et al.* (2006).

Second, the religions (Christendom and Islam) studied in this literature and their Holy Scriptures (Bible and Qua'ran) have existed for centuries. By analysing the changes in interpretations of these texts over time and places enables us to shed more light than in Chapter 6 on the relation between values and economic circumstances. Two conclusions can be derived from such an analysis. First, under similar economic conditions, individuals belonging to the same religion can have very different opinions on the appropriate organization and aim of the economy. This suggests no relation between religious values and economic developments. The second conclusion, however, is that although at a particular point in time opinions can differ a lot, a dominant view can still be derived. Changes in this dominant view are clearly related to the economic situation, and are more likely to be determined by these circumstances than the other way round. This causal direction is found in the description of the religious views on the interest ban, the discussion of Weber's hypothesis about the Protestant ethic and the spirit of capitalism, and research on the making of the Biblical book Deuteronomy.

Third, whereas many studies implicitly treat Holy texts as given or inspired by the particular religion's god, the story of the making of Deuteronomy indicates that these texts are influenced by similar forces as views on present-day events. Both in the present and in Biblical times, politicians' and dominant groups' interests have and had a significant influence on the way a story is and was framed and the conclusions drawn.

Fourth, the history of the origins of Islamic economics highlights the importance of religion for forming the identity of a person and a group. The need for identity building will be felt most urgently if the group is under threat. Such identity building does not necessarily reflect differences in deeply help values.

Finally, often writers and politicians refer to a glorious past and to a bright future to come when creating a cultural view, which serves their interests. Moreover, referring to the historically accepted view appears to be a more successful strategy than attacking the history and values incorporated in a religion.

In the concluding chapter we will discuss some explanations for these findings and consequences for research on culture (including religion) and economics.

Chapter 8

Mapping the landscape of social capital: the need for a two-level approach

Sjoerd Beugelsdijk

Economists are increasingly interested in the concept of social capital. In addition to some other developments in economics, Putnam's (1993) *Making Democracy Work* has triggered the interest of economists in more culturally based factors that influence economic growth. Also, Fukuyama's (1995) study on *Trust* has contributed to the inclusion of social capital in economics. Work by Putnam and Fukuyama, for example, has led Jonathan Temple to conclude that 'some of the most interesting thinking on economic growth is to be found on the borders of political science and sociology' (Temple 1999: 146). Although the way economists use a traditionally sociological concept like social capital can be criticized (Fine 2001), it is probably the most successfully introduced 'new' term in economics in the last decade.

The concept of social capital is intuitively highly attractive and potentially promising. Nevertheless, it can only be fruitfully employed when it can be properly defined, operationalized and shown to have explanatory power (cf. Woolcock 1998). Currently, social capital is many things to many people (Harriss and De Renzio 1997). Social capital provides a terminological umbrella for grouping together an extraordinarily diverse range of casually constructed illustrations (Fine 2001: 78). Overuse and imprecision have rendered it a concept prone to vague interpretation and indiscriminate application. The use of social capital as an umbrella concept risks conflating disparate processes and their distinct antecedents and consequences (Adler and Kwon 2002).

In this chapter we elaborate on the concept of social capital, thereby combining insights from sociology and economics. We try to shed light on the cause and effect structure and the internal dynamics, and try to formulate future research questions. To do so, we claim that it is necessary to break down the concept of social capital on two levels, i.e. the individual (firm) and the aggregate level (nation state or region). This two-level approach is more than just a heuristic device to study social capital. We hold that this two-level distinction is crucial for our understanding and the development of the concept of social capital in economics. In the first part of the chapter social capital is deployed as a cultural construct, whereas in the second part it is constructed in a structural way. This means that in the first part we think of social capital in terms of norms and values and treat social capital in the Putnamian tradition. This part of the chapter can perhaps best be classified under the heading of a normative approach in institutional economics (Scott 1995). This normative conception to institutions emphasizes how values and normative frameworks structure choices and form the basis of a stable social order.

In the second part we take a more social–structural account of social capital, which is more in line with sociologists like Coleman (1988). While the first part may be more familiar to political scientists and economists, the second part is closer to the field of sociologists. In our view it is necessary to discuss both for a proper understanding of the concept. When we think about social capital in the normative way, we refer to it as *aggregate* social capital. We have added the label *individual* in case we discuss social capital in the social–structural way. Acknowledging that the individual level includes individuals and firms, we will concentrate on firms.

The added value of the chapter lies in the synthesis of two seemingly distinct fields of research. Whereas most researchers in the field focus either on the macroeconomic aspects of social capital, or on the effects of social capital at the individual level, we take a broader perspective. By doing so, we aim to structure the current chaos in the literature on social capital.

The remainder of this chapter is structured as follows. We proceed by a short discussion of the different definitions of social capital. We briefly recapitulate Putnam's work and then turn to the cause and effect structure of aggregate social capital. We have chosen to start our discussion at the aggregate level because the popularity of social capital is rooted at this level. We discuss two elements of aggregate social capital: social networks and generalized trust. After our analysis of social capital at the aggregate level, we turn to social capital at the individual-level. We discuss the background of the concept in (economic) sociology. As the literature on social capital at the individual level stems from network theory, we also discuss the conflicting viewpoints of Burt (1992) and Coleman (1988) with respect to the structure of a network. After discussing the concept of open versus closed networks, we discuss the individual level of trust. Trust and the closure of the network are related. We conclude our discussion on social capital at the individual level by elaborating on the cause and effect structure, by making use of the insights from network theory and the literature on trust. Finally, we discuss the relationship between the two levels on which social capital is employed. We conclude with suggestions for further research.

Definitions of social capital

The literature is far from unambiguous and consistent in defining social capital. Generally, researchers date back the concept of social capital to Bourdieu (1986) and Coleman (1988). Bourdieu (1986: 248) defines social capital as 'the aggregate of the actual or potential resources which are linked to possession of a durable network of more or less institutionalized relationships of mutual acquaintance and recognition – or in other words, to membership in a group'. Social capital refers to the personal resources individuals derive from membership in a group.

Coleman (1988) also stresses the function of the social structure of a group as a resource for the individuals of that group. Social capital resides in relationships between individuals in families or communities. In Bourdieu and Coleman's definition of social capital, membership in interpersonal networks enables actors to convert social capital into other forms of capital to improve or maintain their position in society.

Still, there are a number of studies published before Bourdieu and Coleman popularized the concept. For example, Jacobs (1961) used the concept of social capital when describing the relational resources embedded in personal ties in the community. In 1977, Loury described social capital as a set of intangible resources that helps to promote the social development of young people.

Without going into a detailed discussion of the definition of social capital and repeat the work of others (e.g. Durlauf and Fafchamps 2004, Adler and Kwon 2002, Fine 2001, Woolcock 1998), it can be observed that there are important differences in the definitions of social capital. In one group of definitions the concept of social capital is used as part of the theory of human action and it applies primarily at microsociological and microeconomic levels. The unit of analysis is the individual or firm or a group of individuals or firms. The other group including researchers like Inglehart (1997), Putnam (1993), and Fukuyama (1995) deploys social capital as a concept to study institutional and economic performance at the aggregate level. They shift the scale of analysis to nations or regions.

Paxton (1999) describes similar levels of social structure to which social capital adheres. According to her, at the individual level social capital is a private good that like human capital can be used for economic gain or other private outcomes. An example of this can be found in Meyerson's (1994) analysis of Swedish managers and the income effects of their social capital. Closely related is the group level. This basically refers to the idea that members of a group collectively gain by being a member of a group. Clearly this is linked to the individual level. The next level is what Paxton (1999) calls the macrosociological level. Here social capital is seen as a feature of a broader community. For authors like Fukuyama (1995), Putnam (1993, 2000) and many economists the object of research consists of nations or regions. At this aggregate level, it is argued that nations or regions can hold different levels of social capital, which affects the level of democracy and economic performance. In the remainder of this chapter we distinguish between the individual and the aggregate level. As a starting point, let us assume for the sake of the argument that the cause and effect structure at both levels is independent of the cause and effect structure at the other level. Social capital at the individual level consists of the network resources for individuals embedded in these networks. Effects of social capital at this level apply in principle to these actors, being individuals or firms. At the aggregate level outcomes apply to society as a whole. While acknowledging that there is a potential multilevel problem in using this two-level approach, we choose not discuss that here. This multilevel problem is explicitly discussed and reflected upon in Beugelsdijk (2006, 2008) and Beugelsdijk and Maseland (2009).

Social capital at the aggregate level

Whereas the study of social capital can be traced back to a number of authors (e.g. Bourdieu, and Coleman), 'Putnam has become the crown prince of social capital' (Fine 2001: 18). Putnam (1993) argues that the critical factor in explaining the effectiveness of regional governments and economic performance in Italy is to be found in regional differences in social structure. He argues that effective governance hinges critically on traditions of civic engagement and the structure of the civic networks. Putnam argues that in regions where social relationships are more horizontal, based on trust and shared values, participation in social organizations is higher and social capital is higher. He concludes that regions in which the regional government is more successful and the economies are more efficient are characterized by horizontal relations that both favoured and fostered greater networks of civic engagement and levels of organization in society. The reason Putnam specifically studies the degree of civic community membership is that 'citizens in a civic community, though not selfless saints, regard the public domain as more than a battleground for pursuing personal interest' (Putnam 1993: 88).

Referring to the work of Alexis de Tocqueville, Putnam maintains that these civil associations contribute to the effectiveness and stability of a democratic government, because of their 'internal' effects on individual members and their 'external' effects on the wider polity. According to Putnam,

> associations instill in their members a habit of cooperation, solidarity and public-spiritedness. [. . .] Participation in civic organizations inculcates skills of cooperation as well as a sense of shared responsibility for collective endeavors. Moreover, when individuals belong to 'cross-cutting' groups with diverse goals and members, their attitudes will tend to moderate as a result of groups interaction and cross-pressures.
>
> (Putnam 1993: 89–90)

Externally, a dense network of associations may enhance 'interest articulation' and 'interest aggregation', thereby contributing to effective social collaboration.

According to Putnam, effective norms of generalized reciprocity are bolstered by these dense networks of social exchange (Putnam 2000: 136–172). Through reputation effects, honesty is encouraged by dense social networks. 'Social networks allow trust to become transitive and spread: I trust you, because I trust her and she assures me that she trusts you' (Putnam 1993: 169). Trust lubricates cooperation. The greater the level of trust in a society the greater the likelihood of cooperation. And cooperation itself breeds trust. Exactly this steady accumulation of social capital has been a crucial part of the story behind the virtuous circles of civic Italy according to Putnam (1993). As Putnam (2000) writes, people who trust others are generally more civically engaged and build more social capital than the people who distrust. Conversely, the civically disengaged believe themselves to be surrounded by miscreants and feel less constrained to be honest themselves. The causal arrows among civic involvement, reciprocity, honesty and social trust are as tangled as well-tossed spaghetti (Putnam 2000: 137). He even goes further by arguing that there may in fact be two social equilibriums (1993: 177–181). Virtuous circles result in social equilibriums with high levels of cooperation, trust, and civic engagement. Conversely, the absence of these traits in the uncivic community is also self-reinforcing. This process of cumulative causation suggests that there may be at least two broad equilibriums towards all societies, which tend to evolve and once attained, tend to be self-reinforcing.

The above leads Putnam to conclude that 'a society that relies on generalized reciprocity is more efficient than a distrustful society, for the same reason that money is more efficient than barter. Honesty and trust lubricate the inevitable frictions of social life' (Putnam 2000: 135). And 'when each of us can relax her guard a little', transaction costs are reduced (Fukuyama 1995).

The touchstone of social capital is generalized reciprocity. In defining generalized reciprocity we follow Putnam; generalized reciprocity refers to a continuing relationship of exchange that is at any given time unrequited or imbalanced, but that involves mutual expectations that a benefit granted now should be repaid in the future (Putnam 1993: 172). Or more simply, 'I'll do this for you, without expecting anything immediately in return and perhaps without even knowing you, confident that down the road you or someone else will return the favor' (Putnam 2000: 134). He argues that this norm of generalized reciprocity is a highly productive component of social capital. Communities in which this norm is followed are assumed to more effectively restrain opportunism and resolve problems of collective action.

Boix and Posner (1998) describe mechanisms through which social capital is translated into better macro performance. They suggest several processes, among which: (a) social capital contributes to effective governance by facilitating the articulation of citizen's demands. As Fine (2001: 113) states, 'sophisticated voters make the elected more representative and accountable'; (b) social capital reduces the need to secure compliance by creating complex and costly mechanisms of enforcement. It reduces transaction costs in the arena of citizen–government relations, because social capital shapes the expectations citizens have about the behaviour of others; (c) social capital encourages the articulation of collective demands that are to everyone's benefit; (d) social capital reduces the probability of individuals engaging in opportunistic behaviour and the resources devoted to monitoring agents' performance can be invested in more productive ways.

Putnam's studies have been extensively criticized on numerous grounds. Critics have not only pointed to the neglect of negative effects of social capital, the lack of a theoretical mechanism between social capital and economic growth, but also criticized the research method that Putnam has used (Jackman and Miller 1996, Tarrow 1996, Dekker *et al.* 1997, Harriss and De Renzio 1997, Paxton 1999, Boggs 2001, Fine 2001). In contrast with Putnam, Jackman and Miller (1996) find little empirical proof to indicate a systematic relationship between political culture, and political and economic performance. They show that the strong correlation between the overall measure of culture and the institutional performance of Italian regions are an artefact of Putnam's application of the principal components analysis. Boggs's (2001) critique concentrates on *Bowling Alone*. Boggs argues that Putnam's choice of indicators to measure and reflect declining social capital is rather arbitrary. According to Boggs, Putnam's explanatory framework rests upon a foundation of pseudo empiricism, with all the assembled data, charts, and graphs telling us little about the conditions underlying historical change (Boggs 2001: 290).

To conclude, at the aggregate level social capital is about norms and values regarding cooperation. According to Putnam, social capital refers to features of social organization such as networks, norms, and social trust that facilitate coordination and cooperation for mutual benefit (Putnam 1993, 1995, and 2000). Values and norms are a key element of social capital 'because social capital prompts individuals to behave on ways other than the naked greed' (Portes and Sensenbrenner 1993: 1323). In this way social capital resembles community spirit that can be defined as the capacity to act collectively as and when required (Forrest and Kearns 2001).

Where does social capital at the aggregate level come from?

The question arises where aggregate social capital, or in other words, norms of cooperation come from. At the aggregate level the origin of social capital is culturally based and historically grown. The question where norms (and values) come from is one of the classic research subjects in sociology (Portes 1998). Norms and values make up the normative system. In defining norms and values, we follow Scott (1995). Values are conceptions of the preferred or the desirable together with the construction of standards to which existing structures or behaviour can be compared and assessed. Norms specify how things should be done; they define legitimate means to pursue valued ends. The normative system as a whole defines goals or objectives and also designates the appropriate ways to pursue them. Norms of reciprocity or better, norms of cooperation refer to the way certain goals are to be achieved. For Coleman (1988, 1990) social capital in its core represents the extent to which an appropriate solution has been found to the problem of public goods and externalities (Fine 2001). Once these arrangements that prevent free-riding are internalized they are social values and sometimes become norms. These social norms constitute social capital.

Besides motivations stemming from deeply internalized norms through processes of socialization in childhood or through experience later in life (primary and secondary socialization processes), the second broad class of motivations are instrumental (Portes 1998). This latter type is also based on norms, but norms that stem from rational calculation. Instrumental motivation stems from either obligations based on dyadic social exchange or obligations enforced on both parties by the broader community (Adler and Kwon 2002). This latter mechanism builds on the role of reputation in networks.

In reality the distinction between internalized norms and instrumental motivations is not as sharp as suggested above. Sometimes, social capital is motivated by normative commitment of a less direct instrumental nature (Adler and Kwon 2002). In this respect, Putnam stresses the role of generalized reciprocity. According to Putnam, this involves 'not I'll do this for you now, if you do that for me now, but I'll do this for you now, knowing that somewhere down the road you'll do something for me' (1993: 183). This is in line with Axelrod's findings, that the anticipation of future interaction provides an important stimulus for the creation of norms of reciprocity. Platteau (1994) also stresses the importance of generalized morality, widely shared norms and conventions instead of shared norms in a small group, for the development of an efficient market system. These norms cannot be created by fiat and the cultural endowment of a society plays a determining role in this respect.

Boix and Posner (1998) suggest three explanations where norms come from. The first explanation of the origin of social capital refers to experimental research, which shows how stable cooperative relations can come into being spontaneously among otherwise uncooperative actors. The evolution of social norms and conventions can be studied in the framework of evolutionary game theory. Since evolutionary game theory studies populations playing games, the outcome (a convention or norm) can be thought of as a symmetric equilibrium of a coordination game (Mailath 1998). In fact, it was Axelrod (1984) who used the Prisoner's dilemma game to examine the conditions under which individuals who pursue their own interest will develop norms of cooperation (in the absence of a third party or central authority). In this game-theoretical setting, it is argued that as long as the pattern of interaction has no foreseeable end, or in Axelrod's words, 'the future must have a sufficiently large shadow' (1984: 174), actors have no incentive to defect from cooperation. This initiates the building of norms of cooperation, in other words, aggregate social capital.

A second explanation for the origin of social capital builds on the distinction between collaborative interactions that take place in associations that produce public goods, and collaborative interactions that take place in associations that produce private goods. The first obviously suffers from problems of free-riding, whereas in the latter group these incentives to free-ride are limited, if not absent. In line with Putnam, Boix and Posner (1998) argue that associations that produce private goods could over time generate enough social capital to make cooperation possible in arenas where individuals face collective action problems. Though historically implausible, social capital would then emerge through an evolutionary process, starting out in interactions producing private goods and ultimately graduating to groups producing public goods.

The third explanation Boix and Posner (1998) put forward emphasizes the role of a sufficiently powerful third-party enforcer. To overcome the collective action problem, the threat of force or creation of institutions facilitates cooperation.

All three explanations to some extent suffer from the fact that they focus on how cooperative relationships come into being, and not how (international) differences in social capital emerge. Boix and Posner (1998) argue that the degree to which cooperation takes root depends on the pre-existing set of social and political relations in the community. More specificly, the level of social capital depends on the degree of equality and polarization suffered by society. According to these authors, the lack of social capital in the South of Italy, as described by Putnam (1993), is caused by the wide inequalities that characterized social life and fuelled resentments that prevented cooperative relations from crystallizing. In the South, 'cooperation was squashed by a Hobbesian state: the Norman invaders' (Boix and Posner 1998: 689), whereas in the North there was more equality, and cooperation proved relatively easy to sustain. Putnam (1993) devotes considerable attention to the question why civic life is more developed in northern Italy than in the southern regions. In tracing the civic roots of the northern regions, Putnam describes the historically grown rich network of associational life that dates back to the Middle Ages. He argues that the communal republics of northern medieval Italy experienced improvements in economic life and governmental performance due to the norms and networks of civic engagement. The southern regions lacked these norms and horizontal networks, which is according to Putnam one of the major reasons for the lack of social capital in southern Italy.

The dark side of aggregate social capital

Now we know what social capital at the aggregate level is, have suggested where it comes from, and discussed the positive effects it is assumed to have, we turn to the negative effects. Though initially social capital was thought to produce only positive outcomes, increasingly scholars have begun to shed light on the negative effects of social capital.

Acknowledging the potential negative effects of social capital, Putnam (2000) made a distinction between bonding and bridging social capital. Some forms of social capital are relatively inward looking and tend to reinforce exclusive identities and homogenous groups. Other networks are more outward looking and encompass people across diverse social cleavages. More simply, bonding social capital cements only homogenous groups, whereas bridging social capital bridges different communities. Bonding social capital, Putnam argues, is good for undergirding specific reciprocity and mobilizing solidarity. For example, dense networks in ethnic enclaves, provide crucial support for less fortunate members of the community, while furnishing start-up financing, and markets for local entrepreneurs. Bridging networks are better for linkage to external assets and for information diffusion.

Social capital could produce a negative outcome because high within-group social capital could have negative effects for members of the community as a whole (Paxton 1999). By creating strong in-group loyalty, bonding social capital may also create strong out-group antagonism. One can think of the Mafia, whose individual members as a group are characterized by high (bonding) social capital, but the group itself has negative effects on society as such. In general, we expect to see negative effects of community level social capital when there is high within-group trust and cohesion, but low between-group trust. Positive effects of community level social capital are expected to occur when there are positive trusting ties between individuals belonging to different groups (Paxton 1999). It is these crosscutting ties between networks of strong ties that Putnam defines as bridging social capital.

The second negative aspect of social capital is the fact that a dense network and the accompanying community norms can place constraints on individual behaviour. Membership in a tightly-knit or dense social network can subject one to restrictive social regulations and sanctions and limit their individual action. All kinds of levelling pressures keep members in the same situation as their peers and strong collective norms and highly unified communities may restrict the scope of individuals (Brown 1998, Meyerson 1994, Portes and Sensenbrenner 1993). The closure of these types of networks may thus lead to lock-in for the individual members belonging to these groups. But this is not a phenomenon that holds only for individuals in groups. The same processes of lock-in can be found at the regional level. Especially for de-industrialized regions, part of the problem is that they are locked-in to institutional structures that were relevant to an earlier phase of successful economic development but which now constitutes a barrier to moving onto a new path of development (Hudson 1999). Grabher's (1993) study on the Ruhr steel industry and Glasmeier's (1991) study on the Swiss watch-making industry show that closed network structures limit the recognition of the necessity to change and innovate at the regional level.

Finally, negative externalities from intense group membership may arise because of effects described by Olson (1982). In the *Rise and Decline of Nations*, Olson argued that small interest groups have no interest or incentive to work towards the common good of society. But they do have an incentive to engage in costly and inefficient rent-seeking (lobbying for tax breaks, colluding to restrain competition, etc.). And, when these groups become too large and powerful, rent-seeking behaviour and lobbying costs influence economic development negatively.

Thus, the 'wrong' type of social capital can impede economic performance (cf. Fedderke *et al.* 1999, Portes and Landolt 1996). Social capital can be deployed for developmental and destructive purposes, which suggests that aggregate social capital should be optimized and not maximized. This is why Putnam argues that it is 'important to ask how the positive consequences of social capital – mutual support, cooperation, trust, institutional effectiveness – can be maximized and the negative manifestations – sectarianism, ethnocentrism, corruption – minimized' (Putnam 2000: 22).

The individual level of social capital

At the individual level, social capital refers to the network to which an individual or firm belongs. In the field of organization and management studies, the individual-level concept of social capital builds on the relational view, as an extension of the resource-based view. The relational view holds that competitive advantage not only comes from firm-level resources but also from difficult-to-imitate capabilities embedded in dyadic and network relationships (Dyer and Singh 1998). The potential of a firm to create competitive advantage depends not solely on its own resources, but also on its relationships with other firms. According to these authors, idiosyncratic inter-firm linkages may be a source of relational rents and competitive advantage. A relational rent is defined as a supernormal profit jointly generated in an exchange relationship that cannot be generated by either firm in isolation and can only be created through the joint idiosyncratic contributions of the specific alliance partners (Dyer and Singh 1998: 662). Arm's length market relationships are incapable of generating these relational rents because there is nothing idiosyncratic about the exchange relationship.

Nahapiet and Ghoshal (1998) and Tsai and Ghoshal (1998) have provided an insightful overview of social capital at the individual-level. These authors argue that social capital consists of a structural component (an actor's network position), a relational component (trustworthiness and trusting relationships among network actors) and a cognitive component (shared vision).

The cognitive dimension refers to a shared code or shared paradigm that facilitates a common understanding of collective goals and proper ways of acting in a social system (Tsai and Ghoshal 1998). It is unclear if this social system refers to society in general or to a firm's network. Tsai and Ghoshal (1998) leave room for interpretation here.

The structural dimension of social capital refers to an actor's location in a network. Social capital is the resource available to actors as a function of their location in the structure of social relations (Adler and Kwon 2002). It is argued that firms occupying a central network position have superior access to information through their network linkages, which provides a firm with additional information about the nature of and degree of accessibility of the complementary resources of potential partners (Dyer and Singh 1998). The location of an actor in a network of relationships and interactions provides certain advantages like finding a job, obtaining information or accessing specific resources (Tsai and Ghoshal 1998).

The relational dimension of social capital relates to the degree of trust (see also Noorderhaven *et al.* 2003). Advantages of this dimension are the exchange of valuable information, reduced costs of finding exchange partners and lower transaction costs. Trust(-worthiness) is a useful kind of social capital that increases 'the capacity to form new associations' (Fukuyama 1995: 27). Dyer and Singh (1998) distinguish two types of governance mechanisms to limit opportunistic behaviour in partnerships. The first relies on third-party enforcement of agreements, like contracts. The second relies on self-enforcing mechanisms, like trust (direct), reputation (indirect) and embeddedness. According to Dyer and Singh (1998) self-enforcing mechanisms are more efficient than third-party enforcement.

The economic function of social capital is strongly related to the theory of (social) networks. In general, these network approaches build on the notion that economic actions are influenced by the social context in which they take place and that actions can be influenced by the position of actors in social networks (cf. Granovetter 1985).

What networks?

With respect to social capital there are two basic network theories that are relevant for discussion. The first is Burt's theory on the so-called social structure of competition. The second approach we take is the embeddedness perspective that builds on Coleman's ideas of closed networks. Burt (1992) argues that the structure of the player's network and the location of the player in the social structure add up to a competitive advantage. By occupying the structural location between otherwise unconnected nodes (a structural hole), the so-called *tertius gaudens* or the third who profits realizes greater returns on the social capital extant within his network. The social network becomes a social resource (cf. Granovetter 1973).

According to Burt social capital is especially important when competition is imperfect and investment capital is abundant. Under perfect competition social return is a constant in the production function. Where competition is imperfect, social capital is a critical variable. This is in line with Uzzi (1997, 1999), who stated that especially if the transactions between actors are non-reciprocal and are deals in which price is a sufficient statistic, the competitive market mechanism may work. But as conditions change under which the transactions take place, i.e. more tacit elements like quality and service (instead of quantities and prices) are present and important (the weaker the ability of prices to distil information), the more organizations will form embedded ties (Uzzi 1997). Relations go beyond the level of neoclassical concept of buyer–seller relationships, and include trust, altruism, etc.

However, as Coleman (1988) argues, closure of the social structure is important for the existence of effective norms and the trustworthiness of social structures. In Burt's theory the structural hole is the most efficient position one could take in a network. According to Coleman, reputation cannot rise in an open structure, and collective sanctions that would ensure trustworthiness cannot be applied. Therefore, because of the fact that closure creates trustworthiness in a social structure and Burt's theory assumes open structures, it can be argued that Burt's theory cannot effectively handle norms and trustworthiness in relationships. As Brown (1998) puts it, the advantage of Burt's model lies in its generalizability. Its weakness lies in Burt's reluctance to admit environmental causal factors that influence the dynamic, processional aspects of the network's structure.

Summarizing the above discussion on network theory rather bluntly, the structural dimension of social capital builds on the ideas of Burt, whereas the relational dimension mainly builds on Coleman's ideas. The latter assumes closed networks to be important for trustworthiness. We elaborate on the concept of trust in the next section.

Where does trust come in?

Trust is mostly seen as the perception and interpretation of the other's expected dependability. It refers to the confidence that a partner will not exploit the vulnerabilities of the other (Barney and Hansen 1995). As Zaheer *et al.* (1998) summarize, the concept of trust may be framed as an expectation of a partner's reliability with regard to his obligations, predictability of behaviour, and fairness in actions and negotiations while faced with the possibility to behave opportunistically. Trust has to do with signalling that the actor will not play one-shot games and behave opportunistically.

The literature on trust is extensive. Here we only summarize the main insights, relevant for our discussion on social capital. First, we need to distinguish between two important types of trust (Luhmann 1979): a) there is the microlevel (personal or interpersonal), based on the emotional bond between individuals, which is more characteristic of primary and small group relationships, and b) the macrolevel (system, institutionalized or generalized), more abstract relationships where trust is related to the functioning of bureaucratic systems (e.g. legal, political and economic). For our discussion on the two levels of social capital, it is important to follow Luhmann (1979) and distinguish these two basic types of trust. To be more precise, Luhmann makes a distinction between confidence and trust. Confidence relates to bigger systems that we can hardly influence, which can indeed be summarized as institutions (Nooteboom 2002). Trust refers to the social interaction taking place at the interpersonal level. Paxton (1999) makes a similar distinction between concrete trust and abstract trust (a perception of the trustworthiness of the 'average' person). She claims that 'while trust in specific others may be important at more micro-levels of social capital, generalised trust is the important feature of national-level social capital' (Paxton 1999: 99).

In his overview on the trust literature, Nooteboom (2002) follows this distinction between macro sources which apply apart from any specific exchange relation and micro sources arising from specific relations. Whereas the former arise from the institutional environment of laws, norms, and standards, the latter is personalized and therefore yields 'thick' trust.

At the individual level numerous typologies of trust have been developed. For an overview we refer to Nooteboom (2002). In general, he argues that trust is based on rational reasons and psychological causes. Reasons arise from a rational evaluation of the trustee's trustworthiness. This can be based on knowledge of the trustee inferred from reputation, records, norms and standards, or one's own experience. A psychological cause is empathy. This is the ability to share another person's feelings and emotions as if they were one's own, thereby understanding motives of action of the other. Empathy affects both one's own trustworthiness, in the willingness to make sacrifices for others, and one's trust, in the tolerance of behaviour that deviates from expectations. One will more easily help someone when one can identify with his or her needs. One can more easily forgive someone's breach of trust when one can identify with the lack of competence or the motive that caused it. Since one can identify with the other, one may sympathize with his or her action, seeing perhaps that this action was in fact a just response to one's own previous actions (Nooteboom 2002: 81).

Trust is related to networks. Through the role of reputation, social networks can serve as a basis for deterrence-based trust. Burt and Knez (1995) show that, what they call 'third party gossip', amplifies both the positive and the negative in relationships, because it makes actors more certain of their trust (or distrust) in another. Trust is associated with the strength of a relationship. Trusting relationships may develop inside a (closed) network, actors build up a reputation for trustworthiness that may become important information for other actors in the network (Tsai and Ghoshal 1998). If this occurs, the network serves in a way as a system of checks and balances. Networks may then fulfil the function of implicit contracts. Greif's (1994, 2006) study of the medieval Maghribi traders is a clear illustration of these kind of reputation effects.

At the individual level, trust is regarded as a property of individuals or characteristic of interpersonal relationships. Through ongoing interactions firms develop trust around norms of equity or knowledge based trust (Gulati 1998), which can be compared with Zucker's (1986) process based trust. Numerous studies have shown the importance of trust in economic transactions. These studies can also be seen as a critique or extension of Williamson's transaction cost theory (1975, 1985, 1998). Ring and Van de Ven (1992) have shown that informal, personal connections between and across organizations play an important role in determining the governance structures used to organize transactions. Also Nooteboom *et al.* (1997) and Gulati (1995) have shown that both trust and traditional factors from transaction cost economics are relevant for governing inter firm relationships.

Another question is how trust relationships come into being that are not embedded in structures of personal relationships. Shapiro (1987) uses the principal–agent framework to discuss the role of several mechanisms that control trust relationships which are *not* embedded in structures of personal relations. She discusses so-called 'guardians of trust', like a supporting social control framework of procedural norms, organizational forms, and social control specialists. All kinds of mechanisms come to life in an atomistic market when transactions are not embedded in a social network, where trust and personal relationships are present. Or, as Zucker (1986) says, there are markets for trust production.

Trust fulfils several economic functions. First, through third parties, trust provides options for control in social networks. Second, trust is linked with the facilitation of highly uncertain transactions. It reduces the uncertainty of these kinds of transactions, especially the relational risk involved. Uzzi shows that 'trust facilitates the exchange of resources and information that are crucial for high performance but are difficult to value and transfer via market ties' (1996: 678). The third function of trust is related to its information function. As Malecki puts it (2000: 195) 'through the economic and social relationship in the network, diverse information becomes inexpensive to obtain'. When discussing alliances, Gulati (1998: 308) argues that 'trust not only enables greater exchange of information, but it also promotes ease of interaction and a flexible orientation on the part of each partner'. It operates as a mechanism that facilitates communication and cooperation between firms. 'Trust relationships can result in a supplier exceeding contractual requirements, whether by early delivery, higher quality, or some other means of assuring goodwill' (Sako 1992). Nooteboom (1999) even states that too detailed and formal contracts may seriously inhibit the growth of trust. Trust yields more flexibility and economies on the costs of governance (Nooteboom 1996). Another benefit of trust as a vehicle in forming alliances is the reduction of search costs for alliance partners. Firms in social networks of trusting relationships can ally with someone they already know (Gulati 1995: 107).

The cause- and effect structure of social capital at the individual level

Now we have discussed some basic conceptions on network theory and trust we are able to summarize our insights on the cause and effects structure of social capital at the microlevel. We have developed a conceptualization of social capital at the microlevel in terms of network resources. In line with the relational view, it is argued that there are important external sources of capabilities that firms draw upon. Gulati (1999) labels these as 'network resources'. These network resources enable and constrain firms' abilities to acquire competitive capabilities through exposure to information and opportunities (McEvily and Zaheer 1999).

Adler and Kwon (2002) discuss three benefits of social capital. The first is information. Building on the network perspective of Burt, social capital facilitates access to broader sources of information. And in line with Coleman's network thinking, social capital improves information's quality, relevance and timeliness. According to McEvily and Zaheer (1999), exposure to many different external contacts is essential to learning in a competitive environment.

The second kind of benefit is found in influence, control and power. As the costs of sharing know-how in inter-organizational relationships are high, effective mechanisms must be in place to allow knowledge sharing and discourage free-riding (Dyer and Singh 1998). Dyer and Singh claim that self-enforcing governance mechanisms are crucial in this respect. Yli-Renko *et al.* (2001: 591) argue that informal norms of reciprocity and trust may discourage free-riding because (a) relational governance norms are not time-dependent and may appreciate in value as the relationship progresses (cf. Putnam who argues that the use of social capital increases its value), (b) actions are more freely undertaken on behalf of the exchange partner when reciprocal benefits are expected, and (c) the likelihood of violation is diminished when high-quality hard-to-replace relationships exist.

A final benefit of social capital refers to the fact that a closed social network encourages compliance with local – sometimes implicit – rules and customs and reduces the need for formal monitoring. Shared goals and expectations reduce the need for formal monitoring.

However, there are also potential dangers of network relationships. According to Portes and Sensenbrenner (1993: 1338) 'it is important not to lose sight of the fact that the same social mechanisms that give rise to appropriable resources for individual use can also constrain action or even derail it from its original goals'. Other authors also note that more is not necessarily better (e.g. Brown 1998, Woolcock 1998). Relation-specific capital such as trust and tacit understanding develops over time (Tsai 2000: 927). By intensifying the frequency and depth of information exchange, social interaction increases relation-specific common knowledge (Yli-Renko *et al.* 2001). Common knowledge, in turn, increases relation-specific capital. As several authors (e.g. Gulati 1995) have shown, social relationships (in contrast to market or spot relations) are path-dependent.

Relation-specific capital – or as Dyer and Singh (1998) call it 'human cospecialization' – increases as partners develop experience working together. They accumulate specialized information, language and know-how, which allow them to communicate efficiently and effectively. Frequent and close interactions create a common point of view. The potential gains from this capital influence partners in such a way that they tend to focus on existing relationships instead of new ones. If the tendency to stick to existing linkages is dominant social networks can suffocate. Trust-based embedded relations between firms may become too exclusive and durable, thereby yielding rigidities and lack of innovation (Nooteboom 2002).

Engaging in a relationship may result in the development of dedicated linkages that further enhance the benefits from engaging in the joint relationship (Dyer and Singh 1998). The fact that these relational capabilities are partly path-dependent could result in a potential loss of flexibility. Embeddedness may therefore reduce adaptive capacity. This may imply the danger of lock-in effects and path-dependency. These lock-in effects can be strengthened by processes of cognitive dissonance in tight groups (Meyerson 1994, Rabin 1998). Individuals that make up a dense network tend to develop a commitment to one another and to their group. Information that disturbs the consensus of the group's perception of reality is likely to be rejected. A high-quality relationship may reduce the transaction costs associated with managing this relation, but may lead to the expectation that information is provided when needed, so that the incentive to acquire external knowledge is reduced (Yli-Renko *et al.* 2001). In this case, the closure of the network may result in inertia. Besides this, Adler and Kwon (2002) mention that the maintenance of strong ties may be costly. The assumption that strong ties are better than weak ties for reasons discussed above, neglects the costs of building and maintaining the relationship.

Hence, some dimensions of social capital may at times inhibit exchange and combination processes and constrain rather than enable learning (Nahapiet and Ghoshal 1998).

'Structuring the chaos'

The study of social capital extends to multiple levels of analysis. Whereas some researchers focus on the aggregate level of societies, nations and regions (Fukuyama 1995, Putnam 1993, 1995, Knack and Keefer 1997), others have studied social capital at the level of the individual or the firm (Coleman 1988, Gulati 1999, McEvily and Zaheer 1999, Yli-Renko *et al.* 2001, Tsai 2000, Tsai and Ghoshal 1998).

Social capital at the aggregate level is thought of in terms of norms of cooperation. At the individual level social capital is not defined in a normative way, but relates to network resources. Social capital at this level is thought of as a set of resources embedded in relationships. Putnam links trust with the density of associational membership in a society. According to him, trust and engagement are two facets of the same underlying factor, which is social capital. At the aggregate level social capital (norms of cooperation) is reflected in a degree of abstract trust and density of associational activity.

At the individual level trust is an element that is necessary for the existence of social capital. As trust is a self-enforcing mechanism trust not only serves as a cause of social capital but also as an effect of social capital. The social capital of a firm consists of its relationships and network, which may serve as a resource. But for building and keeping this network, trust is crucial. At the aggregate level, social capital is assumed to generate positive effects to society as a whole. At the microlevel, these potential benefits increase a firm's efficiency and productivity.

We have shown that the distinction between these two levels is important. Conflating norms and networks under the same conceptual umbrella makes it difficult to understand causal flows (Fox and Gershman 2000). When discussing the risks of social capital at the aggregate level, Adler and Kwon (2002: 31) state that the costs of the broader aggregate are echoed in the costs at the individual level and they suggest it is merely a matter of summing. However, the insights on social capital at the individual level cannot be applied to the macrolevel through simple aggregation. This would be the reverse ecological fallacy (see Chapter 4). The 'trust' that figures prominently in firm level studies of relationships and embeddedness, is not the generalized (abstract) trust of the political science literature. The reduction of transaction costs because of a trusting relationship cannot simply be translated to the statement that high interpersonal (abstract) trust reduces overall transaction costs in an economy, which positively affects GDP-growth. The leap from individual- to aggregate-functioning is illegitimate, because what may be true for individuals may not be true for the society as a whole (Fine 2001).

In fact, by extending the traditional field of economics into the sociological discipline, researchers in this field of social capital have 'as a by effect' brought on themselves a central theoretical problem in sociology, namely that of the transition from the level of the individual to the macrolevel. Hence, as such this level problem in the field of social capital is not surprising.

Table 8.1 summarizes our main ideas. As discussed in the previous sections, social capital at the aggregate level refers to norms of cooperation. At the individual level a central element of social capital is networks of firms and the resources these networks may provide to a firm. We have also discussed the cause and effect structure and the potential benefits and costs of social capital at both levels. Some keywords are mentioned in Table 8.1.

At the aggregate level, literature on social capital is mostly found in the broader fields of (macro-) sociology, political science and increasingly economics. Researchers like Luhmann (1979), Fukuyama (1995) and Putnam (1993, 1995, 2000) play an important role in the literature on aggregate social capital. At the individual level, the study of social capital attracts sociologists, specifically from the field of organization studies. Traditionally, authors have diverse backgrounds, and most of them have some basic training in (micro-) sociology.

Studies at the aggregate level are mostly theoretical. This is probably caused by internal validity problems. That is, gathering data that measure what you want to measure is difficult, especially when examining the cause and the effect of social capital. So far most studies focused on relating proxies for social capital with economic growth (Knack and Keefer 1997, Zak and Knack 2001) and/or governance performance (Putnam 1993). None of the scarce empirical studies has been able to directly measure social capital in terms of norms of generalized reciprocity. Associational activity and abstract trust can at most be seen as a proxy for norms of cooperation. But there are several problems with these proxies, especially with the measurement of trust (Beugelsdijk 2006, 2008). At the macrolevel trust is measured as the percentage of respondents in each country that reply: 'most people can be trusted', when asked 'Generally speaking, do you think that most people can be trusted or that you can't be too careful in dealing with people?' In Beugelsdijk (2006) we present empirical evidence that this measure of trust is a proxy of the well-functioning of institutions. Trust appears to have a high loading on the first component of a Principle Components analysis. The other variables with a high loading on this first component are measures of institutional strength, such as contract enforceability, rule of law, social infrastructure, corruption, and black market premium. The last two variables have a negative loading, of course. These empirical results underscore the theoretical reasoning that links trust to efficiency at firm level is not the same as the intermediating mechanism between generalized trust and aggregate economic efficiency. By measuring abstract trust we do not consider the quality of the tie. But also, we do not know whether the associations we study are closed or open. Do they allow an individual to build

Table 8.1 Social capital in economics

	Aggregate level (nation/region)	*Individual level*
Definition	Norms of cooperation	Network resources
Reflected in....	Degree of generalized trust Associational activity	Network relationships
Cause (where does social capital come from?)	Culture, development of norms Socialization processes History	Formation capabilities Prior alliances (specific) Trust in partner
Effect	Positive: Civil society More easy provision of collective goods Limit the need for third-party ensurers → reduction of transaction costs Higher economic growth	Positive: Informational advantages Beyond contract advantages
	Negative: Too powerful groups in society (Olson argument, rent-seeking) Exclusionary effects of groups	Negative: Inertia Lock-out of new opportunities Costs of building and maintaining ties
Literature	Macro-Sociology Political science Economics	(Micro) sociology, in specific organisation studies, building on the relational view and social network theory
Type of studies	Mostly theoretical, difficult to prove empirically	Theory and empirics. More empirics, relatively easy to gather data with decent internal validity
Future directions of research	Are there basic cultural differences in norms of cooperation? What causes international differences in norms of cooperation? The interplay between voluntary associations at the microlevel and institutional and cultural features of democracy at the macrolevel	What influences the capacity of firms to engage in networks? That is, what influences the alliance formation capabilities of firms? Is there a trade-off between the costs of strong ties and the reduction of transaction costs?

bridging social capital? (Paxton 1999). According to Paxton (1999), social capital involves two components, a more quantitative component and a more qualitative component. The first component refers to the objective associations between individuals, indicating that individuals are tied to each other in social space. The second component is about the quality of the tie. This means that the ties between individuals must be of a particular type (trusting).

The validity problem of social capital is less prominent at the individual level. By means of surveys researchers are able to capture the social content of a specific relationship and a firm's position in network better than at the aggregate level. Regarding the relational dimension, numerous researchers have tried to measure the degree of trust in specific relationships. For example, in a study on intra-organizational linkages Tsai (2000) measures trustworthiness at the business unit level. Inter-unit trust is measured by asking two questions; 'suppose your unit is looking for business partners inside your organisation for a joint project: which units are you confident that they will do what you require (what you believe they should do) even without writing a contract to clearly specify their obligations?' and 'which units can provide your unit with reliable information?' A related issue is the duration of the relationship. As we argued, the development of relations may take much time before it yields significant impacts on a firm's performance. Building productive social capital takes time. Duration is something that can be directly measured by a survey. Yli-Renko *et al.* (2001) measure the depth of a relationship by a construct labelled 'social interaction'. This construct consists of two items, namely 'we maintain close relationships with the customer' and 'we know this customer's people on a personal level'. Both reflect the degree of social interaction or the depth of the relationship.

The structural dimension of social capital, in other words the position of a firm in a network, is operationalized in at least two ways in the literature. First, researchers have studied the embeddedness of firms in larger social networks. Second, scholars have tried to measure the extent of information available to actors by measuring the centrality of a firm's location in a network (Uzzi 1996). By including the network centrality of a firm, researchers have tried to measure the extent of information available to actors. However, this has mostly been done by measuring the clique overlap centrality or closeness of a firm to the rest of the firm in the inter-firm network, both directly and indirectly (Gulati 1999). The closeness measure is also known as the breadth of ties, i.e. how widespread are the direct and indirect connections to all possible partners in the network? A similar question has been used by McEvily and Zaheer (1999) who operationalize Burt's idea of structural holes and the non-redundancy of ties by asking interviewees 'to write down the initials of the five most important people *not* employed by their company that they can rely on for advice about managing their business'. Moreover, they ask the interviewees to indicate if these people know each other.

The above discussion on validity makes clear that measuring social capital at the microlevel seems somewhat easier than at the aggregate level. This may be exactly the reason why most studies at the aggregate level remain theoretical and why there is a lack of solid empirical studies at this level.

Future research

In Table 8.1 we have tried to propose several directions for future research. Again, we made a distinction between the two levels. At the aggregate level, perhaps the most important direction of future research is related to a possible direct linkage between norms of cooperation and economic growth. Also, there is the question where international or regional differences in norms of cooperation come from. Why are some nations characterized by a high amount of aggregate social capital while others seem to lack norms that promote cooperation? Moreover, more light should be shed on the interplay between voluntary associations at the microlevel and institutional and cultural features of democracy at the macrolevel. The often-heard criticism on the lack of a theoretical mechanism between associational activity and economic growth is less relevant once we see associational activity as a proxy for norms of cooperation. However, more insight in the causal relationship between these norms of cooperation, international differences in it and the economic outcomes in terms of welfare is needed. So far, the assumed causal mechanism between aggregate social capital and economic growth might be too (culturally) deterministic. It might very well be that the above relationship is endogenous (cf. Durlauf 2002). An empirical attempt to relate types of social capital (bonding and bridging) to economic growth in 54 European regions that explicitly takes this endogeneity into consideration is by Beugelsdijk and Smulders (2003). They show that that bridging social capital has a positive effect on growth, whereas bonding social capital has a negative effect on the degree of sociability outside the closed social circle. In other words, they find evidence for Fukuyama's claim that 'the strength of the family bond implies a certain weakness in ties between individuals not related to one another' (Fukuyama 1995: 56).

At the individual level, there are also a number of areas to be explored. The ability to engage in new networks differs across firms. Firms vary in terms of their potential to discover and exploit competitive capabilities through their networks. An important question concerns the alliance formation capabilities of firms. What are the factors that determine if a firm is capable of effectively handling external relationships? Are internal organizational elements related to the capacity to build and maintain external relations? Empirical studies that have tried to shed some light on this are from Ritter (1999) and Beugelsdijk *et al.* (2006). The latter authors show that certain aspects of organizational culture influence the alliance capabilities which in their turn affect the potential benefits generated by an interfirm relationship. In addition, we argued that strong ties might generate all kinds of benefits. At the same time we argued that building and managing a relationship takes time and money. It would be interesting to examine if there is a trade-off in the costs of maintaining strong ties and the reduction of transaction costs.

Perhaps the most important research question in the field of social capital as a whole concerns the relationship between the two levels. The distinction between the two levels as we outlined above is not as strict as it might look after our discussion. Clearly the two levels are interrelated. Norms of generalized reciprocity present in the society as a whole do affect the capability of firms to build and maintain inter-firm relations. An important field of future research is the relationship between the two levels. Is the aggregate level of social capital related to the individual level? It can be argued that in societies in which norms of cooperation are more prevalent it is easier to build individual level social capital. Can international differences in the creation of social capital at the individual level be explained by cultural differences? We already know a great deal about cross-cultural differences in the field of international management (Hofstede 2001), but to our knowledge so far no study explicitly deals with cross-cultural differences and the capabilities of firms to engage in external partnerships and in this way build social capital. As Uzzi (1996: 695) puts it, 'what modern institutions and cultural arrangements need exist if embedded exchange systems are to arise and prosper in a society?'. An institutional environment that encourages trust among trading partners may facilitate the creation of relational rents (North 1990). A clear example is perhaps the fact that Japanese firms seem to have been successful in generating relational rents because of a country-specific culture that fosters trust and cooperation (Dyer and Singh 1998). Cooperating firms in other countries may not be able to obtain the same relational rents and reduction in transaction costs because they lack the 'proper' culture. The institutional environment may be important in the potential to reduce transaction costs to achieve a certain type and level of cooperation. Social capital at the aggregate level may serve as a conditioning factor for social capital at the individual level.

In this chapter we explored the literature on social capital. Our most important aim has been to structure the current chaos in the literature. We tried to do so by making a distinction between the aggregate and the individual level of social capital. The fact that social capital means so many different things makes it a convenient concept for different agendas. As Fine (2001) argues, one of the merits of social capital as a conceptual tool is that it seeks to integrate economic and non-economic analyses or at least complementarities between the two. The social and the capital tend to stand for the non-economic and the economic, respectively. In other words, something that is essentially social might serve as an asset. If we wish to employ social capital as an analytical tool in explaining the economic success of nations or firms, the distinction we made is helpful, perhaps even crucial.

Chapter 9

International relations and coordination

Previous chapters discuss culture as an explanatory factor for differences between countries. A common history and intergenerational transmission of values lead to a configuration of values and attitudes which in their turn gave rise to a particular way of organizing an economy. Within a country, this common culture and institutional framework ease coordination of activities between members. For cross-border transactions, however, the resulting differences between nations and regions with respect to cultures and institutions are expected to have a negative impact. Unfamiliarity with the working of formal institutions and unease with informal procedures (culture) will give rise to an inward looking attitude and thus hamper transactions across borders. Actual transaction costs (defined in a broad sense) are higher than suggested by physical costs and tariffs.

Obstfeld and Rogoff (2000) claim that by explicitly introducing transaction costs in the model they can go far towards explaining six puzzles in international macroeconomics. Among these six puzzles are two home bias puzzles: the home bias in trade puzzle and the home bias in equity portfolios. The home bias in trade puzzle stems from the empirical finding that international goods markets appear to be far more segmented than suggested by theory. The puzzle of home bias in equity portfolios concerns the fact that despite a much expanded world market for equities, stock market investors maintain a puzzling preference for home assets. Some studies explicitly dealing with cultural explanations for these home bias puzzles will be described in this chapter.

The studies on cultural influence on international trade expect a negative influence of cultural differences on international trade. The argument being that cultural differences are expected to negatively affect all international transactions including international trade. From the perspective of a firm this is a partial view only. A firm has at least two strategies by which it can enter a foreign market: trade and foreign Direct Investment (FDI). FDI implies a higher degree of involvement in the foreign society than trade. Consequently, one would expect firms to use trade for the markets with which management is less familiar and FDI for countries with a high degree of similarity in institutions and culture. In this set-up a positive (negative) relation is expected between trade (FDI) and cultural differences between countries. In case a firm decides to invest in a foreign country, management also has to decide on the particular form: greenfield investment, acquisition, merger, and joint venture. Each of these entry modes is characterized by a different degree and form of interest in the foreign country.

In the previous paragraph foreign investments were considered as a way of servicing foreign markets; the perspective of a multinational's management was taken. One can also see foreign investments from the perspective of financial investors, who are seeking for a good trade-off between return and risk. In that case these investments are part of a portfolio selection model. Theoretical models, such as the International Capital Asset Pricing Model (ICAPM), recommend investing in various different assets and countries. The actual portfolios contain a higher share of domestic assets than recommended by these models. Cultural differences between the investor and the country or region the investment is located are brought forward as possible explanations for these biases.

As well as goods and investments, people also cross borders. Cultural differences are expected to be of even more importance for migration and cross-border commuting than for international trade and investments.

When discussing the entry modes of firms, we pay attention to the role of culture and cultural differences for cooperation within a firm or for establishing a new management team when companies merge. Likewise one expects that these cultural factors will influence international cooperation in the field of politics.

Many empirical studies make use of gravity equations. These equations were first used in the 1950s and 1960s. Their popularity increased in the late 1990s when some studies revealed that gravity equations can be interpreted as the reduced form of several structural models of international trade. These theoretical underpinnings gave the gravity equation more legitimacy and enhanced its use considerably. A short description of the gravity equation and its history is presented in Appendix 6 The gravity equation.

The set-up of this chapter is as follows. In the next section we describe various measures of cultural similarity and distance. Thereafter the topics of culture and international relations are dealt with in the order they are described above: the partial view on international trade, international trade and Foreign Direct Investments as alternative ways of entering a foreign market, the mode by which multinational firms enter a foreign country, investors' behaviour, migration, and international political cooperation. Unless stated otherwise, the null hypothesis is that cultural differences will hamper all forms of international transactions.

Measures of cultural distance and similarity

Studies investigating the role of culture for international transactions and cooperation use three types of cultural measures: the characteristic of a particular dimension, the differences between countries with respect to a score on a dimensions, and cultural distance. The distinction between intrusive and natural measures introduced in Figure 4.1 will be used as a guideline.

Obtrusive measures

As far as we know all intrusive measures are obtained by means of questionnaires. Two types of attitudes can be distinguished: attitudes towards others, in particular foreigners and foreign products, and bilateral preferences. Indicators of the first type measure the extent to which respondents prefer their own group or products over others. Some cultural dimensions presented in Chapter 4 can be used for indicating the degree of home bias in a population. A high score on Uncertainty Avoidance, for example, can signal a more hostile attitude towards foreigners and foreign influences, because a more open economy is more vulnerable to external shocks and thus has to absorb a higher level of uncertainty (see De Jong *et al.* 2006; see also literature on entry modes cited in Kogut and Singh 1988). A high degree of international transactions fosters transparency, which is less appreciated by corrupt leaders and managers. Corruption positively correlates with Power Distance, so that one would expect a negative relation between Power Distance and openness.

The Kogut-Singh index is a very frequently used index for representing bilateral cultural differences in studies of international business and economics (see Kogut and Singh 1988). The index is based on the deviation of each of the cultural dimensions of each country j from the home country, h. The deviations are corrected for differences in the variance of each dimension and then arithmetically averaged. Algebraically:

$$CD_{jh} = \sum_{i=1}^{4} \{(I_{ij} - I_{ih})^2 / V_i\} / 4$$

where CD_{jh} is the cultural distance between country j and country h, I_{ij} is country j's score on the ith cultural dimension, I_{ih} is the score of country h on this dimension, and V_i is the variance of the score of the dimension. The number of dimensions is assumed to be 4 in this equation.

The cultural distance can also be calculated as the Euclidean distance (see for example Barkema *et al.* 1997, Brouthers and Brouthers 2001). It computes the distance as the square root of the sum of the squared differences in the scores on each cultural dimension. Formally:

$$CD_{jh} = \sqrt{\sum_{i=1}^{4} \{(I_{ij} - I_{ih})^2 / V_i\}}$$

where the symbols have the same meaning as previously.

The Kogut-Singh index has met with much criticism. Shenkar (2001) criticizes both the conceptual and methodological properties of cultural distance. The latter refers to aspects we have already dealt with in Chapter 4, such as the homogeneity assumption of both the firm and the country, and the fact that use is made of the Hofstede data, which are relatively old. We therefore confine the review to Shenkar's criticism on the concept of distance. The reader should be aware of the fact that Shenkar has the Hofstede-based Kogut-Singh index in mind when writing his criticism.

Distance suggests symmetry: the distance from A to B is the same as from B to A. The *perceived* physical distance, cultural, psychological and emotional distance need not be symmetric. For A the cultural distance to B can be greater than it is for B with respect to A.

Since Hofstede's dimensions are measured only once, the Kogut-Singh index suggests a *constant* cultural difference. In reality, however, culture itself and cultural distances can change through time. In principle, this criticism can be met by regularly organizing similar surveys and updating the index on the basis of the newly available data.

The use of the distance concept assumes a *linear impact* on investment, entry mode and performance.

> The higher the distance between cultures, the higher the likelihood that (a) investment will occur at a later stage in the investment sequence, (b) a less controlling entry mode will be selected, and (c) the worse the performance of foreign affiliates will be.
>
> (Shenkar 2001: 523)

In this way one neglects the possibility that the structure of this pattern can differ depending on, for example, differences in managers' learning curves. Bell (1996) is one of the few authors who incorporates a nonlinear (quadratic in this case) term in the relation.

Implicitly, researchers assume that cultural distance *causes* differences in international transactions. The reverse causation can also be true.

Finally, it is implicitly assumed that *differences in cultures hamper* international transactions. This need not be the case. First, some cultural differences do not matter for international transactions. Second, some cultural differences can be complementary and thus have a positive synergetic effect on the transaction.

Shenkar suggests replacing the 'distance' metaphor by the 'friction' metaphor. His concept of friction shows much similarity with Oliver Williamson's transaction costs. By friction Shenkar means 'the scale and essence of the interface between interacting cultures, and the "drag" produced by that interface for the operation of those systems.' (Shenkar 2001: 528).

Direct observations of a particular country's inhabitants' opinion about citizens of several other countries meet many of the criticisms raised against the Kogut-Singh index. Patriotism is an example of direct observations and indicates the appreciation of domestic persons and issues. Morse and Shive (2006) use the answers to some questions in the World Value Survey and in the International Social Survey Program for measuring patriotism (see Appendix 5 Survey measures of patriotism and attitude towards foreigners). The Eurobarometer forms a source for direct measures of attitudes towards inhabitants of foreign countries. In regressions the answers are used on questions referring to the respondents' opinion on Central European countries becoming members of the EU and about their trust in inhabitants of other countries (See Appendix 5 on Survey Measures). The respondents answering the trust question come from the same countries as those listed in the answer sheet. Consequently, one can calculate the average bilateral trust between the inhabitants of two countries (resulting in a matrix), the average level of trust the inhabitants in a country have in those of the other countries in the sample, and the average trust of the inhabitants from other countries in a particular country.

In addition to these widely held surveys, some individual researchers have asked respondents for their perception of the cultural differences between their home country and a particular foreign country (see e.g. Drogendijk and Slangen 2006, Bell 1996). In this they obtain a measure of the cultural distance as perceived by the person who made the relevant decisions.

Natural (non-intrusive) measures

Similarity is measured by common language, religion or history. Colonial ties are often regarded as reflecting a common history which favours international transactions. In regressions, these factors are represented by dummy variables. A one is assigned to a country pair if the two countries share the same language, dominant religion, and colonial ties.

A few authors use genetic distance as an indicator for cultural differences between groups. This distance is interpreted as a measure of vertically transmitted characteristics, reflecting different historical paths of populations over a long period. The genetic distance is predetermined and thus exogenous to current economic conditions. The differences in genetic material within a local population accounts for about 93 per cent of the variation, whereas the differences between populations is about 7 per cent of the total human variability. The index used for this genetic distance is based on these 7 per cent differences in genetic material between populations (Giuliano *et al.* 2007). By construction it ranges from 0 to 1; the closer to 1, the higher the genetic difference between populations. The pattern of overall genetic variation measured by this index differs substantially from racial divisions (ibid: 7 and 8). In contrast, genetic and geography are correlated. The index of genetic distance shows small jumps for populations opposite to geographical barriers, including mountains and seas. These results suggest that genetic distance measures geographical barriers instead of cultural variables, such as religion and languages (ibid: 13).

Bilateral trade flows

Many investigations of cultural influences on bilateral trade flows use answers on attitudes towards foreigners and foreign influences as indicators of cultural differences. Disdier and Mayer (2007) use the answers of respondents from EU-countries on the question of their attitude to each of ten Central and Eastern European Countries becoming a member of the European Union (see the previous section and Appendix 5). Disdier and Mayer use the percentage of positive answers for these countries for the years 1992, 1994 and from 1997 to 2001 for explaining exports to and imports from these countries to EU-member states. The relation is a gravity equation as this can be derived from a standard new trade model (see also Appendix 6 The gravity equation). Disdier and Mayer assume that the distance between two countries consists of two components: 'freeness of trade' and 'bilateral love'. The first term depends upon transport costs, protection measures and information/communication costs. In the empirical analysis these costs are represented by the distance between the trade partners, a dummy for common border, bilateral exchanges of newspapers, and the share of asylum seekers going to a particular EU member during the period 1988–1993. The latter two variables are assumed to reduce information/communication costs. The 'bilateral love' term reflects the preference for each country's types of pro-ducts. This cultural similarity is represented by a language similarity index and bilateral trade in printed books. The bilateral opinions variable is thought to represent dimensions of both bilateral preferences and bilateral information/communication costs. Bilateral opinion appears to have a statistically significant positive effect on the imports of EU countries from the CEEC, whereas its effect on exports from the EU to these countries is mostly negligible. These results confirm the idea that the bilateral opinions of EU-respondents reflect consumers' preferences. The addition of bilateral opinions to the relation does not have any significant impact on the coefficients of the other variables representing 'freeness of trade' and 'bilateral love'.

A simultaneity problem arises, however, because Disdier and Mayer (2007: Table 4) find that the bilateral opinions are, among others, related to: imports relative to GDP from these CEEC, and exports to these countries (less significant). They, therefore, apply Instrumental Variables estimation to the change in imports (as a percentage of GDP) and the change in the opinion variable. It appears that a more favourable attitude towards these countries becoming members of the EU has a positive influence on the imports from these countries, whereas changes in imports do not have a significant effect on the change of opinions.

For a group of 15 EU-member states[1] Guiso *et al.* (2004) and Den Butter and Mosch (2003) explain bilateral trade by means of mutual trust. Both studies augment a standard gravity equation with the trust variable and some other indicators of cultural or communication differences. In both studies the coefficients of mutual trust are significant in every specification used. Both studies also pay attention to the endogeneity problem of trust: trust might increase as a result of relatively high trade flows. Guiso and co-authors apply an Instrumental Variables Estimation for correcting this bias. As instruments they use the variables found to significantly affect trust. The IV-estimates of the effect of trust on trade are twice as large as the OLS estimates and remain highly significant, suggesting that trust is exogenous to trade. Den Butter and Mosch use the mutual trust variable from the 1996 wave of the Eurobarometer as an explanatory variable for bilateral trade during the period 1993–95 and 1997–99, respectively. They find that the 1996 trust variable is much more significant in the regressions for the period 1997 to 1999 than for the period prior to 1996. From these results they conclude that trust explains trade.

In addition to mutual trust, Dekker *et al.* (2006) uses the Kogut-Singh index, based on Hofstede's four original dimensions, for explaining exports of OECD countries in 1999. They find a significant coefficient for each of these cultural distance variables in a gravity equation. Insofar as culture and institutions are related, the coefficients of the cultural distance variables can partly capture the effect of (the quality of) institutions. They therefore add institutional quality and institutional distance to the relation. Mutual trust's coefficient is reduced but remains significant, whereas the Kogut-Singh index's coefficient becomes insignificant. The original coefficients thus partly reflect the effect of institutions' characteristics.

A few studies use genetic differences as a measure of cultural differences. Giuliano *et al.* (2007) test this with bilateral trade flows within Europe. As well as the genetic distance, they construct an index of transportation costs and a measure of geographical barriers using information on sea, mountain chains and average elevation of countries. The find that 'i) the same factors that determined genetic distance in the past also have a strong influence on current transportation costs; ii) once we properly control for transportation costs, the impact of genetic distance on trade disappears' (ibid: 12). Hence, genetic differences seem to reflect geographical differences that determine transaction costs and not differences in preferences or culture.

Trade by different types of goods

In the previous section no distinction has been made between different types of goods. One can imagine, however, that the importance of communication and similar legal and informal rules differ between different types of goods, especially whether the goods are homogeneous or not. Then Rauch's categorization can be useful. Rauch (1999) distinguishes three types of goods: organized exchange commodities, reference priced commodities and differentiated goods. The organized exchange commodities are listed on organized exchanges. Their quality standards are known worldwide and given the quality standard and the place where the commodity is located, prices provide enough information. Different types of raw material belong to this category. Reference priced commodities are not traded on an organized exchange but are also not branded. Hence, one can mention the prices of the product without referring to the manufacturer. Finally, differentiated products have many characteristics that make them relatively unique. They are often branded and their price depends on quality, local demand and supply, etc. Consequently, buyers and sellers have to search for the item they prefer. This search is enhanced by proximity, common language, and a network of traders one can trust. Because of the differentiation in products, complaints about the quality of the commodity can easily arise. A legal system guaranteeing property rights and contract enforcement is then needed to reduce the deals' insecurity. In sum, trade in differentiated products will flourish if the quality of the institutions is good and communicational and cultural barriers are small.

Some authors have used Rauch's classification of internationally traded goods for studying the different effects of institutions and culture. Linders (2006: Chapter 5) focuses on the role of common language, common religion and institutional quality. Many of the results for the organized exchange commodities are hard to interpret. In all likelihood, the importance of raw materials in this category explains much. Raw material is exported from a particular country just because nature has supplied that country with huge reserves. Hence, the space for free choice is much more limited than is implicitly suggested by theory. Colonial ties might and have (see Linders 2006: 118) a positive effect on the trade in these commodities. We therefore focus on the results for reference priced goods and differentiated goods. Linders finds that the positive effect of common language and common religion are significantly greater for the trade in differentiated goods. The same result is found for institutional quality of the exporting and importing country: they have a significantly larger effect on trade in differentiated goods. Institutional distance negatively effects international trade and this effect is the largest for referenced priced goods: a result contradicting expectations. Guiso *et al.* (2004: Table 5) test the effect of trust on exports in organized exchange commodities and in differentiated goods. They find consistently a larger and a more statistically significant effect of trust on the trade in differentiated commodities. Giuliano *et al.* (2007: 17) find that genetic differences have no effect on trade for both homogenous and differentiated goods if transportation costs are taken into account.

Cheptea (2007) disaggregates trade in cultural goods and non-cultural goods in order to derive a measure of bilateral cultural affinity. Cultural goods, such as newspapers, books, and cinematographic films carry information and preference of the market of origin. Consumers in countries that import large volumes of these goods will be influenced by the preferences incorporated in these products and are expected to import larger volumes of non-cultural goods from the countries from which these cultural goods are imported. In order to investigate whether this cultural affinity effect comes in addition to the traditional measures of closeness, such as common border and common language, Cheptea develops a two step procedure. In the first step bilateral trade in cultural commodities is explained by a gravity equation containing the traditional measures of closeness, such as distance, common border, common language, colonial ties and whether the two countries have been part of one country in recent history. The residuals of these regressions measure the volume of trade in addition to the volume explained by the traditional measures of cultural and social ties between the countries. Cheptea considers these as a measure of cultural affinity. By construction this cultural affinity is not necessarily the same for a given pair of countries. It depends on the trade flows from one country to the other so that the cultural affinity of American consumers for French products can differ from that of French consumers for American products. In the second step, the residuals from the first step regressions are used as explanatory variables in gravity relations explaining bilateral trade in non-cultural products. The coefficients of the first step regressions' residuals indicate the influence of cultural affinity on bilateral trade. The coefficients of cultural affinity are all statistically significant in regressions of trade in non-cultural goods. Moreover, these regressions also contain the traditional measures of cultural ties – common border, common language and cultural ties – indicating that the cultural affinity measure has an additional effect. The influence is largest for trade in advertising material.

International trade and foreign direct investment

The previous studies focused on the effects of cultural and institutional differences on international trade as such. From the perspective of a firm's management this is a partial view only. A firm has at least two strategies by which it can enter a foreign market: trade and Foreign Direct Investments (FDI). In the case of international trade, the firm produces goods at home and sells them abroad. The company needs sales representatives in these countries. In the case of FDI, the company owns a plant in the foreign country, where it produces the good. In this case management has to comply with foreign national law and culture for acquiring and running a factory. This the strategy of servicing a foreign market by trade leads to less involvement in the foreign country than servicing the same market by FDI. Consequently, one would expect firms to use trade for the markets management is less familiar with and FDI for countries with a high degree of similarity in institutions and culture. In this set-up a positive (negative) relation is expected between trade (FDI) and cultural differences between countries.

By means of a gravity equation Lankhuizen, Linders and De Groot (2008) investigate whether cultural and institutional differences have opposite effects on trade and FDI. They find that cultural distance (represented by the Kogut-Singh-index) has a significantly positive influence on exports and a significantly negative one on FDI.[2] The latter effect holds for various measures of FDI activities: stocks, sales and intensity. The size and level of significance of the coefficients increase if measures of institutional quality in the importing and exporting countries and institutional differences are added to the relation. In a fixed effect regression both coefficients of cultural differences are negative with that of FDI being larger (in absolute terms) than that of trade. These results confirm that trade and FDI are substitutes for servicing foreign markets.

Establishment mode choices by multinational firms

Once a company has chosen to invest abroad, its management has to decide on the legal form. This entry mode decision has been investigated by scholars of International Business. As a rule these studies do not investigate the choice between trade and FDI, but between different forms of FDI. A reason for this restriction could be that the transaction cost theory, which is often used in these studies, is regarded as inappropriate for studying the decision to export or to invest. '(T)he proper comparison is between setting up a subsidiary in a country A and licensing a local firm in country A' (Hennart 1989: 215).

An investment in a foreign country can take different forms with different degrees of involvement in the host country's culture. Several modes of entry can be distinguished. Greenfield investments and strategic alliances are forms with a relatively low level of foreign involvement. A Greenfield start is a foreign subsidiary set up from scratch. The company can send in a few people who hire some local employees and gradually build the subsidiary. The local employees can be selected to fit best with corporate culture. Strategic alliances are agreements to collaborate on specific products or markets. Here the risk is limited to this joint project. If a company acquires a foreign firm, it buys all assets and liabilities of that firm, including the contracts with the latter's local employees. The employees are used to the culture of the acquired firm. When integrating local activities into the acquirer's business, tensions between the culture of the two companies can easily arise. Often key people leave the company or are replaced by the acquirer's own managers. Mergers are in essence similar to acquisitions but differ in that both companies are of about equal size. Examples of failing international mergers abound, the Dutch–German mergers of

Hoogovens-Hoesch (Estel) and Fokker-Vereinigte Flugzeugwerke. On the other hand some British–Dutch mergers (Shell and Unilever) flourish still after many decades. Finally, a joint venture is a new business in which two or more companies pool resources. This legal construction can be used because the partners regard it as convenient, but in some (mostly developing or emerging) countries government regulation requires a foreign company to cooperate with a domestic one. The cultural risk of a joint venture is less than that of a merger or acquisition, because a new entity is set-up instead of integrating two existing ones.

Theories about the choice of entry mode do not come up with an unambiguous sign for the influence of cultural differences. According to the transaction costs theory foreign operations increase both the transaction costs of equity mode of entrance and non-equity and thus there are low commitment strategies for entering a foreign country. The Uppsala school, which is also known as the school of internationalization (Johanson and Vahlne 1977) emphasizes the learning process involved in internationalization. A company will start with a low commitment entry mode (exporting and licensing for example) and after it has learned more about the country, it will change to modes that require more commitment, such as subsidiaries. Hence, the relevance of cultural distance (psychic distance in their terms)[3] depends on the particular firm's experience with foreign operations, and one can argue in favour of both a positive and negative effect of cultural distance (CD) on various forms of foreign involvement. An overview of studies on cultural influences on entry modes (Harzing 2004) reveals that indeed for a particular type of entry mode both negative and positive affects of cultural distance have been found.

By far the majority of studies of the cultural influence on the choice and success of different establishment modes use Kogut-Singh's index of cultural distance (see Harzing 2004 for a survey and critical assessment). The entry modes differ with respect to the degree of the parent company's involvement in the project and in the foreign country.

The criticism on these studies can be categorized in three groups: the neglect of other explanatory factors than cultural difference, the use of secondary data for deriving the cultural distance and the focus on cultural distance instead of the different cultural dimensions.[4] By focusing on cultural differences these studies tend to neglect some obvious alternative explanatory factors, such as geographical distance, the firms' previous experience with internationalization, host country effects and home country effects. According to Harzing (2004: 104) 'variables other than CD (Cultural Distance) would seem to offer at least an equally plausible, if not more plausible, explanation for any differences in entry-mode choice'. As mentioned before, the internationalization school already considers a firm's experience with internationalization as important: more experienced companies are likely to choose an entry mode with more commitment, such as an acquisition. Some authors explicitly take this learning into account (e.g. Barkema *et al.* 1997, Vermeulen and Barkema 2001). Other firm specific factors which can be relevant are the type of industry the firm belongs to and the role of foreign operation in the company. In many studies no attention is paid to relevant host country effects, in particular regulation. Some countries, especially developing and emerging countries, restrict the legal modes by which foreign firms are allowed to operate in their country.[5] Often foreign firms are not allowed to acquire wholly owned subsidiaries, and are forced to enter into joint ventures with local partners. It might be that this explains the empirical finding that the incidence of joint ventures increases whereas its success decreases with cultural distance (see for example Barkema and Vermeulen 1997: 854, 855). Home country effects mentioned, are the preference for a particular type of entry mode. It is said that companies from Anglo-Saxon countries favour acquisitions as an entry mode.

By far the majority of the studies on entry modes use the Kogut-Singh index for measuring cultural distance. This measure can be criticized for: the particular measure of distance used (squared differences), the use of Hofstede's dimensions instead of other cultural dimensions, and the fact that these dimensions are secondary data. This last point of critique is based on the observation that the decision to enter a foreign market and the mode by which they enter are determined by managers from the company concerned. Hence, the cultural distance as *perceived* by these managers is relevant and not a measure of distance derived from a questionnaire of other people. A few studies have developed a measure of perceived distance and relate this distance to the entry mode chosen (Bell 1996, Drogendijk and Slangen 2006, Kim and Hwang 1992).

In their study Drogendijk and Slangen use a perceived measure of distance along with four other measures in order to investigate the sensitivity of the results of cultural influence on establishment modes to the use of Hofstede's dimensions. Measures included in Drogendijk and Slangen's study are: the Kogut-Singh index and the Euclidian distance measure (see the Section Measures of cultural distance and similarity) using Hofstede's or Schwartz's cultural dimensions, and a measure of managers' perception of cultural distance. The explanatory variable is a dummy variable which is 1 for greenfields and 0 for acquisitions by Dutch firms. Each of the measures of cultural distance is added to an equation with a series of MNE characteristics (such as MNE's size, diversification, etc.) as explanatory variables. Somewhat to their surprise Drogendijk and Slangen find that the managers' perspective on cultural distance is hardly statistically significant and improves the relation's fit only marginally. Adding each of the measures using Hofstede's and Schwartz's cultural dimensions to the relations improves the fit by approximately the same size. The estimated coefficients of these four indicators of cultural distance are all correctly signed and statically significant. The distances based on Hofstede's dimensions are more significant than those based on Schwartz's dimensions. From these results Drogendijk and Slangen (2006: 373) conclude: '(o)verall, the Hofstede and Schwartz-based measures thus explain establishment mode choices by MNEs equally well'. The Hofstede-based measures and the Schwartz-based measures are only moderately correlated, indicating that they do not reflect the same cultural differences.

The influence of a measure of cultural distance based on Hofstede's dimensions does not decrease over time. On the contrary, regressions by Barkema and Vermeulen (1997: 857) suggest an increase in size and significance of this impact.

A final point of criticism on these studies concerns the focus on *distance*. Consequently, the cultural differences between countries are regarded as barriers to international cooperation. Two qualifications need to be made: i) the degree to which cultural differences hamper transactions will depend on the particular dimension on which the countries differ, and ii) cultural differences need not be negative, they can enhance international transactions. Whether cultural differences hamper international transaction will depend on the particular dimension on which the countries differ. A high score on Uncertainty Avoidance implies that the inhabitants of the country prefer to control every aspect of life as much as possible and hence are hostile to foreign influences. Moreover, differences between countries on this score hamper the functioning of multinationals. The reason is that differences in Uncertainty Avoidance imply different meanings for rules in different countries. Managers and employees in high-UA countries expect and prefer rigid rules, whereas the opposite holds for people from low-UA countries (Hofstede 2001: 442). Although less than differences in Uncertainty Avoidance, large differences with respect to Power Distance are also regarded as hampering international cooperation. Differences on this dimension refer to different expectations with respect to the hierarchy in a firm. In general the mangers from low-PDI countries adapt their behaviour easily in countries with high scores on this index (Hofstede 2001: 442). Barkema and Vermeulen (1997: 855) find that differences in Uncertainty Avoidance and in Long Term Orientation reduce the chance of success of a joint venture. Differences in Masculinity also have a negative but smaller effect. Kogut and Singh (1988: 424) report that Uncertainty Avoidance significantly increases the probability that a firm selects a joint venture or a greenfield investment over an acquisition. Drogendijk and Slangen (2006) studied the influence of the individual dimensions on the decision by Dutch firms to use a greenfield investment or an acquisition as an entry mode. They found that differences in Power Distance and in Individualism account for the significant effects of the Hofstede-based cultural difference measures. For the Schwartz-based measure, the significant effects are caused by differences in Conservatism, Hierarchy and Egalitarian Commitment. Large differences on these dimensions cause management to favour greenfields.

Until now the studies reviewed assume (at least implicitly) that culture, by means of distance or differences, hampers international cooperation. This need not be the case. Hofstede (2001: 447), for example, ascribes the success of the Dutch–British mergers of Shell and Unilever partly to different scores of The Netherlands and Britain on the Femininity/Masculinity index. In his view both feminine (relations maintenance) and masculine (task performance) aspects are required for success in international operations. The masculine British attitude seems to nicely fit with the feminine manner of the Dutch.[6] So, different scores on a particular cultural dimension can even be favourable for international cooperation.

Fons Trompenaars and Charles Hampden-Turner, even go one step further. For each dimension distinguished in their work (Trompenaars and Hampden-Turner 1997, Hampden-Turner and Trompenaars 2000) they argue that differences in scores can be used successfully for wealth creation. The main idea is that foreign countries (and in particular when they differ a lot from one's own) can be seen as mirror images of one's own culture. A cultural dimension refers to a dilemma on a particular aspect of life. Each dimension as such is common to all, but cultures differ in the choice made with respect to this dilemma. By means of stories and cases they illustrate how each of the two extremes functions at its bests and what the consequences are if it is taken too far. Thereafter, they describe vicious and virtues circles of the dimension concerned. Their main idea is that for the successful functioning of a person, organization or country one has to reconcile the dilemma put forward by the dimension at hand. For example, with respect to the Universalism versus Particularism dimension they write: '(n)ot only must universal rules (Universalism) cover more and more exceptions or special cases (Particularism), but these exceptions must be used to improve the universalism of our rules' (Hampden-Turner and Trompenaars 2000: 3). This circular thinking integrates the exceptions into the generally applicable rules. Hampden-Turner and Trompenaars refer to this process as reconciliation: the dilemma has to be reconciled. In Hampden-Turner and Trompenaars (2000) for each dimension they first explore and describe the dilemma or value dimension and then use storytelling and business case studies to describe how this dilemma can be reconciled.

Home bias in portfolio investments

The previous section discussed the role of culture on the managers' investment decision. In this section we focus on the influence of culture on investors' decisions. Several empirical studies reveal a share of foreign equities in portfolios which is much smaller than the optimal share suggested by models of portfolio diversification. For example, based on a simple mean variance analysis, for a typical US investor Lewis (1999: 576, 578) finds an optimal share for foreign assets of 40 per cent or more, whereas the actual share of this type of investment is only 8 per cent. Similar results are found for investors from other countries. The resulting overweight of domestic assets in portfolios has been dubbed the home bias puzzle in portfolios. Within countries a similar pattern has been observed: households and managers of mutual funds hold a higher share of local companies than one would expect from applying first principles of investment theory (see, for example, Grinblatt and Keloharju 2001, Huberman 2001, Coval and Moskowitz 1999).

Several explanations of this home or local bias in portfolio investments have been offered (see Lewis 1999, Karolyi and Stulz 2003, Sercu and Vanpée 2007, for reviews). First, the model used for deriving the benchmark weights is an inadequate description of optimizing investors' portfolio. The high share of domestic assets can serve as a hedge for non-traded goods consumption (Adler and Dumas 1983) or for non-traded goods and leisure (Pesenti and Van Wincoop 2002). Another possibility is that investors are not sure of the optimal benchmark and thus choose a weighted average of different rules (Baele *et al.* forthcoming). Second, international investment can be diminished because of direct barriers to international transactions and high transaction costs such as fees, commissions, and higher spreads of foreign assets. Barriers to international financial transactions have been reduced considerably during the last decades. Consequently this seems no valid argument for the developed countries. Third, the amount and quality of information about foreign assets is significantly less than that of domestic or local investments. Although nowadays many figures can be found by Internet, the interpretation of these figures requires knowledge of local or national conventions and culture. Moreover, investors located in proximity of the companies they have shares in, can physically inspect the operations and frequently meet managers and staff in order to obtain a better understanding of the firms' prospects. Hence, the information argument refers both to the amount of information as well as to the ability to correctly interpret the information acquired. Finally, psychological and behavioural factors might account for the differences between actual and benchmark shares of foreign assets in equity portfolios. Investors prefer domestic or local assets for reasons not captured by the models from which the benchmark is derived. They prefer local investments in local companies because they feel familiar with its operation. The information and behavioural arguments differ from each other in that the first refers to objective facts and their interpretation, whereas the latter refers to perception and preferences. None the less, they are closely related as we will see in the rest of this section. Nowadays, the information and behavioural explanations are considered to be the most important if not only relevant explanations for the home bias in equity portfolios.

Cultural arguments belong to the informational and behavioural explanations for the home bias of equity portfolios. A larger cultural distance can be associated with a lack of information but also with less familiarity and hence a neglect of the opportunities offered. Many other factors can play this dual role too. We therefore also pay attention to some non-cultural factors suggested for informational and behavioural accounts of the bias.

Information about equity can more easily be obtained if the investor lives in the vicinity of the company. Coval and Moskowitz (1999) use this information-based argument for the preference of US mutual fund managers for local companies. In their sample, companies are 9 to 11 per cent closer to these managers than the average firm they could have held. This local equity preference is related to: firm size, leverage, and output tradability. Locally held firms tend to be small and highly levered and they produce goods not traded internationally. The local preference is even higher for regional funds, but less for sector funds and small-caps. Is this information advantage profitable? Yes, according to Coval and Moskowitz (2001). They find that on average active mutual fund managers (so no index funds) generate an additional return of 2.67 per cent per year from local investments. When adjusted for risk this extra return becomes 1.84 per cent. Funds with a relatively high share of local companies earn an even higher rate of return. In addition the local stocks not held by these managers underperform the benchmark, and the purchase of local stocks outperform the sales of these stocks. Fund managers herd more in distant holdings and break away from the herd in their local investments. Furthermore, managers appear to trade far more frequently in their distant holdings than in their local holdings. This suggests that managers adopt relatively long-term strategies in their nearby holdings and have more volatile views on distant holdings. The result is also found by others (Tesar and Werner 1995) for international investors in overseas and domestic investments.

Acquiring correct information about a company is more important for investments that are prone to idiosyncratic risk. Consequently, if the home bias is caused by asymmetric information then one would expect the bias to be largest for equities, and smallest for government bonds, with corporate bonds in between. For German and Swiss managed funds Gehrig (1993) indeed observes a larger bias for equities than for bonds. Portes *et al.* (2001) find that transactions in corporate bonds and equities are more sensitive to information than treasury bonds. To their surprise corporate bonds and equities are equally sensitive to information asymmetries. The volume of telephone call traffic (normalized by the real GDP of the two countries) serves as the information proxy. Although Portes and co-authors stress the information channel they note that telephone call traffic has a cultural component: privileged links between the two countries because of immigration, tourism, etc. In order to capture the latter they include as an explanatory variable the number of tourists of a giving country visiting another. Independently each of both variables has a positive influence on foreign residents' transactions in US corporate bonds and equity. The correlation between the two is high, so that a relation containing both variables delivers unstable coefficients.

If the number of short-term visits by tourists can act as a proxy for information flows, then one would expect that the number of permanent settlements by immigrants would be even an better measure. Some recent studies (Battacharya and Groznik 2008, Foad 2008) therefore use immigration as an information-proxy. Battacharya and Groznik (2008) investigate the influence of immigration to the US on US investment in the immigrants' native countries. They find that US investments in a foreign country are positively correlated with the size of the foreign-origin group of that country living in the USA. The effect is strong for Foreign Direct Investment and modest for equity investment. Physical distance, race, language and religion are not significant. Note that the data refer to total investments in a foreign country and not to the immigrants' own investments abroad. Battacharya and Groznik use data on immigration in the US only.

Foad (2008) constructs a dataset with bilateral immigration and portfolio investment positions of 28 OECD-countries. The immigrants (and thus the foreign assets) originate from 41 countries. An advantage of this dataset is that it enables the researcher to differentiate between the effects of immigration (into a country) and emigration (out of a country) on foreign equity positions. The paper reaffirms the results of previous studies that inward immigration increases the investments from the immigrants' adopted country to their native country. In contrast, when people emigrate from a country, investment from their native country to their new country actually decreases.[7] Hence, it seems that increased information flows are not relevant but that immigration affects foreign equity holdings through immigrants' preferences or immigrants' information advantages. These effects depend, however, on the relative development of sending and receiving countries. Immigration between relatively rich countries increases investments in both the receiving and sending country. When either the sending or receiving country is a low income country, immigration fails to induce foreign investment either because immigrants lack the capital necessary to exploit foreign investment opportunities or the low income country lacks the financial infrastructure to attract foreign investment.

The relevance of both information flows and investors' preferences is also found in Grinblatt and Keloharju's (2001) study on ownership and trade in Finnish firms by Finnish investors. Finland is an interesting case in that both Finnish and Swedish are official languages and the country contains a relatively large Swedish minority. In addition to the investor's mother tongue (Finnish or Swedish), the researchers know the municipality they are living in and their type (household, government, non-profit institution, non-financial corporation, and finance and insurance institution). Information about the company concerns the municipality in which its headquarters are located, the main language used in its annual report (Finnish, Swedish, Finnish and English, and Swedish and English), and its culture. The firms' culture is classified as Finnish or Swedish, which is based on the name and native language of its CEO. Households invest and trade significantly more in companies with headquarters nearby, using the investor's own language and belonging to their own cultural group (Swedish or Finish). The distance effect disappears after about 100 km. Institutional investors are less than households influenced by the distance, language and culture of the firm.

A few studies explain the home bias of equity by a relative preference for some foreign countries (mutual trust) or for the domestic country (patriotism). The mean trust of inhabitants from the investors' countries towards people in destination countries has a significant positive effect on the share of assets from these countries in the portfolio of European mutual funds (Guiso *et al.* 2004). Standard proxies for information – common language, common border and distance – have no significant influence. These results are robust to including press coverage and common origin of law as explanatory variables. Note that these results are found in portfolios managed by professionals, who are expected to be well informed and less guarded about cultural factors than private investors. Consequently, these results can be regarded as an underestimation of the effect of cultural factors on portfolio selection.

Morse and Shive (2006) investigate the relation between the home bias and the degree of patriotism. They use two measures for the home bias: the share of domestic holdings in the portfolio and the domestic holdings in excess of the CAPM-share. The degree of patriotism is derived from the World Values Survey and the ISSP (see Appendix 5). Irrespective of the measure of home bias, the degree of patriotism increases the size of the home bias in equity portfolios. This effect is both statistically and economically significant. A one standard deviation change in patriotism is associated with an \$18 to \$31 billion change in investment abroad. Familiarity, approximated as the percentage of population that is foreign born, reduces the home bias.

A preference by investors for equities they are familiar with is in accordance with the findings of experiments reported in Heath and Tversky (1991). These experiments affirm the competence hypothesis, according to which 'people prefer to bet in a context where they consider themselves knowledgeable or competent than in a context where they feel ignorant or uniformed' (Heath and Tversky 1991: 7). Competence helps people to take credit when they succeed and sometimes provide protection against blame when they fail. Ignorance prevents people from taking credit for success and exposes them to blame in case of failure. If the decision maker has limited understanding of the problem, failure will be attributed to ignorance, whereas success is likely to be attributed to chance. In contrast, if the decision maker is an 'expert', success is attributable to knowledge, whereas failure can sometimes be attributed to chance. Consequently, investors are sometimes willing to forego the advantage of diversification and concentrate on a small number of companies with which they are familiar (Heath and Tversky 1991: 26). Van Nieuwerburgh and Veldkamp (2007) developed a model which claims that such an investment strategy results in extra return. They assume that investors have some prior information on the home assets. Given this prior information, it is more rational to learn more about the home assets than about the foreign assets. In this way investors magnify their comparative advantage in home assets and earn an extra return. Although the assets remain risky, the home investor can exploit fluctuations in asset prices since he has acquired information informing him when the payoff is high or low.

Migration

Until now we have assumed that goods and capital can cross borders, while individuals stay within their national boundaries. Now we turn to the literature on migration as far as this pays attention to culture. Within Europe migration crossing national borders is very low; so low, that some speak of a 'European immobility puzzle'. Similarly the number of workers commuting across borders is just a few per cent of the EU-labour force (see e.g. Van der Velde *et al.* 2005). This high degree of immobility has been approached from three perspectives. These three approaches differ with respect to (implicitly) assumed null hypothesis, which are: mobility, immobility and there is a threshold to be passed before people consider migration or commuting across national borders.[8]

The first approach takes mobility as the starting point and explains why the actual figures of migration and commuting are lower than expected by theory. Explanatory variables are differences in wages and unemployment rates and barriers to migration resulting from institutional and cultural differences. Belot and Ederveen (2006) belong to this group. The economic factors considered are income per capita and unemployment rates. Institutional factors are migration policy (do countries allow a free movement of migrants), housing transaction costs and portability of supplementary pensions. Cultural differences are represented by linguistic distance, religious distance and cultural distance. The latter is represented by the Kogut-Singh-index using Hofstede's cultural dimensions and a similar measure using the two dimensions Inglehart derived from the World Values Survey (see Appendix 1 Various cultural dimensions). Linguistic distance is based on the official languages in a country: the measure is based on the proximity between different words from each language (see Dyen *et al.* 1992). Religious distance is measured as the probability of drawing two individuals, one in each country, who would have different religions. Belot and Ederveen (2006) restrict their analysis to 22 OECD-countries, because they think that the extreme differences between developed and developing countries will determine the migration flows between these two groups of countries (see also Chapter 4 on country selection). They estimate a gravity relation for the period 1990–2003 and find significant negative effects of measures of linguistic, religious and cultural distances, where the latter is proxied by Ingehart's dimensions. An increase of 1 per cent of each of these distances reduces migration by 0.76 per cent (linguistic distance), 0.29 per cent religious distance, and 0.34 per cent (Inglehart's cultural distance). These effects are evaluated at the mean.

Since immobility is the rule, it makes sense to find explanatory factors why people stay where they are. The insiders' advantage approach (Straubhaar 1988, Tassinopoulos and Werner 1999: 11–13) suggests factors that generate particular economic values to being immobile. These factors are related to working practices and to social (leisure-time) practices. A person experiences all kinds of 'sunk benefits' such as working routines, insiders' knowledge and social ties (both at the work place and during leisure time). Hence, people are embedded in their working and social life and value the advantages of these. Moreover, people are risk averse and thus reluctant to move even if they expect to improve their income. In addition they might fear discrimination since they will be part of a minority in the country of destination. Finally migration will almost universally lead to a reduction of entitlements in the social security system of both the parent and host country.

The two previous approaches assume a linear and continuous relationship between the explanatory variables and mobility. As a result the agents are assumed to continuously consider the possibility of staying at home or moving to an unknown region. This is a very questionable assumption. Van der Velde *et al.* (2005), therefore, assume that individuals only consider migration at the moment that the difference between the perceived quality of life in their present place and the new place cross a threshold; the threshold of indifference. People want to claim a part of space as theirs (Van Houtum and Van Naerssen 2002). They create a space of ease and comfort where they feel at home. National borders are then expected 'to act very strongly as the intuitive spatial frames of reference for everyday practices' (Van der Velde *et al.* 2005: 82). These borders constitute a space on this side of the border (We and Here) and one on the other side (They and There). Consequently, for everyday practices such as searching for a job, people tend to look only at this side of the border. The other is only considered when the threshold of indifference is passed. After crossing this threshold of indifference agents actively consider moving. This active search process does not necessarily lead to a decision to move. This will only be the case if it results in surpassing the locational threshold. After one has decided to migrate, one has to choose a route to take. The factors influencing this decision are named the trajectory threshold (Van der Velde and Van Naersen, in press).

Empirical evidence of the relevance of thresholds in people's search strategy is found by Van der Velde *et al.* (2005). They interviewed unemployed in the Netherlands, where the unemployment rate is low and in the neighbouring part of Germany, where the unemployment rate is significantly higher. The number of unemployed considering working at the other side of the border is higher among the German respondents than among the Dutch. Some even did not consider working abroad, although the commuting distance is quite small (30 km or less). These results illustrate the importance of the mindset with respect to the space within which one is searching for a job. The respondents hardly mentioned hard factors such as social security, a different taxation system, health care, or cultural differences between Germany and the Netherlands. The two most important factors for not considering the nearby foreign labour market appeared to be no need to consider the option of working abroad and a lack of information about the foreign labour market (Van der Velde *et al.* 2005: 93).

The study by Van der Velde *et al.* is an example of critical or cultural geography. As in economics, scholars working in this field define culture as 'shared meanings shaping social practices, which are spatially specific and also include the construction of space' (Strüver 2004: 7). These shared meanings are not fixed but common meanings and can change over time. An important author in this field is Paasi, who has focused his research on the social construction of boundaries and on the changing representations of these boundaries, depending on social practices. In his view 'the construction of the territoriality is essentially a process of production and reproduction of mental representations which arise on the basis of diverging social and material interests' (Paasi 1996: 37). These representations make a distinction between us and them. The focus is not on the physical boundaries (the borders on the ground) but on the borders in the mind: the factors influencing the perception of people about their present living environment and about the potential new place. This approach shares with economics and culture the interest in intangible aspects and perceptions as well as the assumption that bounded rationality is a plausible way for modelling the decision-making process of individuals. As a consequence, in some situations people do not consider taking an action but wait and see.

Political coordination and cooperation

In the previous sections we have discussed various aspects of international economic relations and in particular the influence of culture on the international flow of goods, financial assets and people. In these cases, the transactions were *between* regions with different cultures. When discussing the entry modes of firms, we also paid attention to the cultural factors influencing the possibilities for employees and managers to operate in a foreign country and for business people from different cultures to cooperate within a multinational firm. Likewise one would expect cultural factors to influence political relations and cooperation in a similar manner. As in the previous studies, the influence of culture should be studied in addition to other factors, such as political power and economic and political interests.

In his seminal work *Culture's Consequences*, Hofstede (2001) discusses the associations of each of his dimensions with political affairs. Here we concentrate on international politics and international organizations. Of Hofstede's dimensions Power Distance and Uncertainty Avoidance are associated with the political process.[9] Individualism and Masculinity primarily affect issues countries want to defend. In particular, large differences between countries on the scores of these dimensions can complicate international cooperation. Since the scores on the various dimensions differ considerably between the member states of the European Union, the EU can be considered a laboratory of the consequences of cultural diversity for international cooperation. Here we discuss a few examples in which differences in culture within the European Union are claimed to have played a role. Thereafter, attention is drawn to the consequences of cultural differences between external (mostly Western) advisors and developing and transition countries.

When signing the Treaty of Maastricht, the large majority of the European Union's members agreed upon low inflation as the most important goal of monetary policy to be obtained by means of a politically independent central bank. During the period between the signing of the treaty and the establishment of the European Central Bank (ECB), the various domestic central banks acted accordingly. They attached a high value to inflation stabilization; so too did Banque de France. The French government, however, took various initiatives that potentially or directly were intended to undermine the political independence of the ECB. They wanted to establish a European economic government that could serve as a counterbalance to the ECB, to downgrade the importance of the central bankers and to split the term of the ECB's first president. So, although they had agreed upon the ECB's independence, and French monetary policy was in accordance with that of the other European central banks, the previously mentioned events suggest that French politicians had difficulty in accepting the central bank's independence. De Jong (2005) argues that this difficulty in accepting an independent central bank is related to the country's high score on Power Distance, which implies that the French president is the top political leader, who can decide on many issues. Moreover, until the coming to force of the Maastricht Treaty the central bank was dependent on the Ministry of Finance. Hence, monetary policy was to a great extent determined by political forces. Consequently, for the French the independence of the European

Central Bank as agreed upon in the Maastricht treaty, 'is at variance with French centralist tradition' (Szász 1999: 114). Thus, French top politicians had difficulty in accepting that their role had become much less dominant.

The downfall of the Santer's Commission is another example of conflicts arising from different cultural attitudes. A report on corrupt practices was leaked to the European parliament by a Dutch internal auditor of the Commission. The commissionaires most blamed for corrupt practices were from France and Spain. In their native countries these practices would have been acceptable and in accordance with political mores. These corrupt political practices correlate with the countries' high scores on Uncertainty Avoidance, Power Distance and indices of corruption. Within the European Union practices of favouring relatives and friends are considered corrupt and unacceptable.

The cultural factor is also important when officials or private persons from one culture provide advice for economic policy in countries with an entirely different culture. As described in Chapter 6 a period of economic growth is associated and preceded, according to some, by an attitude (such as achievement motivation) that favours economic growth. These are the attitudes of the people from the country itself. Economic development can only be obtained by the people from the country. Hence, policy advice by foreigners will enhance growth only if it fits with the population's own attitude and tradition. Advice by foreigners concerns the institutional structure of the society. Tensions will arise when the institutional structure, suggested by Western agents, is not in accordance with the national culture, which is formed over centuries (so tensions between the different levels of Figure 3.2). The culture of Western advisors differs from that of many developing countries with respect to the dimensions Collectivism/Individualism and Power Distance (Dia 1996: 53–56). Power Distance and Collectivism are (very) high in many non-Western countries (see Figure 1.2 in Dia 1996: 55). The challenge is to create effective institutions by reconciling universal principles for effective management with local culture. 'To be effective, the leadership profile and incentive system required to successfully operationalize these generic rules need to reflect and adapt countries' institutional and cultural contexts.' (Dia 1996: 53). He describes various cases which successfully reconcile local culture with institutional requests for effective management. From these best practices Dia (1996: 20, 21) develops an operational framework for successfully generating effective institutions. Aspects of this framework are: developing existing institutions, listening to stakeholders, the building of grassroots institutions, and networking to share lessons of experience and best practices.

Although Dia's study focuses on Africa, its message is relevant for all countries that obtain external advice or undergo a transition. Pejovich (2003) focuses on the increase in transaction costs if (formal) institutions are not in accordance with culture (informal institutions as he calls them). The free market economy with private property is 'a *way of life* in which each and every individual bears the value consequences of his or her decisions' (Pejovich 2003: 350). A transition from a centrally planned economy to a market economy will be obstructed by the old establishment and the 55 plus group, who fear a loss of vested interests. Pejovich gives several examples illustrating the problems arising when the new formal institutions do not fit with values and interests of the population.

Conclusions

Authors investigating the international exchange of goods, services and assets explicitly make a distinction between factors influencing information and communication channels and those affecting the understanding of foreign institutions and codes of conduct. The latter go under the heading institutional and cultural differences. Variables representing the degree of communication are common language, common border and the coverage of the foreign country in newspapers. Note that in contrast to some researchers investigating differences between countries (see Chapter 5), those investigating international relations explicitly consider language as *not* being part of culture. The internationalization school does explicitly pay attention to language differences but sees it along with cultural differences as part of the psychic distance. Some unambiguously share the criticism we raised in Chapter 5; using the same language does not necessarily enhance the understanding of each others position let alone increase sympathy for it. It can also lead to a widening of the differences between participants. Moreover, in many empirical studies common language and common border become insignificant when other measures of familiarity are used, such as migration and patriotism.

Another observation is that international economists have recently shown interest in the role of non-tangible factors for international trade and flows of Foreign Direct Investment. They, often implicitly, focus on the firms' decision of servicing the foreign market by exports or by goods produced abroad (FDI). Scholars of International Business on the other hand, have a tradition of more than two decades during which they have studied the role of cultural factors for decision-making by multinational firms. They focused, however, on the establishment mode of FDI and did not pay much attention to the export/FDI choice. Only a few investigated the cultural influences on the choice whether to export towards a foreign country or to set-up an affiliation or other form of FDI.

Sometimes genetic differences are used as proxies for cultural differences. Giuliano *et al.* (2007) show that these differences reflect transportation costs resulting from geographical barriers. Thus genetic differences seem to be incorrect proxies for cultural differences.

The studies on the home bias of trade, investments and migration indicate the weakness of approaches starting from an optimizing agent without paying attention to the situation from which the agent makes his or her decision. A more promising theory is the one which starts from the situation from which the decision maker makes a choice and then investigates the likely incentives that make him or her rethink the position.

Chapter 10

Conclusions and recommendations

At the end of this book on culture and economics, we seize the opportunity to draw some concluding remarks and make suggestions for future research.

Conclusions

Values and culture

As has been described in the Introduction some anthropologists use a very broad definition of culture, which includes the complex whole of almost all human activities. Such a concept is regarded as unworkable by economists and some anthropologists, who use a more concise definition of culture. Culture consists of values and practices: rituals, symbols and heroes. The discussion of the various streams of literature on culture and economics in this book reveals that in practice, economists restrict their analysis even further. Only values, the core of culture, are used in economic analysis. These values are regarded as proxies for preferences and are supposed to influence economic institutions and economic outcomes. This almost exclusive use of values and neglect of the other elements of culture, suggests that it is more appropriate to use the term values or value system instead of culture.

Culture, institutions, and performance

Culture and institutions appear to be two closely related concepts. Both are said to enable and constrain economic behaviour. DiMaggio (1994) distinguishes between the constitutive types and effects of culture and the regulatory types and effects of culture. A similar distinction is made by North (1990: 3, 4) with regard to the effects of institutions. These are defined as humanly devised constraints and are thought to structure the way societies evolve over time. By reducing uncertainty institutions provide structure to everyday life. North distinguishes formal from informal institutions, whereby the informal institutions correspond with what is called culture in this book.

The close relationship between culture and institutions is also reflected in empirical studies. Researchers, who have developed cultural dimensions, want to validate the dimensions found by regressing them on variables representing economic and political institutions and economic performance (see Chapter 4). On the other hand those interested in the influence of culture on economic phenomena relate economic institutions to cultural variables (see Chapter 5). Using existing economic theory, the latter formulate hypotheses about the relationship between economic institutions and cultural dimensions. Empirical investigations support many of these hypotheses.

Culture is considerably less often found to be an explanatory factor of economic performance, in particular, economic growth. This difference in results between culture and institutions versus culture and economic development can be attributed to the above mentioned similarity in expected effects of culture and institutions. It can also be considered a validation of the theoretical framework frequently used in this study, according to which culture and institutions are much more closely related than culture and economic performance (see Figure 3.2, for example). Economic performance is determined by both culture and institutions (and governance). The latter two can enforce and compensate each other, so that the net effect of culture on economic development is uncertain. This result is in accordance with the cross-country regressions in which economic development is determined by political institutions: some authors find significant effects of these institutions on economic outcomes, others cannot find any systematic effect (see Acemoglu and Robinson 2008: 267 for some references).

Religion, language, and ethnicity as culture

In some studies culture is approximated with religion, language or ethnicity. In this book we devoted an entire chapter, Chapter 7, to religion as culture. From this analysis we conclude that taking religion as a proxy for culture is very inadequate. The main religions consist of various denominations, which have very different views on the preferred structure of the economy. Even within relatively small religious groups a great diversity of opinions can be found. Iannaccone's (1992) study of evangelical Christians in the United States finds that these Christians share the same opinion on many ethical issues, but differ widely in opinion when it comes to economics. Then attitudes vary from a free market economy to a socialized economy, with characteristics of the previous communist economies. Moreover, the history of the various versions of the Biblical book Deuteronomy suggests that Holy Scriptures themselves are influenced by the power distribution at the time of their writing. Consequently, the opinion reflected in these books is much less stable than is implicitly suggested by those who want to proxy culture by means of religion.[1]

Results reported in Chapter 9 reveal that differences in genes can be ascribed to physical barriers, such as mountains and seas. Being a member of a particular ethnic group does not correspond with a particular set of values. Thus, it is also unclear which values are connected with the different ethnical groups, let alone why. Consequently, ethnicity is of no help for explaining economic institutions and behaviour.

Similarly, groups speaking the same language do not necessarily share the same culture. The cultural differences between the Dutch and the Flemish, Dutch speaking Belgians, can serve as an example. Using Hofstede's measure for culture reveals that the cultural attitudes of the Flemish have much more in common with those of the Walloons, the French speaking Belgians, than with the Dutch (Hofstede 1980: 228, Claes and Gerritsen 2002: 143–163). These differences are regarded as barriers for transactions between the Dutch and Flemish (Van Houtum 1998). So, using language as a measure for culture, in the sense of common values and customs, is in our view inadequate. Nevertheless at some phases of a research project in economics and culture, one has to consider the consequences of language and language differences. The language used in experiments can trigger a particular attitude (Akkerman *et al.* 2007). Researchers should be aware of the possible effects and biases of the language selected in experiments and surveys. Furthermore, in interviews on international transactions, respondents often report their perceived inadequate ability to use a foreign language as a barrier for international transactions or for seeking employment in a neighbouring country. This suggests the need for research on the role of language and differences in language on international transactions.

The practice of equating culture with religion, language or ethnicity implies a view of culture as a whole, the broad and impractical definition used by some anthropologists. The results presented above show convincingly that such a broad concept does not help in understanding the motives and preferences of people, and thus does not contribute to explaining economic phenomena.

When does culture matter?

When can one expect that culture will significantly contribute to explain differences between units? As we have written in the Introduction, there is a tendency to explain the unknown by culture; the larger the differences between the group (society or social class) the researchers belong to and the group under investigation, the larger the chance that culture is used as an explanatory factor (DiMaggio 1994). Consequently, DiMaggio (1994: 47) writes '. . . the more similar the units being compared, the more likely it is safe to ignore culture and rely instead on structural explanations'. Results presented in Chapter 5 argue in favour of the opposite, the more similar the units are the more important cultural differences become (cf. Dekker *et al.* 2006: 39). Studies on the importance of financial markets, for example, find more cultural dimensions as significantly explaining differences within a group of Western countries than when the sample is extended with less developed countries. The reason is that the structural features distinguishing developed from developing countries, such as pension funds and social networks, already explain a great deal of the variance.

Another result is that the influence of culture on a particular economic phenomenon can change over time and can be found if the units have freedom to manoeuvre; that is, can choose different positions. In Chapter 5 we reported a time varying influence of cultural dimensions on the openness of an economy. Openness is measured by an index of economic policy: whether there are restrictions on international trade and capital flows. The cultural dimensions (Uncertainty Avoidance in particular) significantly explain the cross-cultural differences from the end of the 1960s to the end of the 1980s. During the first decades after World War II the lack of industrial infrastructure and of monetary reserves forced all continental European countries to restrict the international flow of goods and capital. After 1990 all industrialized countries agreed upon the idea that a policy of free international flow was to be preferred. In the spirit of DiMaggio (1994: 43), there are no observable differences and thus no role for culture to explain these differences.

Generally, international transactions will be more difficult if cultural differences become larger. Cultural differences can create misunderstanding and irritation. Similarly, a good advice to foreigners is always to take the cultural differences between the advisor and the advised into account.

Politicized culture, power distribution, and trends in values

Although, we have argued above that religion is an inadequate measure of culture in the sense of common values and habits, religion and religious differences are often used by political leaders to create what we have called a politicized culture. Examples are the attempts by Mahathir, the then prime minister of Malaysia, to establish a modern version of Islam which corresponded with his economic policies. Another is the islamization movement originating in India as a reaction to the fear that Hindus would dominate independent India. This movement for an Islamic economy is sometimes presented as built upon Islamic teachings and at other times as a third way between rough capitalism and communism. Finally, the African Renaissance propagated by the South African government of Membeki illustrates that it is not always religion which is used as a vehicle for establishing a national identity.

These examples illustrate the importance of power and power distribution when studying national culture. Leaders are in a much better position to change institutions and to influence common views than ordinary people. Quantitative studies take the average of the respondents' answers as a measure of a group's values and attitudes and thus neglect the different roles played by authorities. Case studies are more appropriate for investigating the role of unequal access to power. As Bernstein (2006) illustrates in the case of the South African Renaissance, using both methods can reveal whether the message brought forward by the leaders has any impact on public opinion. Alesina and Glaeser's study suggest that these invented images can have a long-lasting effect; the idea of the United States as a land abundant with opportunities, was proclaimed during the time of its foundation and still has an impact on public opinion.

The role of history

In several cases history plays an important role in the field of culture and economics. This book reports on many periods during which politicians and other leaders make reference to a beautiful and glorious past to establish a national or religious identity. Mahathir, for example, referred to Malay history in order to create the idea that his policies were a prolongation of previous times (Maseland 2006a, 2006b). The adherents of Islamic economics find their inspiration in Islam's 'Golden Age', which consists of the 39 years that span the leadership of the Prophet Mohammad over the original *umma* and the tenure of the 'rightly guided' four caliphs who succeeded him as the leaders of the *umma*. Why do these leaders refer to past events and not to glorious futures?[2] In a similar spirit Esposito and Mogahed (2007: 114, 115) ascribe the successful protest of Muslim women against a proposal of a commission consisting of highly placed religious and governmental individuals, to the fact that these women argued that the proposal was against the Islamic tradition. All these cases suggest that history and tradition can be powerful arguments for preventing or enhancing change. Why is it that referring to the past and thus pretending continuity seems to be such a convincing argument?

Kuran suggests that these and similar examples underscore cognitive psychologists' findings that individuals attach a higher weight to losses than to gains of comparable size (see e.g. Tversky and Kahneman 1991). These results suggest that 'all else being equal, people are more responsive to a promise of improvement when framed as eliminating a loss than when it is presented as providing a new gain. Accordingly, reformers commonly use historical reference points that make experienced changes look like degenerations' (Kuran 2004a: 96).

Methods are complementary

The history of culture and economics has taught us that culture was part of economics until the mid twentieth century. At the beginning of twentieth century culture was left aside by mainstream economists and became the subject matter of sociology, which became an independent discipline within the social sciences. The *Methodenstreid* preceded this divorce between mainstream economics and culture. In this war two camps were standing opposite to each other: researchers seeking for generally valid rules (laws) and those stressing the uniqueness or contingency of every event/phenomenon.[3]

During the twentieth century similar wars have been fought within sociology and management research. In both cases the opinions differed with respect to the degree of generalization and generalizability of results. Along the same line a different appraisal of quantitative and qualitative approaches can be observed. Those in favour of searching for general roles have a preference for quantitative methods; such as surveys and regression analyses, whereas others favour descriptive techniques. In many aspects these different opinions lead to unholy and unfruitful paradigm wars and separate research lines. In general, quantitative research necessitates the researcher to be quite explicit about the assumptions used. The approach is also well suited for finding generally valid rules (laws). It can disentangle causal relations if adequate longitudinal data are available. In the field of culture and economics, however, longitudinal data on values are generally lacking. Qualitative, descriptive techniques can then be very useful.[4] Typically the phenomena or organizations are extensively described and figures are used but remain scarce. It is not always clear which definition of culture the researcher is using although the studies themselves suggest a relatively broad definition. Another disadvantage can be the lack of objectivity and generalizability of the results. These considerations led to the appraisal of using both techniques 'a combination of a qualitative approach for depth and empathy with a quantitative approach for confirmation' (Hofstede 2001: 393). Fortunately, an increasing number of authors are aware of the necessity and advantages of applying both techniques.

Causality

Many researchers in the field of economics and culture regard causality as an important part of their analysis. They are well aware of the fact that culture, institutions and economic performance are simultaneously determined, so that reverse causality can easily occur. According to colleagues of sociology, sociologists are well aware of the possibility of reverse causality but regard it as impossible to correct for it and thus do not put effort into disentangling the direction of causality but avoid claiming a direction by phrases as 'y is related to x' instead of 'y is determined by x'. Economists, however, recommend using instrumental variables estimators for correcting biases resulting from reverse causality. Instrumental variables should be exogenous to the endogenous variables. Moreover, researchers do not know the speed of the interaction process between culture, institutions and economic performance. Some, Williamson for example, argue that these developments are very slow and can last for centuries. Then one should select variables representing culture in previous centuries. These considerations lead to a two-step estimation procedure which consists of first explaining the current measure of culture by a set of variables representing institutions of previous centuries and second explaining the current phenomenon (income per capita, for example) by among other things the part of current culture, as this can be explained by institutions in previous centuries. Hence, one finds first the extent to which a trace of past institutions and circumstances can be found in the current culture and second the effect of that part of culture that can be explained by these past institutions on the current economic phenomenon.

We want to make some critical remarks with respect to this practice. First, the cross-country or cross-region estimates provide information on the stability of countries' and regions' relative position only. No information is obtained about the trend over time. For example, a positive coefficient in the regression of trust in 2000 on the literacy rate in 1800 indicates that in the year 2000 regions, which had a relatively high literacy rate in 1800, score higher on the trust index than those with a lower literacy rate in 1800. In fact one is testing a relative stability hypothesis. Similarly, Hofstede's suggestion that globalization and other forces of change over time do not change the relative position of national cultures Hofstede (2001: 36). Vinken *et al.* (2004: 21) call this phenomenon 'relative cultural stability'. This concept and the cross-country regressions, however, do not shed light on the change over time and thus the causal relations in the time domain.

Second, this instrumental variables procedure easily leads to an intensive search for appropriate instrumental variables and thus detracts attention from the subject matter. Moreover, the regressions provide information on the extent to which historical institutions and circumstance still have an effect. Implicitly, a quite static view on culture is taken. As has been argued in preceding chapters, culture is dynamic. The interesting questions do not concern influences from the past but factors which dynamically interact with culture. So, if changes over time are noticeable, what are the driving forces of these changes, under which conditions are these changes occurring?, are changes in values preceding those in institutions or vice-versa?, etc. Cross-country regressions using data collected at a particular point in time are inadequate for answering these types of questions.

Actually, studies investigating changes over time in values, institutions and their relations are scarce. Among the authors of cultural dimensions, Ingelhart (1997) is the one who most explicitly investigates cultural change.

He develops the scarcity hypothesis, according to which 'one places greatest subjective value on those things that are in a relatively short supply' (Inglehart 1997: 33). Consequently, generations who grew up with the idea that survival could be taken for granted, attach a greater value to immaterial issues, such as environment and personal development. Vinken *et al.* (2004: 22) regard this explanation as based too much on processes and pay too little attention to the individual and groups of individuals, who are the ones who generate change. Hofstede (2001: 254, 255) compares results from the two waves of his survey, and finds an upward trend in Individualism during those four years. The increase in Individualism is correlated with wealth and in Hofstede's view the causality runs from an increase in wealth to Individualism. People become more individualistic if their material resources increase. Inglehart's attention to changes in trends and Hofstede's attempts were made possible because these authors (and especially Inglehart) could make use of different waves of the survey. The two other studies analyzing cultural change are Allen *et al.* (2007) for some Asian countries and Hagenaars *et al.* (2003) with respect to three waves of the European Values Survey.

Theory and empirical evidence

In this book we have paid little attention to theory. This might reflect the author's expertise and intellectual bias (see the section on Subjectivity). However, it also reflects the state of the art (see also Vinken *et al.* 2004: 22–24). Nowadays there are a few theoretical studies on the mechanism of intergenerational transmission of values and norms (Bisin and Verdier 2001, and some recent references mentioned in Tabellini 2008b: 290).

Tabellini (2008a) builds on this work about intergenerational transmission when studying the scope for cooperation. In his model, cooperation results from material incentives and value. Parents pass values on to their children. These values are derived from the parents' own values (backward looking) and the children's future environment (forward looking). In the equilibrium incentives to cooperate and values interact with each other. A gradual move towards improved values strengthens the incentives to cooperate and vice versa. The individuals' values also shape voters' behaviour and thus influence cooperative decisions. Adding an endogenous policy choice to the model creates a path-dependency, in the sense that the equilibrium depends on initial conditions. When low morality characterizes initial conditions, the equilibrium is characterized by poor values, lax legal enforcement and a lack of cooperation. This model can explain the influence of past institutional structures on present values, and the correlation between present values and present economic institutions. It still has a fatalistic flavour: an economy once started with wrong conditions will never evolve towards a better equilibrium. Here one would like to know whether and under what conditions a switch towards an upward track would be possible. Would an external influence, such as the implementation of the West German institutions in former East Germany be of any help? Therefore, as well as modelling intergenerational transfer of values at the *individual* level, we are also in need of understanding the mechanisms by which *collective* beliefs change. Culture does not refer to an individual's opinion but to the beliefs of a collectivity.

Recommendations for future research

This section sketches a strategy for empirical research in Culture and Economics and some topics we regard as important for future research.

Research strategy for empirical research[5]

What then would be the preferable research strategy for empirical studies? In my view, such a strategy consists of the following phases. First of all one should determine the subject of the study. Is this average economic growth, economic development in a broader sense or fundamental changes in development strategies which result in a higher level of economic development? After the aim of the study is selected, one has to search for potentially explanatory variables in previously published empirical and theoretical studies and material found in the countries concerned. It is here that a broad view is recommended. Although I think that a researcher has to start with an investigation of the plausible economic and political factors, he or she should have an open mind for other factors such as the role of values. Of course a model developed by the researcher himself or herself can also guide the research for relevant factors. Ideally this stage ends with a number of hypotheses about the relationships between the various factors (including the cultural ones).

The next phase consists of an empirical investigation of the hypotheses' relevance. I recommend choosing those method(s) which are most appropriate for testing the hypotheses. Often applying more than one methodology will be the best practice. Cross-country or cross-region regressions can provide information on the validity of general patterns. Case studies, historical investigations and interviews give more detail and are better suited for finding causal relations. Preferably, these methods are empirically oriented and not solely based on reading important texts, since texts can be misleading and do not always inform us about real life (see Alatas 2002: 115). In this way the procedure gives researchers an incentive to consider all possible explanations and thus might prevent a biased cultural view. In the end culture is only one among many possible explanations and maybe not the most important or most prominent one. A parsimonious explanation implies that 'if "hard" variables (economic, biological, technological) predict a country variable better, cultural indexes are redundant' (Hofstede 2001: 68).[6]

The study by Alesina and Glaeser on the differences in welfare systems between Europe and the United States, discussed in Chapter 5, serves as a good example (Alesina and Glaeser 2004). Their analysis starts with all factors mentioned in the literature as possible explanatory variables for the differences of welfare systems between Europe and the United States. After having considered all possible explanatory factors Alesina and Glaeser analyse each of these factors by both quantitative and qualitative methods. Among the latter is a historical analysis of the image of the United States as the land of opportunity, as created by the first migrants and those who had financial interest in attracting immigrants to North America.

Dynamics

In several places, this book has drawn attention to the dynamics of culture and institutions. Whereas researchers accept that culture can change, in practice many are inclined to suggest that it is static or changes only very slowly. As mentioned before, the search for historical events and variables as instruments in regression analyses, distracts attention from the system's dynamics and leads to a static view on culture.

Longitudinal analyses are in our view needed for correct analyses of the dynamics between culture, institutions and economic performance. The study by Allen *et al.* (2007) is a good example. Since, institutional structures and values change slowly it can take a long time before this type of study reveals results. Historical analyses of the change in the dominant view on a particular topic can also be used for investigating this relationship over time. An advantage of a historical study is that the events have already taken place, so that researchers do not have to wait until the data become available. A disadvantage however, is that it can prove to be difficult to obtain information about the exact date a change in dominant opinion emerged.

Another possibility for studying the causal relations is to make use of extraordinary events, such as the experiences of the transition economies. Moreover, the differences in development between the various countries in this area enhance the possibilities of analyzing the influence of values on the developments in institutional structure and economic performance. Can the differences in institutional structures in these countries be attributed to differences in values? What is the causal direction of this relationship? The developments in the former *Demokratische Republik Deutschland* (DDR) form an ideal laboratory for answering questions on the effects of institutional change on values. After the reunification of Germany, the *Länder* of the former DDR were forced to implement all institutions of the previous West Germany. What has been the effect of this abrupt change in the structure of society on the value patterns of its inhabitants? Who were the ones who could adopt their behaviour relatively swiftly? One might expect that education, job opportunities and age were relevant factors in this respect. But still, it is interesting to know the exact relationships and thresholds if any exist. Both survey data and more specific case studies can help in this respect.

Studying the dynamics of a system means that one is studying the evolution over time. Variables determining these movements over time can be quite different from those explaining cross-country differences. In economics, for example, unemployment in a particular period can be explained by among other things the increase in wages during previous periods. In general, institutions will not have changed during the sample period, so that they are unable to explain the development of unemployment over time. Differences in institutions are, however, important candidates for explaining differences in unemployment across countries. When investigating the effect of culture one should be aware of these differences. A related issue is the use of cross-country regressions. These regressions reveal only the relative position of countries. No information on the trend is provided.

Empirical findings can inspire theoretical models for explaining movements over time. Based upon the discussions in this book we recommend not using models that assume rational behaviour in the sense that agents know the model. This would contradict the reason for considering the role of culture in economic analysis. A promising approach takes the situation agents are in as starting point and investigates under which conditions they decide to change institutional structures (much like the cultural geographic approach of migration in Chapter 9). Institutional changes are costly, especially in terms of time and expenses, for creating and mobilizing a majority that is willing to implement changes in institutions. These costs can be regarded to be sunk and thus create hurdles. I expect that an important part of theory has to consist of explaining when and how these hurdles are passed. Possible reasons and mechanisms could be: differences between what people want and their actual situation, external pressure, and an important leader or group of leading persons.

The possible role of leaders brings us to the importance of power and the distribution of power when studying the forces changing a culture. Culture is not neutral; 'in virtually every society, it legitimates the established social order – partly because the dominant elite try to shape it to help perpetuate their rule' (Inglehart 1997: 26). In this respect Kuran's concept of preference falsification could prove to be useful. Preference falsification is 'the act of misrepresenting one's genuine wants under perceived social pressures' (Kuran 1995: 3). The effects of it can go both ways (ibid: 16). Expressed preferences have social consequences and the social climate may transform the preferences people are trying to hide: their private preferences. Due to limited cognitive capacity individuals have to rely on the knowledge of others, which opens the possibility of influential groups manipulating public opinion and through the resulting social pressure to determine private opinion as well. This process can result in a situation where previously known facts or ideas are suppressed and forgotten. By means of a few selected cases, Kuran illustrates that his framework can be used to explain stability in preferences and disruptive changes in regimes and preferences.

Individual and group

Culture is about a collectivity. This group consists of many individuals. The behaviour of the group, however, will not be equal to the sum or average of the individuals. Hence, reasoning valid at the individual level cannot be applied at the level of the group. This reverse ecological fallacy (see Chapter 4), incorrectly treats groups as king-sized individuals. Nevertheless, the behaviour and values of individuals will have relevance for the functioning of the group and vice versa. In particular, Chapter 8 on social capital has extensively discussed the different meanings and effects of social capital at the level of the individual, firm and society.

Many aspects of culture have a multilevel nature. The interactions between the different levels form an under-researched area. In which way do particular institutions help or hamper beliefs and behaviour at the individual level? For example, under which conditions does a particular institution help or hinder the formation of trust between individuals? Conversely, when will changes in opinions of individuals lead to a change at a higher level of society?

Subjectivity

In this book we have studied the influence of culture on economic institutions and economic performance. This analysis revealed that a universally valid model of the economy does not exist; cultural elements of the group (often the nation) are of importance too. Of course this subjectivity does not pertain only to national organizations. One might expect that the researchers themselves are also influenced by the environment to which they have been exposed during their formative years. Consequently, theories may have national cultural elements that hamper their applicability across borders. In management studies many ideas and proposals for effective management are developed by professors from American business schools. Whereas these ideas work well within the American and related cultures, they might appear to be ineffective in quite different cultures (see Hofstede 2001: Ch. 8 for similar studies). In general, pleas for foreign solutions to a domestic problem often fail, because the national cultural context is not taken into account. Institutions are not changed in a vacuum but are embedded in value systems as we have argued in this book. A good example is Hillary Clinton's failed attempt to overhaul the American health care system according to principles of solidarity used in continental Europe.

Another consequence of this notion of subjectivity is that disciplines and the treatment or focus by a specific researcher contains subjective elements. Americans score high on Individualism. This could be a reason why in psychology, which focuses on individual's behaviour (except for Sigmund Freud), Americans are the most important scholars, whereas in sociology, which studies groups and their behaviour, Europeans play a more prominent role (see Hofstede 2004: 276). In this book much attention is paid to empirical quantitative research. Qualitative research and theory get less attention. In my view this reflects the present situation of the literature on culture and economics. Of course it could also be, and to a certain extent certainly is, a predisposition of my own resulting from the fact that I have been educated as an econometrician. Consequently, I am more inclined to pay attention to quantitative studies than to qualitative ones, and feel more familiar with the former. Does this imply an entirely subjective view on research and an everything-goes attitude? No, but it reflects an awareness of the subjectivity of an academic researcher's view and methods and a call to study the same object from different angles. This position is nicely summarized in the following quotation from the man who through his writings attracted my attention to the relevance of culture for economic analysis, Geert Hofstede (2004: 272)

> What I tell my students is: *dimensions do not exist*! Culture does not exist either. Dimensions and culture in general are *constructs*, products of our minds that help us to simplify the overwhelming complexity of the real world, so as to understand and predict it. They are useful as they do this, and redundant when they don't. And because the real world is so complex, there is not just one way to simplify it. Different authors' minds produce different sets of dimensions.

Appendix 1
Various cultural dimensions

In this appendix we briefly describe the most frequently cited studies which have used survey data for deriving cultural dimensions. The studies considered are those by Hofstede, Schwartz, the GLOBE-team, Trompenaars, and Inglehart. For each study we sketch the characteristics of the respondents, the sample size and some other features of the research design. Thereafter the individual dimensions are briefly described. These descriptions are based on the corresponding author's publications. From these descriptions the reader can already derive that conceptually some dimensions of the different studies are correlated. We do not describe these correlations but refer to Hofstede (2001, esp. Appendix 6, and 2006) for correlations between the dimensions.

Hofstede

The cultural dimensions of Hofstede were obtained from the data of a survey which was conducted in two rounds, in 1968–69 and in 1972–73, and embraced about 120,000 native employees of subsidiaries of IBM in 40 countries. Fifty-nine questions were selected for further analysis. They were of two types: perceptions (subjective evaluations of an aspect or problem of the work situation; for example 'How often does your manager expect a large amount of work from you?'); and personal goals and beliefs (statements related to an ideal job or to general issues in industry; for example 'How important is it for you to have opportunity for high earnings?' or whether a respondent agrees with the statement 'Competition between employees usually does more harm than good'). Twenty-two questions concerned the importance of various work goals (such as monetary reward, interesting work, and use of skills). These scores were factor-analyzed, leading to two factors, which could be called individual–collective and ego–social. Two other dimensions were identified through an eclectic analysis, combining theoretical reasoning with correlation analysis. In particular, Hofstede looked at questions related to hierarchical relationships and to work stress, because from theoretical considerations he thought they were important. He found that answers to several other questions correlated with answers to those two questions.

Hofstede thus identified four dimensions on which national cultures differ. A country could be given a score on each of the dimensions on the basis of scores on each of the questions related to this dimension. Analysis of the work of other authors shows that the results of many surveys on specific issues correlate with countries' scores on dimensions. So a range of additional values and orientations related to a particular dimension could be identified. The first dimension is Power Distance, which measures the extent to which the less powerful members of organizations and a society accept and expect that power is distributed unequally. The second dimension is Uncertainty Avoidance which measures the extent to which members of society feel either comfortable or uncomfortable in unstructured situations. The basic problem involved is the degree to which societies try to control the uncontrollable. The third dimension is Individualism versus Collectivism. It measures the degree to which individuals are supposed to look after themselves or are integrated into groups, such as families. The fourth dimension found by Hofstede is Masculinity versus Femininity, which deals with the relative emphasis in society on caring for others and quality of life on the one hand, and achievement and success on the other. Feminine societies stress equality and solidarity and feel that the needy should be helped; managers in these societies strive for consensus. Masculine societies stress competition and feel that the strong should be supported; conflicts are resolved by fighting them out; managers make decisions on their own. An independent study with Asian researchers found an extra dimension, namely long-term versus short-term orientation, which refers to the extent to which a culture programmes its members to accept delayed gratification of their material, social and emotional needs (see Chinese Culture Connection 1987).

Schwartz

Another major study of values is conducted by the Israeli psychologist Schwartz. He and his colleagues developed a survey intended to include all the distinct goals likely to be recognized across cultures. The survey included 56 single values which were drawn from the values identified by previous researchers and found in religious and philosophical writings about values in many countries. Respondents rate their importance 'as a guiding principle in their lives' on a nine-point scale. The authors established that 45 of these values had reasonably equivalent meanings across nations, so they used only these variables. By now, more than 60,000 respondents from 63 nations have completed the survey. The dimensions, however, were identified using samples from 38 nations. Schwartz uses two types of samples – schoolteachers and university students.

For each society, the mean importance rating of each of the 45 values was computed. The correlation coefficients were computed and were analyzed with the statistical technique called the smallest space analysis. This technique represents the values as points in multidimensional space, such that the distances between points reflect the empirical relations among the values as measured by the correlations between their importance ratings. The groups of points which were empirically close to each other and substantively related were interpreted as representing value categories of related values. Once these categories were established, scores for their importance were computed for each country as averages of the scores for each value included in the category. Seven such value categories were identified, which were combined in three dimensions.

The first dimension, autonomy/embeddedness, concerns the relationship of the individual and the group. In embedded cultures, people are viewed as embedded in the collectivity. In autonomy cultures people are viewed as autonomous entities who find meaning in life in their own uniqueness and who are encouraged to express and act upon their preferences, feelings and motives. Schwartz distinguishes two types of autonomy. Intellectual autonomy encourages individuals to pursue their ideas (important values are curiosity, broadmindedness, and creativity). Affective autonomy encourages individuals to pursue affectively positive experiences for themselves (important values are pleasure, exciting life, and varied life).

The second dimension, hierarchy/egalitarianism, deals with the ways to guarantee responsible behaviour that preserves the social fabric. Hierarchical cultures rely on hierarchical systems of ascribed roles to insure responsible behaviour. Important values are: social power, authority, humility, and wealth. In egalitarian cultures people recognize one another as moral equals who share basic interests as human beings. Important values are equality, social justice, responsibility, and honesty.

The third dimension deals with the relation of humankind to the natural and social world. The orientation Schwartz named mastery encourages active self-assertion in order to master, change and exploit the natural and social environment to attain personal or group goals (important values are ambition, success, daring, competition). The polar response to this problem is to accept the world as it is, trying to fit in rather than to change or exploit. This cultural orientation, labelled harmony has unity with nature, protecting the environment, world at peace as important values.

GLOBE

In the beginning of the 1990s, Robert J. House started a project on the acceptance and effectiveness of different leadership styles around the world. This project became the Global Leadership and Organizational Behavior Effectiveness Research Program (GLOBE), in which about 170 researchers from 62 countries collaborated. During the years 1994–97 data were collected from 17,370 middle managers in 951 local organizations belonging to one of three industries – food processing, financial service, and telecommunication – in 62 societies.

The items used in the questionnaire were derived from the literature. This resulted in 371 cultural and 382 leadership items. PhD students and country investigators sorted the culture items into theoretical categories represented by the a priori dimensions of culture. Items were deleted, if less than 80 per cent of the sorters categorized them in the categories for which they were theoretically intended. In addition to the sorting, items were deleted because the country investigators found words or phrases that were ambiguous or impossible to be adequately translated into the native language As a result of sorting and editing about 50 per cent of the items were deleted. Two independent pilot studies were conducted to assess the psychometric properties of the culture scales and to empirically develop leadership scales. A sample of 17,370 middle managers from 62 different societies formed the basis of the dimensions presented by the GLOBE team. Various statistical procedures were used to investigate the validity and reliability of the scales obtained. The data were corrected for cultural response bias. Archival data were used to assess the degree to which the societal level scales are meaningful indicators of the constructs they are intended to measure. Both quantitative and the corresponding objective correlates, as well as content analysis of the Culturgrams of the societies, were used. The 1998 Culturgrams provide comparable and consistent four page descriptions of the societies. Implicit and explicit concepts were derived from these descriptions. In addition, the researchers investigated correspondence with the dimensions developed by Hofstede and Schwartz and of questions from the World Values Survey.

The questions in the GLOBE-project differ in three respects from those of the other studies described in this appendix. First, a distinction is made between values and practices. The questions used for measuring practices refer to the present situation (As Is questions), whereas those of the values are phrased in terms that the respondents find the phenomenon should be (the Should Be questions). For seven cultural dimensions they found practices and values to be negatively correlated. For In-Group Collectivism, this correlation is insignificant and for Gender Egalitarianism it is positive and significant. Hofstede (2006: 886) thinks that the negative correlations between 'As Is' and 'Should Be' items originates from the fact that respondents refer to values when describing practices. 'They tended to criticize their society from an ideological point of view (from "things are A but should rather be B" to "things are B but should rather be A").' (Hofstede 2006: 886). The GLOBE team (Javidan *et al.*, 2006) responds to this hypothesis by grouping the countries into four quartiles based on their cultural practices scores. They find that

> generally the most notable relationship between values and practices is manifested in societies with practices scores in the extreme regions, either high or low. For example, societies with Future Orientation practices scores in the fourth quartile (lowest) show the highest upward move in their aspirations.
>
> (Javidan *et al.* 2006: 901)

All societies have an upward aspiration but this aspiration is higher in societies with a low Future Orientation practices. Cultural practices are associated with many societal phenomena. Cultural values are associated with leaders' reported effectiveness. These differences between values and practices ask for a more detailed understanding of cultures and their consequences. (Javidan *et al.* 2006: 903). A recent paper by Van Hoorn and Maseland (in press) frames the results in terms of utility and argues that the answers to many questions in these studies (those of Inglehart, GLOBE-project) measure marginal utility, whereas the authors started from the point of thinking in terms of the level of utility.

Second, GLOBE's questions about values differ from those of the other studies in that the other studies ask respondents for their *own* preferred end states, whereas GLOBE asks respondents to give their preferences about the behaviour of *others*. Hofstede (2006) and Smith (2006) see no logical reason why these two different wordings measure the same values. 'If I want to be powerful, it does not follow that I want others to be powerful' (Smith 2006: 917). Fischer (2006) presents results that indicate when these two forms of questions correlate. He argues in favour of a strong positive correlation between self and cultural ratings for values that are formed during one's childhood. These values are well internalized. A moderate positive correlation between self and culture referent ratings is expected for values referring to the relationship between individuals and others and their environment. No correlation is expected between these types of rating for values referring to maintaining and preserving the social order. The various cultural dimensions are taken from Schwartz's study. In contrast to Schwartz, Fishers asks students from ten cultures to answer the questions in terms of 'for people in my country' instead of 'for myself'. For the ten cultures these scores are compared to the values provided by Schwartz, which are based on questions referring to one's own values. This procedure confirms the expected positive correlation between values internalized early in one's life (embeddedness and affective autonomy). No correlation was found between the self and society referent ratings for the other dimensions. Hence, whether the answers on these two types of questions correspond with each other seems to depend on the dimensions investigated.

Finally, GLOBE makes a distinction between values and practices in the respondents' *organization* and in their *society*. Two different versions of the questionnaire were used for obtaining independent measures of these organizational and societal items. One version contained 78 questions asking about the organization, the other contained the same questions for the society. Both versions contained the same 112 leadership attributes questions. Half of the respondents in each organization completed the organizational culture questionnaire, and the other half completed the societal culture questionnaire.

GLOBE's dimensions

Performance Orientation is the extent to which a community encourages and rewards setting challenging goals, innovation and performance improvement. All countries report a high score for the value of Performance Orientation. Performance Orientation practices correlate with economic health and high levels of economic prosperity. Inhabitants of these societies encourage competitiveness and support a public sector that facilitates prosperity.

Future Orientation is almost universally valued with industrialized and higher-income countries having comparatively low scores on values. Values and practices have a strong negative correlation. Societies with relatively high scores on practices have well-developed collective institutions, and leaders have confidence in the abilities of their members and in their collective safety, and expect their members to be innovative and tolerant of change. High scores on practices correspond with better economic and social health, more scientific advancement, more democratic ideals, more empowered gender status and greater domestic savings.

Gender Egalitarianism refers to the way in which societies divide roles between men and women. The more gender egalitarian a society, the less it relies on biology to determine women's and men's social role. Inhabitants of societies with more gender egalitarian practices achieve greater longevity, knowledge and standards of living. These characteristics are also found in countries with a high score on the value, which also corresponds with economic wealth and a high level of life satisfaction. High gender egalitarianism goes with a distrust for democracy and a desire for less government.

Assertiveness measures the extent to which people practice or value assertiveness, aggressiveness, dominance, toughness and tenderness. Values were positively related to success in science and technology and respect for family and friends, and negatively to voluntarily helping others and transcending selfish interests. No significant correlations between practices and these societal features were found.

Institutional Collectivism measures the degree to which institutions at the societal level encourage and reward collective action. Practices are positively correlated with economic prosperity, public sectors supporting economic success, competitiveness, and success in basic sciences. Values negatively correlate with practices and hence also with the societal features associated with the latter.

In-group Collectivism assesses the degree to which individuals express pride, loyalty and interdependence in their family. In-group Collectivism practices and values are negatively correlated with economic prosperity, public support for prosperity, competitiveness, and success in basic sciences, although these correlations become insignificant after controlling for GNP per capita.

Power Distance refers to the degree to which members of an organization or society expect and agree that power should be shared unequally. High scores on Power Distance practices are negatively correlated with economic prosperity, competitiveness, public support for prosperity, success in basic research, life expectancy, human development index, societal health, general satisfaction, and gender equality. Values only correlate positively with public support for economic competitiveness and the competitiveness index.

Humane Orientation is the degree to which an organization or society encourages and rewards individuals for being fair, altruistic, friendly, generous, caring, and kind to others. Human Orientation practices are found in less-developed countries, where a large share of the population lives in rural areas, with difficult climatic conditions. The score decreases if pre-industrial societies go through exceptionally stressful conditions.

Uncertainty Avoidance is the extent to which members of groups seek orderliness, consistency, structure, formalized procedures and laws to cope with their daily lives. High Uncertainty Avoidance practices correspond with economic prosperity, government support for economic prosperity, societal support for competitiveness, scores on the competitiveness index, life expectancy, general satisfaction and scores on the human development index. Values correlate negatively with practices and thus often with the corresponding societal items too.

Trompenaars

In the beginning of the 1980s, Trompenaars composed a questionnaire of 79 items addressing seven hypothesized dimensions of cultural values. By the mid 1990s, the raw dataset contained 50,000 cases from over 100 countries. The calculated dimensions were based on a subset of managers from multinational and international companies, so that some 30,000 comparative cases were drawn from 55 countries (Trompenaars and Hampden-Turner 1997: 245). In this work, seven dimensions are distinguished, whereas in a later work (Hampden-Turner and Trompenaars 2000) six dimensions (dilemmas as they are called) remain. Some have questioned whether the dataset of Trompenaars contains seven (or six) independent dimensions. A survey of this discussion can be found in Hofstede (2001: 221–223). Appendix 2 to Trompenaars and Hampden-Turner (1997) contains a response. The six dimensions (dilemmas) distinguished in Hampden-Turner and Trompenaars (2000) are as follows.

Universalism versus Particularism. Universalism refers to abiding by generally valid rules, codes and laws and the use of generalization. Particularism is characterized by making exceptions, making decisions depending on circumstances and preferring the quality of the relation.

Individualism versus Communitarism. Characteristics of Individualism are, competition, self-reliance, self-interest, and personal growth and fulfilment. Communitarism refers to cooperation, social concern, altruism and public service and societal legacy.

Specificity versus Diffuseness refers to how precisely and minutely cultures *de-fine* (put an end to) the constructs they use and to what extent they prefer diffuse, patterned wholes, put together in overall configurations and systems. In a specific culture one distinguishes between facts and fantasy, clarifies issues by separating what we know from what we conclude, and values high 'keeping your words'. Diffuse thinking is alert to remote consequences and the need of balance and sees quality as a characteristic of whole products.

Achieved and Ascribed status. Cultures emphasizing achieved status value high an individual's achievement, and the keeping of a promise made. Ascribed status is given to persons before they achieve. It can make its recipients public-inspired: feel they have to return to the society that lavished them. Ascribed status is related to reputation and to mutual trust.

Inner versus Outer direction. Inner direction conceives of virtues as *inside* each person; in a person's will, soul, conviction, principles, and core beliefs. Inner-directed cultures put private conscience on the helm, and support individual innovations. Outer direction conceives of virtues *outside* a person in natural rhythms, in nature, aesthetic environments and relationships. Outer directed cultures are in touch with the living environment and resonate with all nature.

Sequential versus synchronous time. This dimension refers to varying emphases on past, present and future. Sequential time sees time as an arrow, as clock time. It creates a sense of urgency: 'time is money'. Older people are undervalued; they have little sequential time left. In synchronous time events repeat themselves. In a society this corresponds with parallel production and just-in-time delivery. Elderly are respected for their wisdom, and capacity to integrate and synthesize a lifetime of experience.

Inglehart

An important ongoing study programme of values via public opinion surveys was started in the early 1980s by the European Value Systems Study group, a group of social scientists. The first round was conducted in the 1980s and covered 24 countries. From 1990 the study was extended to other continents and renamed the World Value Survey. Eventually it covered about 60,000 respondents from 43 societies. It includes more than 360 questions about various areas of life. Examples are, 'How important is religion in your life?' 'Do you believe in heaven?' 'Divorce is never justifiable' 'Government ownership of business should be increased'. Inglehart (1997) applies a principle components factor analysis on the responses of a hundred key questions from all areas. Two factors accounted for 51 per cent of variance. Inglehart named these factors 'key cultural dimensions'.

The first dimension reflects the polarization between Traditional Authority and Secular–Rational Authority. Respondents in societies that score high on Traditional Authority find religion, God and the family are important, and are proud of their nation. The Secular–Rational Authority pole is characterized by achievement motivation, thrift, an interest in politics and an acceptance of abortion being OK (Inglehart 1997: Fig. 3.2).

The second dimension consists of the poles Survival Values and Well-being Values. Survival Values are opinions such as: rejection of outgroups, a woman needs to give birth to children; children need both parents, and appreciation of technology and of hard work. Well-being Values consist of post-materialist values: homosexuality is OK, friends are important, affect balance, and a high satisfaction with life.

The scores on both dimensions correlate strongly with per capita GDP. The richer countries score high on both Secular-Rational Authority and Well-being Values (Inglehart 1997: Fig. 3.5). Inglehart related a shift from Traditional Authority towards Secular-Rational Authority to modernization, and a shift from survival towards well-being, to what he calls 'post-modernization', a substitution of material goals by expressive, psychological goals.

Trust

The trust question in the World Values Survey is used in many studies. We therefore list this question here, although it is not a cultural dimension, constructed from the answers to different questions, as the other dimensions listed in this appendix. This question reads (Inglehart 1997: 399):

Generally speaking, would you say that most people can be trusted or that you can't be too careful in dealing with people?

1. Most people can be trusted
2. Can't be too careful
3. Don't know

The variable used as the trust-variable in many cross-country studies is the percentage of respondents in a country answering most people can be trusted.

The validity of this trust variable has been questioned. There is ambiguity with respect to who are meant by 'most people' (Delhey and Newton 2005). Are these family, relatives, friends and neighbours and where does this circle end? One can also imagine that what the group respondents have in mind when answering this question differs systematically between countries. Another ambiguity results from the use of the phrases 'can be trusted' and 'can't be too careful' in one sentence. Miller and Mitamura (2003) argue that these phrases refer to two different items, namely trust and caution, which are neither synonyms nor each others opposites. In an experiment Miller and Mitamura find that when the question only refers to trust, American students have a higher level of generalized trust than Japanese students, whereas the World Values Survey reports a higher level of trust for Japanese than for American respondents. This ambiguity might also hamper the use in cross-country comparison if inhabitants of one society needs to be more cautious than in another.

Other forms of critique refer to the use of this question at the macro-level; as a measure of generalized trust. First, this question measures attitudes at the individual level. Can these be translated to a higher level? This multilevel problem is dealt with extensively in Chapter 8 on social capital. Another issue is the high correlation found between trust and the quality of institutions. Van Oorschot *et al.* (2006), for example, find a significant correlation of more than 0.6 between trust in institutions and generalized trust. Beugelsdijk (2006) finds that generalized trust correlates high with various measures of institutional quality. This could reflect the assumption of some researchers that good institutions breed trust. However, it undermines the use of trust as a cultural variable independent of institutions.

Sources of large surveys

More information about the European Values Survey and the World Values Survey can be found on the websites www.europeanvalues.nl and www.worldvaluessurvey.org. Appendix 5 in Inglehart (1997) contains the complete 1990 World Values Survey questionnaire. Since 2001 the European Social Survey (ESS) is operating. This survey contains among others the questions used for deriving Schwartz's dimensions. More information on the ESS can be found on the website www.europeansocialsurvey.org.

Appendix 2
Some experiments

Ultimatum game

In the ultimatum game (UG), two anonymous players are allotted a sum of real money (the stake) in a one-shot interaction. The first player (player 1) can offer a portion of this sum to a second player, player 2 (. . .). Player 2, before hearing the actual amount offered by player 1, must decide whether to accept or reject each of the possible offers, and these decisions are binding. If player 2 specified acceptance of the actual offer amount, then he or she receives the amount of the offer and player 1 receives the rest. If player 2 specified a rejection of the amount actually offered, both players receive zero. If people are motivated purely by self-interest, player 2 will always accept any positive offer; knowing this, player 1 should offer the smallest nonzero amount. Because this is a one-shot anonymous interaction, player 2's willingness to reject provides one measure of costly punishment, termed second-party punishment.

Source: Henrich *et al.* (2006: 1768)

Dictator game

The dictator game (DG) is the same as the Ultimatum Game except that player 2 cannot reject. Player 1 merely dictates the portions of the stake received by himself or herself and player 2. In this one-shot anonymous game, a purely self-interested individual would offer zero; thus, offers in the DG provide a measure of a kind of behavioral altruism that is not directly linked to kinship, reciprocity, reputation, or the immediate threat of punishment.

Source: Henrich *et al.* (2006: 1768)

Trust game

In the Trust game two players, 1 and 2, receive an initial sum, M. Player 1 can then send a sum, $x (0 \leq x \leq M)$, to player 2. The sum sent by 1 will be tripled by the experimenter when player 2 receives it. Player 2 can then send back a sum, $y (0 \leq y \leq 3x)$, to player 1. The amount sent by player 1 is taken as a measure of trust and the fraction returned by player 2 is considered to measure trustworthiness.

Source: Holm and Danielson (2005: 508)

Appendix 3
Construction of cultural items from the World Values Survey

The question from the World Values Survey used by Granato *et al.* (1996) and Marini (2004) is the following:

Here is a list of qualities which children can be encouraged to learn at home.

Which if any, do you consider to be especially important? Please choose up to five.

a) Good manners
b) Independence
c) Hard work
d) Feeling of responsibility
e) Imagination
f) Tolerance and respect to other people
g) Thrift, saving money and things
h) Determination, perseverance
i) Religious faith
j) Unselfishness
k) Obedience

The national percentage of respondents choosing each value has been used for constructing the following cultural indices, where each capital between bracket refers to the percentages used in the calculation of the two cultural indices.

Limited good syndrome: obedience (O), religious faith (F), tolerance and good manners

Achievement syndrome: independence (I), thrift (T), determination (D) and hard work

Generalized trust syndrome: responsibility (R)

Post-materialistic syndrome: imagination and usefulness

The two cultural indices used in the multivariate regressions are

$$CI_1 = T + D - (O + F)$$
$$CI_2 = I + R - O$$

CI_1 is the Achievement motivation used in Granato *et al.* (1996) and CI_2 is the modified cultural index used in Marini (2004).

Source: Marini (2004: 776–778)

Appendix 4
Some Biblical texts on interest

Old Testament
Exodus 22: 25 If thou lend money to any of my people that is poor by thee, thou shalt not be to him as an usurer, neither shalt thou lay upon him usury.

Leviticus 25: 35–36
35 And if thy brother be waxen poor, and fallen in decay with thee; then thou shalt relieve him; yea, though he be a stranger, or a sojourner; that he may live with thee.
36 Take thou no usury of him, or increase: but fear thy God: that thy brother may live with thee.

Deuteronomy 23: 19 and 20
19 Thou shalt not lend upon usury to thy brother; usury of money, usury of victuals, usury of anything that is lent upon usury.
20 Unto a stranger thou mayest lend upon usury; but unto thy brother thou shalt not lend upon usury: that the Lord thy God may bless thee in all that thou settest thine hand to in the land whither thou goest to possess it.

New Testament
Matthew 25: 27 Thou oughtest therefore to have put my money to the exchangers, and then at my coming I should have received mine own with usury.

Luke 19: 23 Wherefore then gavest not thou my money into the bank, that at my coming I might have required my own with usury?

(Translation: Authorized King James version)

Appendix 5
Survey measures of patriotism and attitude towards foreigners

Patriotism

The questions from the World Value Survey are

- How proud are you to be (substitute nationality)?
- Would you be willing to fight for your country?
- Do you think employers should give jobs to nationals first over immigrants?

The questions from the International Social Survey Program are

- How close do you feel to your country?
- How much do you agree that you would rather be a citizen of (insert country).
- How important is it to feel a member of a country?
- Would you support your country even if it is in the wrong?

Attitude toward foreigners

The Eurobarometer contains a few questions asking the respondents' opinion about (the inhabitants of) a series of countries. The first question asks for the EU-inhabitants opinion about a series of listed countries becoming members of the EU. The question reads:

For each of the following countries, would you be in favour or against it becoming part of the European Union?

Several waves of the Eurobarometer contain questions about the respondents' trust in people from other countries. This question is:

I would like to ask you a question on about how much trust you have in people from various countries. For each, please tell me whether you have a lot of trust, some trust, not very much trust or no trust at all.

Appendix 6
The gravity equation

The gravity equation originates from physics, where it formulizes the idea that gravitational forces exerted between two bodies depend on these bodies' mass and distance. The larger the masses, the smaller the distance, the larger are the gravitational forces. In the 1960s this relation was introduced for analyzing international trade flows by Tinbergen (1962) and Linnemann (1966). During the following decades, it was used in regional sciences (Klaassen *et al.* 1972, for example) but neglected in the field of international trade. This neglect can be attributed to the lack of a theoretical foundation. From the mid 1990s onwards some authors showed that the gravity equation can be derived as the reduced form of new trade models (Redding and Venables 2004; Anderson and Van Wincoop 2003) and of the Heckscher-Ohlin trade theory under perfect competition (Deardorf 1998). This resulted in an increased interest for the gravity equation, to the extent that it has been called the workhorse of applied international economics (Eichengreen and Irwin 1998). In this appendix we briefly discuss the original gravity equation, some theoretical models for which it can serve as a reduced form and a few issues relevant to estimating these equations. This description's intention is not to be complete but to provide the reader with some awareness of the value and problems of using gravity equations in empirical analysis.

The traditional gravity equation relates bilateral trade flows to *GDP* levels of the countries and their geographical distance.

$$X_{ij} = K\frac{Y_i^{\alpha}Y_j^{\beta}}{D_{ij}^{\delta}}$$

Where X_{ij} is the value of bilateral trade between countries i and j, K is a scalar, Y_i and Y_j are the levels of *GDP* of countries i and j, respectively, and Dij is the distance between countries i and j. Anderson and Van Wincoop (2003) show that this basic gravity equation is not correctly specified, as it does not incorporate the multilateral resistance term, which is the average barrier to trade.

Redding and Venables (2004) show, that the gravity equation can be considered the reduced form of a standard new trade theory model. In this model firms operate under increasing returns to scale and produce differentiated products. On the demand side, each firm's product is differentiated from that of other firms and is used both in consumption and as an intermediate good. In both uses there is a constant elasticity of substitution. Each country's demand for a particular differentiated good is derived given the total expenditures of the country concerned. At the supply side there are three types of input: an internationally immobile primary factor (labour), an internationally mobile primary factor, and a composite intermediate good. A Cobb-Douglas production technology is used, transport costs are of the iceberg type, and firms maximize profits. Under these conditions the value of bilateral trade is made up of three components: the exporting country's supply capacity, the importing country's market capacity and the bilateral transport costs. Formally:

$$X_{ij} = \frac{n_i p_i^{1-\sigma} Y_j P_j^{\sigma-1}}{T_{ij}^{\sigma-1}}$$

where σ is the elasticity of substitution, n_i and p_i are the number of varieties and prices in country *i*, Y_j and P_j are the expenditure and price level in country *j* and T_{ij} represents bilateral trade costs. The first product is country *i*'s exporting capacity, the second country *j*'s market capacity. Replacing these two capacities by the countries' Gross Domestic Product delivers equation (A-1). Of course Gross Domestic Product is a very rough approximation of the supply and market capacity. Some authors (e.g. Disdier and Mayer 2007), therefore use a fixed effects specification when estimating this relation. In fixed effects estimations, the two capacities are replaced by dummy variables representing each exporting and importing country.

Rauch provides a very simple account for using the gravity equation in studies of international trade. He derives this relation from the assumption 'that every country consumes its own output and that of every other country in proportion to its share of world demand' (Rauch 1999: 11). The resulting relation for bilateral trade is then:

$$X_{ij} = s_i GDP_j + s_j GDP_i$$

where s_i, s_j is the share of country *i*, *j*, respectively in world spending, $s_i = GDP_i / GDP_w$, where GDP_w is world gross domestic product. Assuming balanced trade then leads to

$$X_{ij} = 2GDP_i GDP_j / GDP_w$$

This is the basic gravity equation, without taken distance into account. Rauch views this relation as a 'starting point for further analysis of trade rather than as something that itself needs to be explained' (Rauch 1999: 11).

In empirical studies a relation is estimated which is obtained by taking logarithms of the nonlinear gravity equation. Variables representing cultural dimensions or cultural differences are added to this basic equation, so that a typical relation estimated in studies on cultural barriers to international transactions is of the form:

$$\ln(X_{ij}) = \ln(\alpha_0) + \alpha_1 \ln(Y_i) + \alpha_2 \ln(Y_j) + \alpha_3 \ln(D_{ij}) + \alpha_4 \ln(CD_{ij}) + \alpha_5\, COM_{ij} + \ln(\varepsilon_{ij})$$

where ln(.) is the logarithm operator and D_{ij}, CD_{ij}, and COM_{ij} are, respectively, the physical distance, the cultural distance and common characteristics of the countries i and j, and ε_{ij} is disturbance term.

This relation and the corresponding data have some characteristics which make Ordinary Least Squares (OLS) estimation invalid. First, the observations are clustered by country. As a consequence OLS underestimates the standard errors of the coefficients of the country characteristics and can give rise to biased estimates if unobserved effects and the explanatory variables correlate. Anderson and Marcuillier (2002) use a technique which corrects the standard errors. For cross-section data Egger (2005) presents alternative techniques for correcting both the level of significance and the bias of the estimates. In case the dataset contains both a time and a cross-section dimension, Lankhuizen, De Jong and Pelzer (2008) suggest using a multi-level random effects model. Second, Santos Silva and Tenreyro (2006) argue that the original nonlinear version is likely to be plagued by heteroskedasticity. Under these conditions estimates obtained from a log-linearized model are severely biased. They recommend estimating the original multiplicative model by a pseudo-maximum-likelihood estimator. Third, when the sample contains countries outside Europe and North-America a relatively large part of the observations is very small or zero, indicating that the size of bilateral flows is small. Then one has to decide whether to exclude these observations from the sample, to use a Tobit model that takes these zero flows into account, or to apply a two-part estimation procedure, where one relation estimates the cut-off point above which a country exports, and the other is a standard gravity equation (Hallak 2006). Sensitivity analysis of various methods reveals that the results can differ a lot, especially when the percentage of zero flows is relatively large (Coe *et al.* 2007, Linders 2006: Appendix 5B). A motivated choice of the estimation procedure is warranted in these situations.

Notes

1 Introduction

1 See also DiMaggio (1994: 29), who mentions development, economic history and the economics of organization as the specialized subfields of economics where culture is regarded as relevant.

2 It is remarkable that culture plays a dominant role in international business but is almost entirely neglected in international economics. This illustrates the different trajectories both sub-disciplines have followed after their start at the end of the 1970s, when each obtained its own journal: the *Journal of International Business Studies* and the *Journal of International Economics*. International business is characterized by many empirical studies and almost no formal models. International economics focuses to a large extent on formal mathematical models and empirical analyses derived from these models. The latter approach has a tendency to neglect the context and thus culture.

3 These definitions are from Hofstede (2001: 10).

2 A history of thought about culture and economy

1 McKinley's proclamation reads: 'The mission of the United States is one of the benevolent assimilation, substituting the mild sway of justice and right for arbitrary rule. In the fulfilment of this high mission, supporting the temperate administration of affairs for the greatest good of the governed, there must be sedulously maintained the strong arm of authority to repress disturbance and to overcome all obstacles to the bestowal of the blessings of good and stable government upon the people of the Philippine Islands under the flag of the United States.'

2 Za'ba (1927: 45) for example, claims that 'Malays excel only in a lifestyle of ease, in the ability to waste our time, in not being bothered by any kind of activity. Easy food, easy sleep, easy spending and the indulgence of desires. Such a lifestyle is useless: the lives of animals are more meaningful than this.'

3 Although Weber's subsequent works like '*The Religion of China: Confucianism and Taoism*' (1915) are more suspect in this last respect.

4 Early exponents of the German Historical School, such as Wilhelm Roscher, were more prone to believe in universal structures that were lying underneath the specific mechanisms governing the various economic systems one could observe in the real world.

5 In this sense, Menger and the Austrian School around him never made the complete step towards an entirely formal economics. Economics to Menger was always also to some extent substantive (Barkai 1996).

6 Though without the explicit moral connotation of the word 'ideal'.

3 The re-emergence of culture in economics

1 Another account of the revival of cultural explanation in economics can be found in Chapter 1 of Jones (2006). Maseland (undated) also distinguishes 'Economy as culture' and 'Social science as culture' approaches.
2 The rest of this section is based on Rizvi (2003) and Sent (2006).
3 Technically this path is selected by imposing a transversality condition, well-known from dynamic programming and optimal control problems. A transversality condition is a condition with respect to the way the process ends.
4 The text on the old and new behavioural economics is based on Sent (2004).
5 List (2004) found that consumers with intense market experience behave more in accordance with neoclassical utility than consumers with almost no market experience. The latter behaved largely in accordance with prospect theory.
6 Values were considered an object of study by authors belonging to related disciplines such as sociology, see for example, McClelland (1961) and literature referred to in Hill (2000).
7 This distinction can also be found in Maseland (2008).
8 Lal (1998) thinks that a change in culture takes at least a generation or two.
9 See Inglehart (1997: 33–36) for a theory of intergenerational value change.
10 This paragraph is based on Bowles (1998).

4 Methods and methodology of culture and economics

1 Rituals are collective activities that are technically unnecessary. Heroes are persons who possess characteristics that are highly prized in a culture and thus serve as models for behaviour. Symbols are words, gestures, pictures and objects that carry often complex meanings recognized as such only by those who share the culture (Hofstede 2001: 10).
2 Note that this argument is often brought forward to criticize large-scale survey research which derives quantitative measures of national cultural dimensions. Rarely one finds similar criticism of descriptive studies taking one or more nations as the unit of analysis. It seems as if this criticism is triggered by the quantification of culture instead of the unit of analysis.
3 A brief description of organizational cultures is found in Hofstede (2001: 391–415).
4 See Hanges, Dickson and Sipe (2004) for an introduction into hierarchical linear modelling and the way it is applied by the GLOBE-team
5 The acronyms are derived from the phonemic and phonetic classifications in linguistics. The phonetic classification is universal, whereas the phonemic is the specific.
6 For example, in the first edition of his Culture's Consequences, Hofstede restricted the analysis to countries where at least four out of his seven occupational categories had eight or more respondents. This resulted in a minimum of 58 respondents in Singapore (Hofstede 2001: 52).
7 Note that the trade-off should be included in one single question. Using two separate questions, each asking for the respondents' opinion on the importance of one particular item, is not helpful as the respondents' answers are highly correlated. Respondents are inclined to answer that both items are important. Including both items in one question forces them to make a choice (see Van Lelyveld 2000: Ch. 5).
8 An extensive description of the response bias correction procedure used by the GLOBE-team can be found in Appendix B of House *et al.* (2004).

9 Holm and Danielson (2005: 505) draw a comparison with medical sciences, where researchers also want to understand the microbiological mechanisms that cause a substance's effects.
10 This list is based on Levitt and List (2007), which also provides a list of references for each of the features discussed.
11 The term natural field experiment is from the taxonomy developed in Harrison and List (2004). This article describes the differences between different types of laboratory and field experiments.
12 To a great extent, the text on advantages and disadvantages of unobtrusive methods relies on Chapter 1 of Kellehear (2001).
13 Weber (1985) provides a brief introduction into content analysis.
14 See Gupta, Sully de Luque and House (2004: 155–162) for a description of the method used.
15 The cultural difference between The Netherlands and Dutch-speaking Belgium are also found in later studies, which were held in 1990, 1998, and 2001, respectively. See, Claes and Gerritsen (2002: 145). These studies use the same questions as Hofstede or the Value Survey Module, which is based on the same principles. Research using different methods find similar cultural differences between Belgium and The Netherlands, see Inglehart (1997: 370, 382).
16 See Verbeek (2004: Ch. 5) for more details.

5 Cultural and cross-country differences in institutions

1 They also study the fertility rate for which similar results as for female labour force participation are found.
2 For more details of the selection procedure we refer to Fernández and Fogli (2007: 9).
3 This procedure to consider all cultural variables corresponds to Schwartz's advice to avoid partial relations and to investigate the whole set of relations (Schwartz 1992: 54, 55). Both significant and non-significant associations are relevant for a critical test of any theory.
4 Licht *et al.* (2005) also consider a group of Asian countries as an outlier.
5 In Chapter 7 we discuss the (in)appropriateness of dominant religion and language as proxies for culture.
6 The rest of this section is based on De Jong *et al.* (2006).
7 Shane (1995) and Elenkov and Manev (2005) use the number of respondents as independent observations, whereas the cultural dimensions refer to nations only. Hence, in these studies the multilevel structure of the dataset is not taken into account, which in all likelihood leads to an overestimation of the country variables coefficients' significance (see Chapter 4).

6 Culture and economic performance

1 The Extreme Bounds Analysis is first introduced by Leamer (1983). It consists of estimating a series of equations in which two groups of explanatory variables are distinguished. The first group consists of variables that are always included in the regression, whereas the second group is the conditioning group. Each regression differs from the others in that another subset of conditioning variables are included in the regression. In this way one obtains as much estimated coefficients and corresponding standard deviations of the variable of interest as the number of estimated regressions. These estimates are used for investigating the likelihood that this coefficient is significant form zero and has a particular sign (positive in

the case of the regressions of growth and trust). See Levine and Renelt (1992) for an application and Sali-i-Martin (1997) for an alternative criterion.

2 The trust variable is extensively discussed in Chapter 8.

3 A similar result is found by De Mooij with respect to the adoption of the Internet. Among a group of European countries, Internet was adopted fastest in countries that score low on Uncertainty Avoidance. Once Internet was no new phenomenon any more, other cultural variables became stronger (De Mooij 2004: 252).

4 Long-term orientation was not included in the regressions because it is not available for all countries concerned. Similar regressions with the cultural dimensions of GLOBE as explanatory variables only found Uncertainty Avoidance as a significant explanatory factor in some regressions explaining GDP per capita.

5 This list of advantages of regional data can be found in Beugelsdijk and Van Schaik (2005a: 306).

6 Besides the use of regions, Tabellini's study is interesting for its extensive argumentation and validity tests of instrumental variables estimators.

7 Tabellini (2008b, Table 11) presents similar estimates for the variable trust and respect.

8 According to the associationism such cultural engineering by a legitimate leader can enhance economic performance (see Casson 1993: 441).

9 The description of Malaysia is based on Maseland (2006a: Ch. 5).

10 The text on African Renaissance is based on Bernstein (2006).

11 The scores on Uncertainty Avoidance are from Hofstede (2001). The figures on GDP per capita and the Human development index are from World Bank (2004).

7 Religion as culture

1 This and similar definitions of culture are found in Hofstede (1980: 21), DiMaggio (1994: 25) and Inglehart (1997). See also Chapter 1 for various definitions of culture.

2 Ter Haar and Ellis (2006: 356) distinguish four channels: practices, organization, values, and spiritual experiences. The first two constitute the network feature and the last two the values aspect distinguished in the main text.

3 Examples of studies investigating this network effect of religion are Lewer and Van den Berg (undated) and Blum and Dudley (2001). Lewer and van den Berg investigate the influence of religion on bilateral trade flows. Blum and Dudley interpret Weber's hypothesis of the Protestant ethics and economic growth in terms of information networks.

4 This also implies that we do not deal with the literature on the economics of religion, which explains religious phenomena, such as church attendance, by economic theories. A review of this literature can be found in Iannaccone (1998) and some examples in Fase (2005: especially 60–96).

5 The flexibility appeared to be pro-growth in case of the Islamic law of sale (Kuran 2007).

6 This paragraph is based on Kuran (2004c).

7 Beugelsdijk (2006) argues that the World Values Survey measure of trust used in these aggregate studies is likely to proxy the well-functioning of institutions instead of trust.

8 In contrast to De Haan and Sturm (2000), Alon and Chase do not investigate the sensitivity of their results by adding to the list of independent variables, explanatory variables found in other studies.

9 Some argue that in the short run bribe paying can function as lubricants in cases of bad economic institutions.
10 The idea that money should perform the function of a means of exchange can also be found by Gesell (1949 [1931]: 179): 'Das Geld ist Tauschmittel, nichts anderes'.
11 The aim of protecting the poor formed also the basis of discussions about a just price. Although prices could adjust according to market conditions, they should correspond to the labour and costs of the producer (Tawney 1962 [1926]: 40).
12 This description is based on the English translation of Weber (2001 [1930]) and the German version Weber (2006 [1920]).
13 Compare Alesina and Glaeser (2004) and the section on welfare in Chapter 5.
14 In Tawney's case, Fase (2005) even writes about the Weber–Tawney hypothesis.
15 We only list the contents of the variables and not the specific transformation used in the regressions.
16 The items of each biblical concept of poverty can be found in Sakwa (2006: 32). The relations between biblical concepts and elements of poverty alleviation are summarized in Sakwa (2006: Table 7.1).

9 International relations and coordination

1 The number of countries is restricted by data availability.
2 Note that for trade this result is opposite to the one reported in Dekker *et al.* (2006: 81). There the coefficient was negative or insignificant, whereas it is now positive.
3 Johanson and Vahlne (1977: 24) define psychic distance as 'the sum of factors preventing the flow of information from and to the market. Examples are differences in language, education, business practices, culture and industrial development'.
4 Unless stated otherwise, the paragraphs on the criticism of this type of studies is based on Harzing (2004). The way the arguments are presented is the present author's choice.
5 Kim and Hwang (1992) take these legal restrictions into account by excluding the cases from their analysis where government regulations imposed restrictions on the mode to entry.
6 In his view this success is also due to the fact that the smaller country holds a majority of the shares and the companies have two headquarters (Hofstede 2001: 446).
7 In addition the effect of common border and common language become insignificant.
8 This grouping of explanations is taken from Van der Velde *et al.* (2005).
9 Unless stated otherwise the text of this section is based on Hofstede (2001: 431–440).

10 Conclusions and recommendations

1 The text is mainly based on results within Christianity. Esposito and Mogahed (2007) report a similar high degree of geographical, racial and cultural diversity for the Muslim world.
2 It should be noted that Mahathir also referred to future prosperity in his works.
3 This distinction corresponds with the distinction between formalism and substantivism (see for example, Jones 2006: 6).
4 Some researchers use methods closely related to journalism and literature. In this respect it is telling that in 2007 the most important prize in Dutch literature,

the PC Hooftprijs was awarded to Prof. Dr. Abram de Swaan, a sociologist belonging to the Amsterdam School of Sociology. Members of this school are adherents of descriptive, almost literary, studies of social developments.

5 The suggested phases show some similarity with the stages discussed in DiMagio (1994: 34).

6 For the same reason, Hofstede included GNP per capita in many regressions. 'My reasoning is that if I can explain phenomena across societies by differences in wealth, I don't need culture' (Hofstede 2004: 277).

Bibliography

Acemoglu, D. and Robinson, J. A. (2008) 'Persistence of power, elites and institutions', *American Economic Review*, 98(1): 267–293.

Acemoglu, D., Johnson, S. and Robinson, J. A. (2001) 'The colonial origins of comparative development: an empirical investigation', *American Economic Review*, 91(5): 1369–1401.

Adler, M. and Dumas, B. (1983) 'International portfolio choice and corporation finance: a synthesis', *Journal of Finance*, 38(3): 925–984.

Adler, N. J. (1983) 'A typology of management studies involving culture', *Journal of International Business Studies*, 14: 29–47.

Adler, P. S. and Kwon, S. W. (2002) 'Social capital: prospects for a new concept', *Academy of Management Review*, 27: 17–40.

Akkerman, D., Harzing, A.-W. and van Witteloostuijn, A. (2007) 'Cultural imprinting and language priming: competitive versus cooperative behavior in a prisoner's dilemma game'. Unpublished Manuscript, Faculty of Economics and Business, University of Groningen.

Akoko, R. M. (2007) *'Ask and You Shall be Given': Pentecostalism and the economic crisis in Cameroon*, Leiden: African Studies Centre.

Alatas, S. H. (2002) 'Religion, values and capitalism in Asia', in C. W. J.-L. Wee (ed.) *Local Cultures and the 'New Asia'*, Singapore: ISEAS, 107–128.

Albert, M. (1993) *Capitalism versus Capitalism: How America's obsession with individual achievement and short-term profit has led it to the brink of collapse*, New York: Four Wall Eight Windows.

Alesina, A., Glaeser, E. L. and Sacerdote, B. (2001) 'Why doesn't the U.S. have a European-style welfare state?', *Brookings Papers on Economic Activity*, Fall, 187–278.

Alesina, A. F. and Glaeser, E. L. (2004) *Fighting Poverty in the US and Europe: a world of difference*, Oxford: Oxford University Press.

Allen, F. and D. Gale (2000) *Comparing Financial Systems*, Cambridge, MA/London: MIT Press.

Allen, M. W., Ng, S. H., Ikeda, K., Jawan, J. A., Sufi, A. H., Wilson, M. and Yang, K.-S. (2007) 'Two decades of change in cultural values and economic development in eight Asian and Pacific island nations', *Journal of Cross-Cultural Psychology*, 38: 247–269.

Alon, I. and Chase, G. (2005) 'Religious freedom and economic prosperity', *The Cato Journal*, 25(2): 399–406.

Amable, B. (2003) *The Diversity of Modern Capitalism*, Oxford: Oxford University Press.

American Economic Association (1899) 'Discussion – The President's Address', *Economic Studies: publication of the American Economic Association*, 4(1): 108–111.

Anderson, J. E. and Marcouillier, D. (2002) 'Insecurity and the pattern of trade: an empirical investigation', *Review of Economics and Statistics*, 84: 341–352.

Anderson, J. E. and Van Wincoop, E. (2003) 'Gravity with gravitas: a solution to the border puzzle', *The American Economic Review*, 93: 170–192.

Aristotle (1992) *The Politics*, trans. T. A. Sinclair, revd T. J. Saunders, Harmondsworth: Penguin.

Ascherson, N. (1995) *Black Sea*, New York: Hill and Wang.

Austen, S. (2003) *Culture and the Labour Market*, Cheltenham, UK: Edward Elgar.

Axelrod, R. (1984) *The Evolution of Cooperation*, New York: Basic Books.

Baele, L., Pungulescu, C. and Ter Horst, J. (forthcoming) 'Model uncertainty, financial market integration, and the home bias puzzle', *Journal of International Money and Finance*, (forthcoming).

Banfield, E. C. (1958) *The Moral Basis of a Backward Society*, Chicago: The Free Press.

Barkai, H. (1996) 'The Methodenstreit and the Emergence of Mathematical Economics', *Eastern Economic Journal*, 22(1): 1–19.

Barkema, H. G., Shenkar, O., Vermeulen, F. and Bell, J. H. (1997) 'Working abroad, working with others: how firms learn to operate international joint ventures', *Academy of Management Journal*, 40(2): 426–442.

Barkema, H. G. and Vermeulen, F. (1997) 'What differences in the cultural backgrounds of partners are detrimental for international joint ventures?', *Journal of International Business Studies*, 28(4): 845–864.

Barney, J. B. and Hansen, M. H. (1995) 'Trustworthiness as a source of competitive advantage', *Strategic Management Journal*, 15: 175–190.

Barro, R. J. and McCleary, R. C. (2003) 'Religion and economic growth across countries', *American Sociological Review*, 68(5): 760–781.

Barth, J. R., Caprio, G. and Levine, R. (2006) *Rethinking Bank Regulation: till angels govern*, Cambridge: Cambridge University Press.

Bates, R. H., Greif, A., Levi, M., Rosenthal, J.-L. and Weingast, B. R. (1998) *Analytical Narratives*, Princeton, NJ: Princeton University Press.

Battacharya, U. and Groznik, P. (2008) 'Melting pot or salad bow: some evidence from US investments abroad', *Journal of Financial Markets* (forthcoming).

Bell, J. H. J. (1996) 'Joint or single venturing?: an eclectic approach to foreign entry mode choice'. Unpublished PhD dissertation, Tilburg University.

Belot, M. and Ederveen, S. (2006) 'Cultural and institutional barriers in migration between OECD countries'. Unpublished Manuscript, The Hague: CPB.

Berger, H., de Haan, J. and Sturm, J.-E. (2006) 'Does money matter in the ECB strategy?: new evidence based on ECB communication', CESifo Working Paper no. 1652.

Bernstein, A. (2006) 'Culture and development: questions from South Africa', in L. E. Harrison and P. L. Berger (eds) *Developing Cultures: case studies*, New York/London: Routledge, 23–41.

Beugelsdijk, S. (2006) 'A note on the theory and measurement of trust in explaining differences in economic growth', *Cambridge Journal of Economics*, 30: 371–387.

Beugelsdijk, S. (2008) 'Trust, institutions and the "generally speaking question"; a reply to Uslander', *Cambridge Journal of Economics*, 32: 633–638.

Beugelsdijk, S., de Groot, H. L. F. and van Schaik, A. B. T. M. (2004) 'Trust and economic growth: a robustness analysis', *Oxford Economic Papers*, 56: 118–134.

Beugelsdijk, S. and Maseland, R. (2009) *Culture in Economics; history, methodological reflections and contemporary applications* (forthcoming).

Beugelsdijk, S. and Smulders, S. (2003) 'Bonding and bridging social capital: which type is good for economic growth?', in W. Arts, L. Halman and J. Hagenaars (eds) *The Cultural Diversity of European Unity*, Leiden: Brill, 147–184.

Beugelsdijk, S., Koen, C. I. and Noorderhaven, N. G. (2006) 'Organizational culture and relationship skills', *Organization Studies*, 27: 833–854.

Beugelsdijk, S. and van Schaik, A. B. T. M. (2005a) 'Social capital and growth in European regions: an empirical test', *European Journal of Political Economy*, 21: 301–324.

Beugelsdijk, S. and van Schaik, A. B. T. M. (2005b) 'Differences in social capital between 54 western European regions', *Regional Studies*, 39(8): 1053–1064.

Bisin, A. and Verdier, T. (2001) 'The economics of cultural transmission and the dynamics of preferences', *Journal of Economic Theory*, 97: 298–319.

Black, B. (1999) 'National culture and labour-market flexibility', *International Journal of Human Resource Management*, 10: 592–605.

Black, B. (2001a) 'National culture and industrial relations and pay structures', *Labour*, 15(2): 257–277.

Black, B. (2001b) 'Culturally coded? The enigma of flexible labour markets', *Employee Relations*, 23(4): 401–416.

Black, B. (2005) 'Comparative industrial relations theory: the role of culture', *International Journal of Human Resource Management*, 16(7): 1137–1158.

Black, B. (2006) 'Equity culture'. Unpublished Manuscript, Queens University Belfast.

Blanchard, O. J., Froot, K. A. and Sachs, J. D. (eds) (1994) *The Transition in Eastern Europe*, Vol. 1 *Country Studies* and Vol. 2 *Restructuring*, Chicago/London: University of Chicago Press.

Bloningen, B. A. and Wang, M. G. (2005) 'Inappropriate pooling of wealthy and poor countries in empirical FDI studies', in T. Moran, E. Graham and M. Blomström (eds) *Does Foreign Direct Investment Promote Development?*, Washington, DC: Peterson Institute for International Economics, 221–244.

Blum, U. and Dudley, L. (2001) 'Religion and economic growth: was Weber right?', *Journal of Evolutionary Economics*, 11: 207–230.

Bodley, J. H. (1994) Cultural Anthropology: tribes, states and the global system, available at www.wsu.edu/gened/learn-modules/top_cultures/culture-definitions/bodley-text.html.

Boggs, C. (2001) 'Social capital and political fantasy: Robert Putnam's bowling alone', *Theory and Society*, 30: 281–297.

Boix, C. and Posner, D. N. (1998) 'Social capital: explaining its origins and effects on government performance', *British Journal of Political Science*, 28: 686–693.

Bond, M. H. and Yang, K.-S. (1982) 'Ethnic affirmation versus cross-cultural accommodation: the variable impact of questionnaire language on Chinese bilinguals from Hong Kong', *Journal of Cross-Cultural Psychology*, 13: 169–185.

Bornschier, V. (2005) *Culture and Politics in Economic Development*, London: Routledge.

Botero, J. C., Djankov, S., La Porta, R., Lopez-de-Silanes, F. and Shleifer, A. (2004) 'The regulation of labour', *The Quarterly Journal of Economics*, 119(4): 1339–1382.

Bourdieu, P. (1986) 'Forms of capital', in J. G. Richardson (ed.) *Handbook of Theory and Research for the Sociology of Education*, New York: Greenwood Press, 251–258.

Bourdieu, P. (1998a) *L'essence du néolibéralisme*, Le Monde Diplomatique, 3rd March 1998.

Bourdieu, P. (1998b) 'A reasoned utopia and economic fatalism', *New Left Review*, I, 227: 125–130.

Bowles, S. (1998) 'Endogenous preferences: the cultural consequences of markets and other economic institutions', *Journal of Economic Literature*, 36(1): 75–111.

Boyd, R. and Richerson, P. J. (1985) *Culture and the Evolutionary Process*, Chicago: University of Chicago Press.

Brouthers, K. D. and Brouthers, L. E. (2001) 'Explaining the national cultural distance paradox', *Journal of International Business Studies*, 32(1): 177–189.

Brown, T. F. (1998) 'Theoretical perspectives on social capital', Working Paper, Program for Comparative and International Development, John Hopkins University.

Burt, R. (1992) 'The social structure of competition', in N. Nohria and R. Eccles (eds) *Networks and Organizations, Structure, Form and Action*, Boston, MA: Harvard Business School Press.

Burt, R. and Knez, M. (1995) 'Kinds of third-party effects on trust', *Rationality and Society*, 7: 255–292.

Calmfors, L. and Driffill, D. J. (1988) 'Bargaining structure, corporatism and macro-economic performance', *Economic Policy*, 6: 14–59.

Carlin, W. and Mayer, C. (2003) 'Finance, investment, and growth', *Journal of Financial Economics*, 69: 191–226.

Carroll, C. D., Rhee, B.-K. and Rhee, C. (1994) 'Are there cultural effects on savings? Some cross-country evidence', *The Quarterly Journal of Economics*, 109(3): 685–699.

Casson, M. (1993) 'Cultural determinants of economic performance', *Journal of Comparative Economics*, 17: 418–442.

Chang, H.-J. (2008) *Bad Samaritans: the myth of free trade and the secret history of capitalism,* New York: Bloomsbury Press.

Cheptea, A. (2007) 'Trade and cultural affinity', paper presented at the Annual Conference of the Royal Economic Society, April 2007, Warwick.

Chinese Culture Connection (1987) 'Chinese values and the search for culture-free dimensions of culture', *Journal of Cross-Cultural Psychology*, 18: 143–174.

Claes, M. T. and Gerritsen, M. (2002) *Culturele Waarden en Communicatie in Internationaal Perspectief (An International Perspective on Cultural Values and Communication)*, Bussum: Uitgeverij Coutinho.

Coe, D. T., Subramanian, A. and Tamirisa, N. T. (2007) 'The missing globalization puzzle: evidence of the declining importance of distance', *IMF Staff Papers*, 54(1): 34–58.

Coleman, J. (1988) 'Social capital in the creation of human capital', *American Journal of Sociology* 94: S95–S120.

Coleman, J. (1990) *Foundations of Social Theory*, Cambridge, MA: Harvard University Press.

Coval, J. D. and Moskowitz, T. J. (1999) 'Home bias at home: local equity preference in domestic portfolios', *Journal of Finance*, 54(6): 2045–2073.

Coval, J. D. and Moskowitz, T. J. (2001) 'The geography of investment: informed trading and asset prices', *Journal of Political Economy*, 109(4): 811–841.

Crouch, C. (1993) *Industrial Relations and European State Traditions*, Oxford: Clarendon Press.

Cuesta, J. (2004) 'From economist to culturalist development theories: how strong is the relation between cultural aspects and economic development?', Working Papers Series No. 400, The Hague: Institute of Social Studies.

Cukierman, A. (1992) *Central Bank Strategy, Credibility and Independence*, Cambridge, MA: MIT Press.

Damaska, M. R. (1986) *The Faces of Justice and State Authority: A Comparative Approach to the Legal Process*, New Haven: Yale University Press.

De Haan, J. and Sturm, J.-E. (2000) 'On the relationship between economic freedom and economic growth', *European Journal of Political Economy*, 16: 215–241.

De Jong, E. (1988) 'Expectation formation: criteria and an assessment', *De Economist*, 136: 435–468.

De Jong, E. (2002) 'Why are price stability and statutory independence of central banks negatively correlated?: the role of culture', *European Journal of Political Economy*, 18: 675–694.

De Jong, E. (2005) 'Conflicts about the ECB: the role of culture', paper presented at the annual meeting of the European Public Choice Society, Durham, UK, March–April 2005.

De Jong, E. and Semenov, R. (2004) 'A theory on the cultural determinants of stock market development: its strength and limits'. Unpublished Manuscript, Radboud University Nijmegen.

De Jong, E. and Semenov, R. (2006a) 'Cultural determinants of ownership concentration across countries', *International Journal of Business Governance and Ethics*, 2: 145–165.

De Jong, E. and Semenov, R. (2006b) 'Determinants of corporate ownership concentration: firm and country effects'. Unpublished Manuscript, Radboud University Nijmegen.

De Jong, E., Smeets, R. and Smits, J. (2006) 'Culture and openness', *Social Indicators Research*, 78: 11–136.

De Mooij, M. (2004) *Consumer Behaviour and Culture: consequences for global marketing and advertising*, Thousand Oaks: Sage Publications.

Deardorff, A. V. (1998) 'Determinants of bilateral trade: does gravity work in a neoclassical world?', in J. A. Frankel (ed.) *The Regionalization of the World Economy*, Chicago: University of Chicago Press, 7–28.

Dekker, P., Ederveen, S., de Groot, H., van der Horst, A., Lejour, A., Straathof, B., Vinken, H. and Wennekers, C. (2006) 'Cultural diversity, economics and policy', in P. Dekker, S. Ederveen, H. de Groot, A. van der Horst, A. Lejour, B. Straathof, H. Vinken and C. Wennekers, *Diverse Europe*, The Hague: CPB, 37–105.

Dekker, P., Koopmans, R. and Van den Broek, A. (1997) 'Voluntary associations, social movements and individual political behaviour in Western Europe: a micro-macro puzzle', in J. W. van Deth (ed.) *Private Groups and Public Life: social participation, voluntary associations and political involvement in representative democracies*, London: Routledge.

Delhey, J. and Newton, K. (2005) 'Predicting cross-national levels of social trust: global pattern of Nordic exceptionalism?', *European Sociological Review*, 21(4): 311–327.

Demirgüc-Kunt, A. and Levine, R. (2001) *Financial Structure and Economic Growth: a cross-country comparison of banks, markets and development*, Cambridge, MA: The MIT Press.

Den Butter, F. A. G. and Mosch, R. H. J. (2003) 'Trade, trust and transaction costs', Tinbergen Institute Discussion Paper, TI 2003-82/3, Amsterdam.

Denzau, A. T. and North, D. C. (1994) 'Shared mental models: ideologies and institutions', *Kyklos* 47: 3–31.

Dia, M. (1996) *Africa's Management in the 1990s and Beyond: reconciling indigenous and transplanted institutions*, Washington DC: The World Bank.

Dieckmann, O. (1996) 'Cultural determinants of economic growth: theory and evidence', *Journal of Cultural Economics*, 20(4): 297–320.

DiMaggio, P. (1994) 'Culture and economy', in N. J. Smelser and R. Swedberg (eds) *Handbook of Economic Sociology*, Princeton, NJ: Princeton University Press, 27–57.

Disdier, A.-C. and Mayer, T. (2007) 'Je t'aime, moi non plus: bilateral opinions and international trade', *European Journal of Political Economy*, 23: 1149–1159.

Drogendijk, R. and Slangen, A. (2006) 'Hofstede, Schwartz, or managerial perception? The effects of different cultural distance measures on establishment mode choices by multinational enterprises', *International Business Review*, 15: 361–380.

Durlauf, S. (2002) 'On the empirics of social capital', *The Economic Journal*, 112: F459–F479.

Durlauf, S. N. and Fafchamps, M. (2004) 'Social capital', NBER Working Paper Series No. 10485.

Durlauf, S. N., Kourtellos, A. and Tan, C. M. (2005) 'How robust are the linkages between religiosity and economic growth?'. Unpublished Manuscript, Department of Economics, University of Wisconson-Madison.

Dyen, I., Kruskal, J. B. and Black, P. (1992) 'An Indoeuropean classification: a lexicostatistical experiment', *Transactions of the American Philosophical Society*, 82(5), iii–132.

Dyer, J. H. and Singh, H. (1998) 'The relational view: cooperative strategy and sources of interorganisational competitive advantage', *Academy of Management Review*, 23: 660–679.

Earley, P. C. (1993) 'East meets West meets Mideast: further explorations of collectivistic and individualistic work groups', *Academy of Management Journal*, 36(2): 319–348.

Egger, P. (2005) 'Alternative techniques for estimation of cross-section gravity models', *Review of International Economics* 13(5): 881–891.

Eichengreen, B. and Irwin, D. A. (1998) 'The role of history in bilateral trade flows', in J. A. Frankel (ed.) *The Regionalization of the World Economy*, Chicago: University of Chicago Press, 33–57.

Elenkov, D. S. and Manev, I. V. (2005) 'Top management leadership and influence on innovation: the role of sociocultural context', *Journal of Management*, 31(3): 381–402.

Engen, D. (2004) The economy of Ancient Greece, in R. Whaples (ed.) *EH.Net Encyclopedia*, Online Available: <http://eh.net/encylcopedia/article/engen.greece>

Esposito, J. L. and Mogahed, D. (2007) *Who Speaks for Islam?: what a billion Muslims really think*, New York: Gallup Press.

Etounga-Manguelle, D. (2000) Does Africa need a cultural adjustment program?, in L. E. Harrison and S. P. Huntington (eds) *Culture Matters: how values shape human progress*, New York: Basic Books, 65–77.

Fase, M. M. G. (2005) 'On economics and religion', *De Economist* 153(1): 85–106.

Fedderke, J., De Kadt, R. and Luiz, J. (1999) 'Economic growth and social capital: a critical reflection', *Theory and Society*, 28: 709–745.

Fernández, R. and Fogli, A. (2007) 'Culture: an empirical investigation of beliefs, work and fertility'. Unpublished Manuscript, January 2007.

Fernández, R., Fogli, A. and Olivetti, C. (2004) 'Mothers and sons: preference formation and female labor force dynamics', *The Quarterly Journal of Economics*, 119(4): 1249–1299.

Fine, B. (2001) *Social Capital versus Social Theory: political economy and social science at the turn of the millennium*, New York: Routledge.

Fischer, R. (2006) 'Congruence and functions of personal and cultural values: do my values reflect my culture's values?', *Personality and Social Psychology Bulletin*, 32: 1419–1431.

Foad, H. (2008) 'Familiarity breeds investment: immigration and equity home bias'. Unpublished Manuscript, Department of Economics, San Diego State University, February 2008.

Forder, J. (1998) 'The case for an independent European Central Bank: a reassessment of evidence and sources', *European Journal of Political Economy*, 14: 53–71.

Forder, J. (1999) 'Central bank independence: reassessing the measurements', *Journal of Economic Issues*, 33: 23–40.

Forrest, R. and Kearns, A. (2001) 'Social cohesion, social capital and the neighbourhood', *Urban Studies*, 38: 2125–2143.

Fox, J. (1991) *Regression Diagnostics*, Newbury Park, CA: Sage.

Fox, J. and Gershman, J. (2000) 'The World Bank and social capital: lessons from ten rural development projects in the Philippines and Mexico', *Policy Sciences* 33: 399–419.

Franke, R. H., Hofstede, G. and Bond, M. H. (1991) 'Cultural roots of economic performance: a research note', *Strategic Management Journal*, 12: 165–173.

Friedman, M. (1962) *Capitalism and Freedom*, Chicago: University of Chicago Press.

Fukuyama, F. (1995) *Trust: the social virtues and the creation of prosperity*, New York: The Free Press.

Ganeshamoorthy, M. (2003) '*The Political Economy of Trade Liberalization in Developing Countries: the Sri Lankan case*', Nijmegen Studies in Development and Cultural Change, No. 41, Nijmegen: NICCOS, Saarbrücken: Verlag für Entwicklungspolitik Saarbrücken GmBH.

Geertz, C. (1969) 'Religion as a cultural system', in D. R. Cutler (ed.) *The World Year Book of Religion: the religious situation*, vol. I, London: Evans Brothers, 639–688.

Geertz, C. (1993) *The Interpretation of Cultures: selected essays*, London: Fontana Press.

Gehrig, T. (1993) 'An information based explanation of the domestic bias in international equity investment', *Scandinavian Journal of Economics*, 95(1): 97–109.

Gesell, S. (1949 [1931]) *Die natürliche Wirtschafstordnung*, 9th Edition, Lauf bei Nürnberg: Rudolf Zitzmann Verlag, available at <http://www.geldreform.de>

Giddens, A. (1974) *Max Weber over Politiek en Sociologie*, [trans. H. O. van den Berg], Meppel: Boom.

Giddens, A. (2001) 'Introduction' to M. Weber *The Protestant Ethic and the Spirit of Capitalism*, Abingdon/New York: Routledge Classics, Routledge, vii–xxiv.

Giuliano, P. (2007) 'Living arrangements in Western Europe: does cultural origin matter?', *Journal of the European Economic Association*, 5(5): 927–952.

Giuliano, P., Spilimbergo, A. and Tonon, G. (2007) 'Genetic, cultural and geographical distance', Available Online at <http://www.economics.harvard.edu/faculty/giuliano/files/Genetics_August2007.pdf>.

Glasmeier, A. (1991) 'Technological discontinuities and flexible production: the case of Switzerland and the world watch industry', *Research Policy*, 20: 469–485.

Grabher, G. (1993) 'The weakness of strong ties: the lock-in of regional development in the Ruhr area', in G. Grabher (ed.) *The Embedded Firm: on the socio-economics of industrial networks*, London: Routledge, 255–277.

Gramsci, A. (1980 [1977]) *Grondbegrippen van de Politiek: hegemonie, staat, partij*, trans. M. Horn), Nijmegen: Socialistische Uitgeverij Nijmegen.

Granato, J., Inglehart, R. and Leblang, D. (1996) 'The effect of cultural values on economic development: theory, hypotheses, and some empirical tests', *American Journal of Political Science*, 40(3): 607–631.

Granovetter, M. (1973) 'The strength of weak ties', *American Journal of Sociology*, 78: 1360–1380.

Granovetter, M. (1985) 'Economic action and social structure: the problem of embeddedness', *American Journal of Sociology*, 91: 481–510.

Greif, A. (1994) 'Cultural beliefs and the organization of society: a historical and theoretical reflection on collectivist and individualist societies', *Journal of Political Economy*, 102: 912–950.

Greif, A. (2006) *Institutions and the Path to the Modern Economy: lessons from medieval trade*, Cambridge: Cambridge University Press.

Grier, R. (1997) 'The effect of religion on economic development: a cross national study of 63 former colonies', *Kyklos*, 50(1): 47–61.

Grinblatt, M. and Keloharju, M. (2001) 'How distance, language, and culture influence stockholdings and trades', *The Journal of Finance*, 56(3): 1053–1073.

Guiso, L., Sapienza, P. and Zingales, L. (2003) 'People's opium? religion and economic attitudes', *Journal of Monetary Economics*, 50: 225–282.

Guiso, L., Sapienza, P. and Zingales, L. (2004) 'Cultural biases in economic exchange', NBER Working Paper 11005.

Guiso, L., Sapienza, P. and Zingales, L. (2006) 'Does culture affect economic outcomes?', *The Journal of Economic Perspectives*, 20(2): 23–48.

Gulati, R. (1995) 'Does familiarity breed trust? the implications of repeated ties for contractual choice in alliances', *Academy of Management Journal*, 38: 85–112.

Gulati, R. (1998) 'Alliances and networks', *Strategic Management Journal*, 19: 293–317.

Gulati, R. (1999) 'Network location and learning: the influence of network resources and firm capabilities on alliance formation', *Strategic Management Journal*, 20: 397–420.

Gupta, V., Sully de Luque, M. and House, R. J. (2004) 'Multisource construct validity of GLOBE scales', in R. J. House, P. J. Hanges, M. Javidan, P. W. Dorfman and V. Gupta (eds) *Culture, Leadership and Organizations: the Globe study of 62 societies*, London: Sage, 152–177.

Hagenaars, J., Halman, J. and Moors, G. (2003) 'Exploring Europe's basic values map', in W. Arts, J. Hagenaars and L. Hermans (eds) *The Cultural Diversity of European Unity: findings, explanations and reflections from the European Values Study*, Leiden: Brill, 23–58.

Hall, P. A. and Gingerich, D. W. (2004) 'Varieties of capitalism and institutional complementarities in the macroeconomy: an empirical analysis', MPIfG Discussion Paper 04/5, Cologne: Max Planck Institute for the Study of Societies.

Hall, P. A. and Soskice, D. (eds) (2001) *Varieties of Capitalism: the institutional foundations of comparative advantage*, Oxford: Oxford University Press.

Hallak, J. C. (2006) 'Product quality and the direction of trade', *Journal of International Economics*, 68: 238–265.

Hampden-Turner, C. M. and Trompenaars, F. (2000) *Building Cross-Cultural Competence: how to create wealth from conflicting values*, Chichester: John Wiley.

Hanges, P. J., Dickson, M. W. and Sipe, M. T. (2004) 'Rationale for GLOBE statistical analyses: societal rankings and test of hypotheses', in R. J. House, P. J. Hanges, M. Javidan, P. W. Dorfman and V. Gupta (eds) *Culture, Leadership and Organizations: the Globe study of 62 societies*, London: Sage, 219–233.

Harrison, G. W. and List, J. A. (2004) 'Field experiments', *Journal of Economic Literature*, 42(4): 1009–1055.

Harrison, L. E. and Berger, P. L. (eds) (2006) *Developing Cultures: case studies*, New York/London: Routledge.

Harrison, L. E. (1992) *Who Prospers? How cultural values shape economic and political success*, New York: Harper Collins, Basic Books.

Harrison, L. E. and Huntington, S. (2000) *Culture Matters: how values shape human progress*, New York: Basic Books.

Harriss, J. and De Renzio, P. (1997) '"Missing link" or analytically missing?: the concept of social capital', *Journal of International Development*, 9: 919–937.

Harzing, A.-W. (2003) 'The role of culture in entry mode studies: from neglect to myopia', *Advances in International Management*, 15: 75–127.

Harzing, A.-W. and Maznevski, M. and country collaborators (2002) 'The interaction between language and culture: a test of the cultural accommodation hypothesis in seven countries', *Language and Intercultural Communication*, 2(2): 120–139.

Hayek, Friedrich (1980 [1948]) *Individualism and Economic Order*, Chicago: University of Chicago Press.

Heath, C. and Tversky, A. (1991) 'Preference and belief: ambiguity and competence in choice under uncertainty', *Journal of Risk and Uncertainty*, 4: 5–28.

Heath, W. C., Waters, M. S. and Watson, J. K. (1995) 'Religion and economic welfare: an empirical analysis of state per capita income', *Journal of Economic Behaviour and Organization*, 27: 129–142.

Heinemann, F. and Ullrich, K. (2005) 'Does it pay to watch the central banker's lips?: the information content of ECB wording', ZEW Discussion Paper No. 05–70, ZEW, Mannheim.

Hennart, J.-F. (1989) 'Can the "new forms of investment" substitute for the "old forms"?: a transaction costs perspective', *Journal of International Business Studies*, 20(2): 211–234.

Henrich, J. (2000) 'Does culture matter in economic behaviour? ultimate game bargaining among the Machinguenga of the Peruvian Amazon', *The American Economic Review*, 90(4): 973–979.

Henrich, J., McElreath, R., Barr, A., Ensminger, J., Barrett, C., Bolyanatz, A., Cardenas, J. C., Gurven, M., Gwako, E., Henrich, N., Lesorogol, C., Marlowe, F., Tracer, D. and Ziker, J. (2006) 'Costly punishment across human societies', *Science*, 312 (23 June 2006): 1767–1770.

Hill, M. (2000) '"Asian values" as reverse Orientalism: Singapore', *Asian Pacific Viewpoint*, 41(2): 177–190.

Hodgson, G. M. (2006) 'What are institutions?', *Journal of Economic Issues*, 40(1): 1–25.

Hofstede, G. (1980) *Culture's Consequences: international differences in work-related values*, Beverly Hills, CA: Sage.

Hofstede, G. (2001) *Culture's Consequences: comparing values, behaviours, institutions and organizations across nations*, 2nd edn, Beverly Hills: Sage.

Hofstede, G. (2004) 'EpiDialoge', in H. Vinken, J. Soeters and P. Essers (eds) *Comparing Cultures: dimensions of culture in a comparative perspective*, Leiden: Brill.

Hofstede, G. (2006) 'What did GLOBE really measure? researchers' minds versus respondents' minds', *Journal of International Business Studies*, 37: 882–896.

Hofstede, G. and Hofstede, G. J. (2005) *Cultures and Organizations: software of the mind*, 2nd edn, New York: McGraw-Hill.

Hofstede, G., Neuijen, B., Ohayv, D. D. and Sanders, G. (1990) 'Measuring organizational cultures: a qualitative and quantitative study across twenty cases', *Administrative Science Quarterly*, 35: 286–316.

Holm, H. and Danielson, A. (2005) 'Tropic trust versus Nordic trust: experimental evidence from Tanzania and Sweden', *The Economic Journal*, 115 (April): 505–532.

Hooghe, M., Reeskens, T., Stolle, D. and Trappers, A. (2006) 'Ethnic diversity, trust and ethnocentrism and Europe; a multi level analysis of 21 European countries', paper presented at the 102nd Annual Meeting of the American Political Science Association, Philadelphia, 31 August–3 September 2006.

Hope, O. K. (2003) 'Firm-level disclosures and the relative roles of culture and legal origin', *Journal of International Financial Management and Accounting*, 14(3): 218–248.

House, R. J., Hanges, P. J., Javidan, M., Dorfman, P. W. and Gupta, V. (eds) (2004) *Culture, Leadership and Organizations: the Globe study of 62 societies*, London: Sage.

Hox, J. (2002) *Multilevel Analysis: techniques and applications*, Mahwah, NJ: Lawrence Erlbaum.

Huberman, G. (2001) 'Familiarity breeds investment', *The Review of Financial Studies*, 14(3): 659–680.

Hudson, R. (1999) 'What makes economically successful regions in Europe successful? Implications for transferring success from West to East', EGRG Working Paper 99/01.

Iannacone, L. R. (1992) 'Heirs to the Protestant ethic? The economics of American fundamentalists', in M. E. Marty and R. Scott Appleby (eds) *Fundamentalisms and the State: remaking politics, economics, and militance*, Chicago: University of Chicago Press, 342–366.

Iannacone, L. R. (1998) 'Introduction to the economics of religion', *Journal of Economic Literature*, 36 (September): 1465–1496.

Inglehart, R. (1997) *Modernization and Postmodernization: cultural, economic and political change in 43 societies*, Princeton, NJ: Princeton University Press.

Inglehart, R. and Baker, W. E. (2000) 'Modernization, cultural change, and the persistence of traditional values', *American Sociological Review*, 65(1): 19–51.

Jackman, R. W. and Miller, A. R. (1996) 'A renaissance of political culture?', *American Journal of Political Science*, 40(3): 632–659.

Jacobs, J. (1961) *The Death and Life of Great American Cities*, New York: Vintage Books.

Jaggi, B. and Low, P. Y. (2000) 'Impact of culture, market forces and legal system on financial disclosures', *The International Journal of Accounting*, 35(4): 495–519.

Jansen, D.-J. and De Haan, J. (2007) 'Were verbal efforts to support the euro effective?: a high-frequency analysis of ECB statements', *European Journal of Political Economy*, 23: 245–259.

Javidan, M., House, R. J., Dorfman, P. W., Hanges, P. J. and Sully de Lucque, M. (2006) 'Conceptualizing and measuring cultures and their consequences: a comparative review of GLOBE's and Hofstede's approaches', *Journal of International Business Studies*, 37: 897–914.

Johanson, J. and Vahlne, J.-E. (1977) 'The internationalization process of the firm – a model of knowledge development and increasing foreign market commitments', *Journal of International Business Studies*, 8(1): 23–32.

Jones, E. L. (1988) *Growth Recurring: economic change in world history*, Oxford: Clarendon Press.

Jones, E. L. (2006) *Cultures Merging: a historical and economic critique of culture*, Princeton, NJ: Princeton University Press.

Kahneman, D. and Tversky, A. (1979) 'Prospect theory: an analysis of decision under risk, *Econometrica*, 47(2): 263–291.

Karasek, R. A. (2004) 'Job socialization: the carry-over effects of work on political and leisure activities', *Bulletin of Science, Technology and Society*, 24(4): 284–304.

Karolyi, A. and Stulz, R. M. (2003) 'Are financial assets priced locally or globally?', in G. Constantinides, M. Harris and R. M. Stulz (eds) *Handbook of the Economics of Finance*, North Holland: Elsevier.

Kellehear, A. (2001) 'Unobtrusive methods: an introduction', available online at <http://www.allen-unwin.com/Academic/unobtrus.pdf>

Kemmelmeier, M. and Cheng, B. Y.-M. (2004) 'Language and self-construal priming: a replication and extension in a Hong Kong sample', *Journal of Cross-Cultural Psychology*, 35: 705–712.

Kenworthy, L. (2001) 'Wage-setting measures: a survey and assessment', *World Politics*, 54(1): 57–98.

Kim, W. C. and Hwang, P. (1992) 'Global strategy and multinationals' entry mode choice', *Journal of International Business Studies*, 23(1): 29–53.

Klaassen, L. H., Wagenaar, S. and Van der Weg, A. (1972) 'Measuring psychological distance between the Flemings and the Walloons', *Papers of the Regional Science Association*, 29, 45–62.

Kluckhohn, C. (1951) 'The study of culture', in D. Lerner and H. D. Lasswell (eds) *The Policy Sciences*, Stanford, CA: Stanford University Press, 86–101.

Knack, S. and Keefer, P. (1997) 'Does social capital have an Economic payoff?: a cross-country investigation', *The Quarterly Journal of Economics*, 112(4): 1251–1288.

Knowles, J. and Postlewaite, A. (2005) 'Do children learn to save from their parents?'. Unpublished Manuscript, Department of Economics, Philadelphia: University of Pennsylvania.

Kogut, B. and Singh, H. (1988) 'The effect of national culture on the choice of entry mode', *Journal of International Business Studies*, 19(3): 411–432.

Kok Hwa, B. S. (1997) 'Singapore, a modern Asian city-state: relationship between cultural and economic development'. Unpublished PhD thesis, University of Nijmegen.

Kunio, Y. (2006) 'Japanese culture and post-war growth', in L. E. Harrison and P. L. Berger (eds) *Developing Cultures: case studies*, New York: Routledge, 83–100.

Kuran, T. (1995) *Private Truths, Public Lies: the social consequence of preference falsification*, Cambridge, MA: Harvard University Press.

Kuran, T. (2004a) *Islam and Mammon: the economic predicaments of Islamism*, Princeton, NJ: Princeton University Press.

Kuran, T. (2004b) 'Why the Middle East is economically underdeveloped: historical mechanism of institutional stagnation', *Journal of Economic Perspectives*, 18(3): 71–90.

Kuran, T. (2004c) 'The economic ascent of the Middle East's religious minorities: the role of Islamic legal pluralism', *Journal of Legal Studies*, 33 (June): 475–515.

Kuran, T. (2007) 'Economic underdevelopment in the Middle East: the historical role of culture, institutions and religion'. Unpublished Manuscript, Durham: Duke University.

Kwok, C. C. Y. and Tadesse, S. (2006) 'National culture and financial systems', *Journal of International Business Studies*, 37: 227–247.

La Porta, R., Lopez-De-Silanes, F., Shleifer, A. and Vishny, R. W. (1997a) 'Legal determinants of external finance', *Journal of Finance*, 52: 1131–1150.

La Porta, R., Lopez-De-Silanes, F., Shleifer, A. and Vishny, R. W. (1997b) 'Trust in large organizations', *The American Economic Review*, 87(2): 333–338.

La Porta, R., Lopez-De-Silanes, F., Shleifer, A. and Vishny, R. W. (1998) 'Law and finance', *Journal of Political Economy*, 106(6): 1113–1155.

La Porta, R., Lopez-De-Silanes, F., Shleifer, A. and Vishny, R. W. (1999) 'The quality of government', *Journal of Law, Economics and Organization*, 15: 222–279.

La Porta, R., Lopez-De-Silanes, F., Shleifer, A. and Vishny, R. W. (2000) 'Investor protection and corporate governance', *Journal of Financial Economics*, 58: 3–27.

Lal, D. (1983) *The Poverty of Development Economics*, London: The Institute of Economic Affairs.

Lal, D. (1985) 'The misconceptions of 'development economics', *Finance and Development*, 22: 10–13.

Lal, D. (1998) *Unintended Consequences: the impact of factor endowments, culture, and politics on long term economic performance*, Cambridge, MA: MIT Press.

Landes, D. S. (1999) *The Wealth and Poverty of Nations: why some are so rich and some so poor*, London: ABACUS.

Landes, D. S. (2006) 'Why Europe and the West? why not China?', *Journal of Economic Perspectives*, 20(2): 3–22.

Lankuizen, M., De Jong, E. and Pelzer, B. (2008) 'Estimating the knowledge-capital model for multiple parents and hosts: taking the cross-classified structure of the data into account', Radboud University Nijmegen: NiCE Working Paper 08-105.

Lankhuizen, M., Linders, G.-J. and De Groot, H. L. F. (2008) 'Cultural distance and the mode of serving foreign markets: an empirical investigation of the trade-off between FDI and exports'. Unpublished Manuscript, Department of Spatial Economics, Free University of Amsterdam, Amsterdam.

Leamer, E. E. (1983) 'Let's take the con out of econometrics', *The American Economic Review*, 73(1): 31–43.

Lee, R. and Ackerman, S. (1997) *Sacred Tensions: modernity and religious transformation in Malaysia*, Columbia: University of South Caroline Press.

Leung, K. and Bond, M. H. (1989) 'On the empirical identification of dimensions for cross-cultural comparisons', *Journal of Cross-Cultural Psychology*, 20: 133–151.

Levine, R. and Renelt, D. (1992) 'A sensitivity analysis of cross-country growth regressions', *The American Economic Review*, 82(4): 942–963.

Levitt, S. D. and List, J. A. (2007) 'What do laboratory experiments measuring social preferences reveal about the real world?', *Journal of Economic Perspectives*, 21(2): 153–174.

Lewer, J. J. and Van den Berg, H. (undated) Religion and globalization: do religious countries trade more? Unpublished Manuscript.

Lewis, K. K. (1999) 'Trying to explain home bias in equities and consumption', *Journal of Economic Literature*, 37: 571–608.

Licht, A. N., Goldschmith, C. and Schwartz, S. H. (2001) 'Culture, law, and finance: cultural dimensions of corporate governance'. Unpublished Working Paper.

Licht, A. N., Goldschmith, C. and Schwartz, S. H. (2005) 'Culture, law, and corporate governance', *International Review of Law and Economics*, 25: 229–255.

Linders, G.-J. (2006) 'Intangible barriers to trade: the impact of institutions, culture, and distance on patterns of trade'. Unpublished PhD thesis, Free University Amsterdam, Amsterdam.

Linnemann, H. (1966) *An Econometric Study of International Trade Flows*, Amsterdam: North Holland.

List, J. A. (2004) Neoclassical theory versus prospect theory: evidence from the marketplace, *Econometrica*, 72(2): 615–625.

Loury, G. (1977) 'A dynamic theory of racial income differences', in P. A. Wallace and A. M. laMond (eds) *Women, Minorities, and Employment Discrimination*, Lexington, MA: D. C. Health, 153–186.

Luhmann, N. (1979) *Trust and Power*, Chichester: John Wiley.

Luttmer, E. F. P. (2001) 'Group loyalty and the taste for redistribution', *Journal of Political Economy*, 109(3): 500–528.

Lynn, M. and Gelb, B. D. (1996) 'Identifying innovative national markets for technical consumer goods', *International Marketing Review*, 13(6): 43–57.

MacKinnon, J. G. and White, H. (1985) 'Some heteroskedasticity consistent covariance matrix estimators with improved finite sample properties', *Journal of Econometrics*, 29: 53–57.

McCleary, R. C. and Barro, R. J. (2006) 'Religion and economy', *Journal of Economic Perspectives*, 20(2): 49–72.

McClelland, D. C. (1961) *The Achieving Society*, Princeton, NJ: D. Van Nostrand Reinhold.

McEvily, B. and Zaheer, A. (1999) 'Bridging ties: a source of firm heterogeneity in competitive capabilities', *Strategic Management Journal*, 20: 1133–1156.

McKinley, W. (1898) 'Benevolent assimilation', *Proclamation of U.S. President William McKinley*, 21 December 1898.

McSweeney, B. (2002) 'Hofstede's model of national cultural differences and their consequences: a triumph of faith – a failure of analysis', *Human* Relations, 55: 89–117.

Mailath, G. J. (1998) 'Do people play Nash equilibrium? lessons from evolutionary game theory', *Journal of Economic Literature*, 36: 1347–1374.

Malecki, E. J. (2000) 'Network models for technology based growth', in Z. Acs (ed.) *Regional Innovation, Knowledge and Global Change*, London: Pinter, 187–204.

Mangeloja, E. (2005) 'Economic growth and religious production efficiency', *Applied Economics*, 37: 2349–2359.

Marini, M. (2004) 'Cultural evolution and economic growth: a theoretical hypothesis with some empirical evidence', *The Journal of Socio-Economics*, 33: 765–784.

Marschan-Piekkari, R. and Welch, C. (eds) (2004) *Handbook of Qualitative Research Methods for International Business*, Cheltenham: Edward Elgar.

Marx, K. (1978 [1867]) *Het Kapitaal, Vol. 1* (trans. I. Lipschitz), Haarlem: De Haan.

Maseland, R. K. J. (2006a) 'Embedding economics: the constitution of development and reform in Malaysia and the Philippines'. Unpublished PhD thesis, Radboud University Nijmegen.

Maseland, R. K. J. (2006b) 'Path-dependence from present to past: the embeddedness of the EDSA-Revolution in Philippine history'. Unpublished Manuscript, Radboud University Nijmegen.

Maseland, R. K. J. (undated) 'Cultural and Economics: theoretical perspectives'. Unpublished Manuscript, Radboud University Nijmegen.

Maseland, R. K. J. (2008) 'Taking economics to bed: about the pitfalls and possibilities of cultural economics', in W. Eisner and H. Hannapi (eds) *Varieties of Capitalism and Institutional Deals*, Cheltenham: Edward Elgar: 197–219.

Meyerson, E. M. (1994) 'Human capital, social capital and compensation: the relative contribution of social contacts to managers' incomes', *Acta Sociologica*, 37: 383–399.

Miller, A. S. and Mitamura, T. (2003) 'Are surveys on trust trustworthy?', *Social Psychology Quarterly*, 66.1: 62–70.

Morse, A. and Shive, S. (2006) 'Patriotism in your portfolio'. Unpublished Manuscript, Ann Arbor: University of Michigan.

Murrell, P. (1995) 'The transition according to Cambridge, Mass.', *Journal of Economic Literature*, 32 (March): 164–178.

Nahapiet, J. and Ghoshal, S. (1998) 'Social capital, intellectual capital and the organizational advantage', *Academy of Management Review*, 23: 242–266.

Nash, M. (1964) 'Social prerequisites to economic growth in Latin America and Southeast Asia', *Economic Development and Cultural Change*, 12(3): 225–242.

Ng, S. H., Hossain, A., Ball, P., Bond, M. H., Hayaski, K., Lim, S. P., O'Driscoll, M. P., Shinha, D. and Yang, K. S. (1982) 'Human values in nine countries', in R. Rath, H. S. Asthana, D. Sinha and J. B. P. Sinha (eds) *Diversity and Unity in Cross-Cultural Psychology*, Lisse, The Netherlands: Swets and Zeilinger, 196–205.

Noland, M. (2005) 'Religion and economic performance', *World Development*, 33(8): 1215–1232.

Noorderhaven, N. G. and Tidjani, B. (2001) 'Culture, governance, and economic performance: an explorative study with a special focus on Africa', *International Journal of Cross Cultural Management*, 1(1): 31–52.

Noorderhaven, N. G., Koen, C. and Beugelsdijk, S. (2003) 'Organizational culture and network embeddedness', CentER Discussion Paper 91, Tilburg University.

Nooteboom, B. (1996) 'Trust, opportunism and governance: a process and control model', *Organization Studies*, 17(6): 985–1010.

Nooteboom, B. (1999) 'Innovation, learning and industrial organization', *Cambridge Journal of Economics*, 23: 127–150.

Nooteboom, B. (2002) *Trust; Forms, Foundations, Functions, Failures and Figures*, Cheltenham: Edward Elgar.

Nooteboom, B., Berger, H. and Noorderhaven, N. G. (1997) 'Effects of trust and governance on relational risk', *Academy of Management Journal*, 40: 308–338.

North, D. C. (1990) *Institutions, Institutional Change and Economic Performance*, Cambridge: Cambridge University Press.

Obstfeld, M. and Rogoff, K. (2000) 'The six major puzzles in international macroeconomics: is there a common cause?', NBER Working Paper 7777.

Olson, M. (1982) *The Rise and Decline of Nations*, New Haven: Yale University Press.

Paasi, A. (1996) *Territories, Boundaries and Consciousness: the changing geographies of the Finnish-Russian border*, Chichester: John Wiley.

Paldam, M. (2001) 'Corruption and religion: adding to the economic model', *Kyklos*, 54(2/3): 383–414.

Paxton, P. (1999) 'Is social capital declining in the United States? A multiple indicator assessment', *American Journal of Sociology*, 105: 88–127.

Pejovich, S. (2003) 'Understanding the transaction costs of transition: it's the culture stupid', *The Review of Austrian Economics*, 16(4): 347–361.

Perotti, E. and Schwienbacher, A. (2006) 'The political origin of pension funding'. Unpublished Manuscript, University of Amsterdam, 20 December 2006.

Pesenti, P. and Van Wincoop, E. (2002) 'Can nontradables generate substantial home bias?', *Journal of Money, Credit and Banking*, 34(1): 25–50.

Platteau (1994) 'Behind the market stage, where real societies exist, Part II: the role of moral norms', *Journal of Development Studies*, 30(3): 753–817.

Polanyi, K. (1944) *The Great Transformation*, New York: Rinehart.

Portes, A. (1998) 'Social capital: its origins and applications in modern sociology', *Annual Review of Sociology*, 24: 1–24.

Portes, A. and Landolt, P. (1996) 'The downside of social capital', *The American Prospect*, 26: 18–21.

Portes, A. and Sensenbrenner, J. (1993) 'Embeddedness and immigration: notes on the social determinants of economic action', *American Journal of Sociology*, 98(6): 1320–1350.

Portes, R., Rey, H. and Oh, Y. (2001) 'Information and capital flows: the determinants of transactions in financial assets', *European Economic Review*, 45(4–6): 783–796.

Punnett, B. J. and Shenkar, O. (eds) (2004) *Handbook for International Management Research*, 2nd edn, Ann Arbor: University of Michigan Press.

Putnam, R. (with Leonardi, R. and Nanetti, R. Y.) (1993) *Making Democracy Work*, Princeton, NJ: Princeton University Press.

Putnam, R. (1995) 'Bowling alone: America's declining social capital', *Journal of Democracy*, 6: 65–78.

Putnam, R. (2000) *Bowling Alone: the collapse and revival of American community*, New York: Simon and Schuster.

Rabin, M. (1998) 'Psychology and economics', *Journal of Economic Literature*, 36: 11–46.

Raghuram, S., London, M. and Larsen, H. H. (2001) 'Flexible employment practices in Europe: country versus culture', *International Journal of Human Resource Management*, 12(5): 738–753.

Rajan, R. and Zingales, L. (1998) 'Financial dependence and growth', *American Economic Review*, 88(3): 559–586.

Rauch, J. E. (1999) 'Networks versus markets in international trade', *Journal of International Economics*, 48(1): 7–35.

Redding, G. (2005) 'The thick description and comparison of societal systems of capitalism', *Journal of International Business Studies*, 36: 123–155.

Redding, S. and Venables, A. J. (2004) 'Economic geography and international inequality', *Journal of International Economics*, 62(1): 53–82.

Ring, P. and Van de Ven, A. (1992) 'Structuring cooperative relationships between organizations', *Strategic Management Journal*, 13: 483–498.

Ritter, T. (1999) 'The networking company. Antecedents for coping with relationships and networks effectively', *Industrial Marketing Management*, 28: 467–479.

Rizvi, S. A. T. (2003) 'Post-war Neoclassical Microeconomics', in W. J. Samuels, J. E. Biddle, and J. B. Davis (eds) *A Companion to the History of Economic Thought*, Oxford: Blackwell, 377–394.

Robbins, L. (1932) *An Essay on the Nature and Significance of Economic Science*, London: Macmillan.

Rodinson, M. (1980 [1966]) *Islam and Capitalism*, Middlesex, UK: Penguin Books.

Roe, M. (2000) 'Political preconditions to separating ownership from corporate control', *Stanford Law Review*, 53: 539–606.

Röell, A. (1996) 'The decision to go public: an overview', *European Economic Review*, 40: 1071–1181.

Rokeach, M. (1973) *The Nature of Human Values*, New York: Free Press.

Rosa, C. and Verga, G. (2007) 'On the consistency and effectiveness of central bank communication: evidence from the ECB', *European Journal of Political Economy*, 23: 146–175.

Rosenstein-Rodan, P. (1943) 'Problems of Industrialization of Eastern and South-Eastern Europe', *The Economic Journal*, 53(210/211): 202–11.

Roth, A. E., Vesna, P., Masahiro, O.-F. and Shmuel, Z. (1991) 'Bargaining and market behaviour in Jerusalem, Ljubljana, Pittsburgh, and Tokyo: an experimental study', *American Economic Review*, 81(5): 1068–1095.

Sako, M. (1992) *Prices, Quality and Trust: interfirm relations in Britain and Japan*, Cambridge: Cambridge University Press.

Sakwa, M. M. (2006) *Bible and Poverty in Kenya: an empirical exploration*, Leiden: Brill.

Sakwa, M. M., De Jong, E., Schilderman, J. B. A. M. and Van der Ven, J. A. (2005) 'The Impact of religion on the means and goals of poverty alleviation: an empirical attitudinal approach'. Unpublished Manuscript, Radboud University Nijmegen.

Sala-i-Martin, X. X. (1997) 'I just ran two million regressions', *American Economic Review*, 87(2): 178–183.

Samuelson, P. A. (1974) *Foundations of Economic Analysis*, Cambridge Mass.: Harvard University Press.

Samuelsson, K. (1961) *Religion and Economic Action: a critique of Max Weber*, trans. from the Swedish by E. Geoffrey French and edited and with an introduction by D. C. Coleman), New York: Harper Torchbooks.

Santos Silva, J. M. C. and Tenreyro, S. (2006) 'The log of gravity', *The Review of Economics and Statistics*, 88(4): 641–658.

Scheuch, E. K. (1996) 'Theoretical implications of comparative survey research: why the wheel of cross-cultural methodology keeps on being reinvented', in A. Inkeles and M. Sasaki (eds) *Comparing Nations and Cultures: readings in cross-disciplinary perspective*, Prentice Hall, NJ: Englewood Cliffs, 57–73.

Schneider, F. and Wagner, A. F. (2001) 'Institutions of conflict management and economic growth in the European Union', *Kyklos*, 54(4): 509–532.

Schwartz, S. H. (1992) 'Universals in the content and structure of values: theoretical advances and empirical tests in 20 countries', *Advances in Experimental Social Psychology*, 25(1): 1–65.

Schwartz, S. H. (1994) 'Beyond individualism/collectivism: new cultural dimensions of values', in U. Kim, H. C. Triandis, C. Kagitçibasi, S. C. Choi and G. Yoon (eds) *Individualism and Collectivism: theory, method, and applications*, Thousand Oaks, CA: Sage, 85–119.

Scott, R. W. (1995) *Institutions and Organizations*, London: Sage.

Semenov, R. (2000) 'Cross-country differences in economic governance: culture as a major explanatory factor'. Unpublished PhD thesis, Tilburg University.

Sent, E.-M. (1998) 'Bounded rationality', in J. Davis, W. Hands and U. Mäki (eds) *Handbook of Economic Methodology*, Cheltenham and Northampton: Edward Elgar, 36–40.

Sent, E.-M. (2004) 'Behavioral economics: how psychology made its (limited) way back into economics', *History of Political Economy*, 36(4): 735–760.

Sent, E.-M. (2006) 'Pluralisms in economics', in S. Kellert, H. Longino and K. Waters (eds) *Scientific Pluralism*, Minnesota Studies in the Philosophy of Science, 2006, 80–101.

Sercu, P. and Vanpée, R. (2007) 'Home bias in international equity portfolios: a review', Discussion Paper AFI 0710, Faculty of Economics and Applied Economics, Katholieke Universiteit Leuven.

Shalev, M. (2007) 'Limits and alternatives to multiple regression in comparative research', *Comparative Social Research*, 24: 261–308.

Shane, S. (1995) 'Uncertainty avoidance and preference for innovation championing roles', *Journal of International Business Studies*, 26: 47–68.

Shane, S. and Venkataraman, S. (1996) 'Renegade and rational championing strategies', *Organization Studies*, 17: 751–771.

Shane, S., Venkataraman, S. and MacMillan, I. (1995) 'Cultural differences in innovation championing strategies', *Journal of Management*, 21(5): 931–952.

Shapiro, S. P. (1987) 'The social control of impersonal trust', *American Journal of Sociology*, 93(3): 623–658.

Shenkar, O. (2001) 'Cultural distance revisited: towards a more rigorous conceptualization and measurement of cultural differences', *Journal of International Business Studies*, 32(3): 519–535.

Shleifer, A. and Vishny, R. W. (1997) 'A survey of corporate governance', *Journal of Finance*, 52(2): 737–783.

Small, M. (1998) *Our Babies, Ourselves: how biology and culture shape the way we parent*, New York: Anchor Books.

Smith, A. (1976 [1759]) *The Theory of Moral Sentiments*, D. Raphael and A. Macfie (eds), Oxford: Oxford University Press.

Smith, A. (1981 [1776]) *An Inquiry into the Nature and Causes of the Wealth of Nations*, Indianapolis: Liberty Fund.

Smith, P. B. (2006) 'When elephants fight, the grass gets trampled: the GLOBE and Hofstede projects', *Journal of International Business Studies*, 37: 915–921.

Spierings, N., Smits, J. and Verloo, M. (2006) 'Are Islam and gender equality inherently incompatible?'. Unpublished Manuscript, Radboud University Nijmegen.

Straubhaar, T. (1988) *On the Economics of International Labour Migration*, Bern: Haupt.

Strüver, A. (2004) 'Stories of the "boring border": the Dutch–German borderscape in people's minds'. Unpublished PhD thesis, Radboud University Nijmegen.

Stulz, R. and Williamson, R. (2003) 'Culture, openness, and finance', *Journal of Financial Economics*, 70: 313–349.

Svaleryd, H. and Vlachos, J. (2005) 'Financial markets, the pattern of industrial specialization and competitive advantage: evidence from OECD countries', *European Economic Review*, 49: 113–144.

Szász, A. (1999) *The Road to European Monetary Union*, London: MacMillan Press.

Tabellini, G. (2005) 'Culture and institutions: economic development in the regions of Europe', CESifo Working Paper No. 1492.

Tabellini, G. (2008a) 'The scope of cooperation: values and incentives', *The Quarterly Journal of Economics*, 123(3): 905–950.

Tabellini, G. (2008b) 'Institutions and culture', *Journal of the European Economic Association*, 6(2–3): 255–294.

Tarrow, S. (1996) 'Making social science work across space and time: a critical reflection on Robert Putnam's making democracy work', *The American Political Science Review*, 90: 389–398.

Tassinopoulos, A. and Werner, H. (1999) 'To move or not to move – migration of labour in the European Union', IAB Labour Market Research Topics 35.

Tawney, R. H. (1962 [1926]) *Religion and the Rise of Capitalism: a historical study*, Clouchester, MA: Peter Smith.

Temple, J. (1999) 'The new growth evidence', *Journal of Economic Literature*, 37: 112–156.

Ter Haar, G. and Ellis, S. (2006) 'The role of religion in development: towards a new relationship between the European Union and Africa', *The European Journal of Development Research*, 18(3): 351–367.

Tesar, L. L. and Werner, I. M. (1995) 'Home bias and high turnover', *Journal of International Money and Finance*, 14(4): 467–492.

Teulings, C. and Hartog, J. (1998) *Corporatism or Competition: labour contracts, institutions and wage structures in international comparison*, Cambridge: Cambridge University Press.

Therborn, G. (1992) 'Lessons from "corporatist" theoretizations', in J. Pekkarinen, M. Pohjola and B. Rowthorn (eds) *Social Corporatism: a superior economic system?*, Oxford: Oxford University Press: 24–43.

Tinbergen, J. (1962) *Shaping the World Economy: suggestions for an international economic policy*, New York: Twentieth Century Fund.

Trompenaars, F. and Hampden-Turner, C. (1997) *Riding the Waves of Culture: understanding cultural diversity in business*, 2nd edn, London: Nicholas Brealey.

Tsai, W. (2000) 'Social capital, strategic relatedness and the formation of intra-organizational linkages', *Strategic Management Journal*, 21: 925–939.

Tsai, W. and Ghoshal, S. (1998) 'Social capital and value creation: the role of intrafirm networks', *Academy of Management Journal*, 41: 464–476.

Tversky, A. and Kahneman, T. (1991) 'Loss aversion and riskless choice: a reference dependent model', *The Quarterly Journal of Economics* 106(4): 1039–1061.

Tylor, E. B. (1958 [1871]) *Primitive Culure: researches into the development of mythology, philosophy, religion, art and custom*, Vol. 1: 'Origins of Culture', Gloucester, MA: Smith.

Usunier, J.-C. (1998) *International and Cross-Cultural Management Research*, London: SAGE.

Uzzi, B. (1996) 'The sources and consequences of embeddedness for the economic performance of organizations: the network effect', *American Sociological Review*, 61: 674–698.

Uzzi, B. (1997) 'Social structure and competition in interfirm networks: the paradox of embeddedness', *Administrative Science Quarterly*, 42: 35–67.

Uzzi, B. (1999) 'Embeddedness in the making of financial capital: how social relations and networks benefit firms seeking financing', *American Sociological Review*, 64: 481–505.

Van de Vijver, F. and Leung, K. (1997) *Methods and Data Analysis for Cross-Cultural Research*, Thousand Oaks/London: SAGE.

Van der Toorn, K. (2007) *Scribal Culture and the Making of the Hebrew Bible*, Harvard: Harvard University Press.

Van der Velde, M., Janssen, M. and Van Houtum, H. (2005) 'Job mobility in the Dutch–German regional labour market: the threshold of indifference', in G. van Vilsteren and E. Wever (eds) *Borders and Economic Behaviour in Europe:a geographical approach*, Assen: Royal Van Gorcum, 77–95.

Van der Velde, M. and Van Naerssen, T. (in press) 'People borders and trajectories: a model to approach migration in the enlarged Europe', in M. van der Velde and T. Naerssen (eds) *East-West Migration in a New Europe*, Rome: Home of Geography.

Van Hoorn, A. and Maseland, R. (in press) 'Explaining the negative correlation between values and practices: a note on the Hofstede–GLOBE debate, *Journal of International Business Studies.*

Van Houtum, H. (1998) '*The Development of Cross Border Economic Relations: a theoretical and empirical study of the influence of the state border on the development of cross-border economic relations between firms in border regions of the Netherlands and Belgium*', Amsterdam: ThelaThesis.

Van Houtum, H. and Van Naerssen, T. (2002) 'Bordering, ordering, othering', *Tijdschrift voor Economische en Sociale Geografie*, 93(2): 125–136.

Van Lelyveld, I. P. P. (1999) 'Inflation or unemployment? who cares?' *European Journal of Political Economy*, 15: 463–484.

Van Lelyveld, I. P. P. (2000) Inflation, institutions, and preferences. Unpublished PhD thesis, University of Nijmegen.

Van Nieuwerburgh, S. and Veldkamp, L. (2007) 'Information immobility and the home bias puzzle', NBER Working Paper Series No. 13366.

Van Oorschot, W., Arts, W. and Gelissen, J. (2006) 'Social capital in Europe; measurement and social and regional distribution of a multifaceted phenomenon', *Acta Sociologica*, 49(2): 149–165.

Van Raaij, W. F. (1987) 'Cross-cultural research methodology as a case of construct validity', in K. Hunt (ed.) *Advances in Consumer Research*, 5: 693–701.

Veblen, T. (1998 [1898]) 'Why is economics not an evolutionary science?' *Cambridge Journal of Economics*, 22: 403–414.

Veblen, T. B. (1953 [1899]) *The Theory of a Leisure Class: an economic study of institutions* (with an introduction by C. Wright Mills); New York: The New American Library.

Veblen, T. (1897) 'Review of Antonio Labriola, *Essais sur la conception materialiste de l'histoire*', *Journal of Political Economy*, 5: 390–391.

Verbeek, M. (2004) *A Guide to Modern Econometrics*, 2nd edn, Chichester: John Wiley.

Vermeulen, F. and Barkema, H. G. (2001) 'Learning through acquisitions', *Academy of Management Journal*, 44(3): 457–476.

Vinken, H., Soeters, J. and Ester, P. (2004) 'Cultures and dimensions: classic perspectives and new opportunities in "dimensionalist" cross-cultural studies', in H. Vinken, J. Soeters and P. Ester (eds) *Comparing Cultures: dimensions of culture in a comparative perspective*, Leiden/Boston, MA: Brill, 5–27.

Weber, E. U. and Hsee, C. (1998) 'Cross-cultural differences in risk perception, but cross-cultural similarity in attitudes towards risk', *Management Science*, 44(9): 1205–1217.

Weber, M. (2006 [1920]) *Die protestantische Ethik und der Geist des Kapitalismus*, Erftstadt: area verlag gmbh.

Weber, M. (2001 [1930]) *The Protestant Ethic and the Spirit of Capitalism* (with an Introduction by A. Giddens), Abingdon/New York: Routledge Classics.

Weber, R. P. (1985) *Basic Content Analysis*, Beverly Hills: Sage.

Weintraub, E. R. (2002) *How Economics Became a Mathematical Science*, Durham/London: Duke University Press.

Welsch, R. E. (1980) 'Regression sensitivity analysis and bounded-influence estimation', in J. Kmenta and J. Ramsey (eds) *Evaluation of Econometric Models*, New York: Academic Press, 153–167.

White, H. (1980) 'A heteroskedasticity-consistent covariance matrix estimator and a direct test for heteroskedasticity', *Econometrica*, 48: 817–838.

Williamson, J. (ed.) (1990) *Latin American Adjustment: how much has happened?*, Washington, DC: Institute for International Economics.

Williamson, O. E. (1975) *Markets and Hierarchies, Analysis and Antitrust Implications*, New York: Free Press.

Williamson, O. E. (1985) *The Economic Institutions of Capitalism*, New York: Free Press.

Williamson, O. E. (1998) 'Transaction cost economics: how it works; where it is headed', *De Economist*, 146: 23–58.

Williamson, O. E. (2000) 'The new institutional economics: taking stock, looking ahead', *Journal of Economic Literature*, 38(3): 595–613.

Woolcock, M. (1998) 'Social capital and economic development: toward a theoretical synthesis and policy framework', *Theory and Society*, 27: 151–208.

World Bank (2004) *Human Development Report 2004: cultural liberty in today's diverse world*, Washington DC: World Bank.

Yli-Renko, H., Autio, E. and Sapienza, H. J. (2001) 'Social capital, knowledge acquisition, and knowledge exploitation in young technology-based firms', *Strategic Management Journal*, 22: 587–613.

Za'ba (1927) 'Kemiskinan Orang Melayu', reprinted in Ungku Abdul Aziz (1975) *Jejak-Jejak Di Pantai Zaman*, Kuala Lumpur: Universiti Malaya, 43–56.

Zaheer, A., McEvily, B. and Perrone, V. (1998) 'Does trust matter? exploring the effects of interorganisational and interpersonal trust on performance', *Organization Science*, 9: 141–159.

Zak, P. J. and Knack, S. (2001) 'Trust and growth', *The Economic Journal*, 111: 295–321.

Zarzeski, M. T. (1996) 'Spontaneous harmonization effects of culture and market forces on accounting disclosure practice', *Accounting Horizons*, 10(1): 1837.

Zucker, L. G. (1986) 'Production of trust: institutional sources of economic structure, 1840–1920', *Research in Organizational Behaviour*, 8: 53–111.

Index

Page numbers in *Italics* represent Tables. Page numbers in **Bold** represent Figures